Perspectives

on Management

*A Multidisciplinary
Analysis*

Perspectives on Management

A Multidisciplinary Analysis

EDITED BY
MICHAEL J. EARL

OXFORD UNIVERSITY PRESS

1983

Oxford University Press, Walton Street, Oxford OX2 6DP
London Glasgow New York Toronto
Delhi Bombay Calcutta Madras Karachi
Kuala Lumpur Singapore Hong Kong Tokyo
Nairobi Dar es Salaam Cape Town
Melbourne Auckland
and associated companies in
Beirut Berlin Ibadan Mexico City Nicosia

Oxford is a trade mark of Oxford University Press

Published in the United States
by Oxford University Press, New York

© *Michael J. Earl 1983*

British Library Cataloguing in Publication Data
Perspectives on management.
1. Management
I. Earl, Michael J.
658   HD31
ISBN 0-19-827257-x

Typeset by Burgess & Son (Abingdon) Ltd Abingdon Oxfordshire
and Printed in Great Britain
at the University Press, Oxford

Contents

1. EDITOR'S INTRODUCTION   1

2. BRITISH MANAGEMENT AND INDUSTRIAL
   RELATIONS: THE SOCIAL ORIGINS OF A
   SYSTEM   6

   ALAN FOX, *Sometime Lecturer in Industrial Sociology, University of
   Oxford and Fellow of the Oxford Centre for Management Studies*

2. ENTREPRENEURSHIP AND ECONOMIC
   HISTORY: THE STATE OF THE DEBATE   40

   PETER MATHIAS, *Chichele Professor of Economic History, Oxford
   University; Fellow of All Souls College, Oxford*

3. MANAGEMENT AND ECONOMIC
   PERFORMANCE   55

   DONALD HAY, *Fellow and Tutor in Economics, Jesus College,
   Oxford*

4. MANAGERIAL BEHAVIOUR: HOW RESEARCH
   HAS CHANGED THE TRADITIONAL PICTURE   82

   ROSEMARY STEWART, *Fellow of the Oxford Centre for
   Management Studies, Oxford*

5. ACCOUNTING AND MANAGEMENT   99

   MICHAEL EARL, *Fellow of the Oxford Centre for Management
   Studies, Oxford*

6. PERSPECTIVES ON CORPORATE
   GOVERNANCE: INTELLECTUAL INFLUENCES
   IN THE EXERCISE OF CORPORATE
   GOVERNANCE   143

   BOB TRICKER, *Director, The Corporate Policy Group, Oxford;
   Fellow, Nuffield College, Oxford*

7. MANAGEMENT IN GOVERNMENT   170

   NEVIL JOHNSON, *Nuffield Reader in the Comparative Study of
   Institutions, University of Oxford; Fellow of Nuffield College, Oxford*

8. THE MEANING OF MANAGEMENT AND THE
    MANAGEMENT OF MEANING: A VIEW FROM
    SOCIAL ANTHROPOLOGY   197

DAN GOWLER, *Lecturer in Management Studies, University of
Oxford; Fellow, Oxford Centre for Management Studies*

KAREN LEGGE, *Senior Lecturer, Department of Social and
Economic Studies, Imperial College of Science and Technology,
University of London*

9. PERSPECTIVES ON MANAGEMENT   234

MICHAEL EARL, *Fellow of the Oxford Centre for Management
Studies, Oxford*

Editor's Introduction

Management may be said to be a recent phenomenon since it is only in this century that a significant segment of the working population has been employed as managers, most management technologies have been invented, and management has become a subject for serious study. As an activity, of course, management has been practised for as long as man has been 'deciding and doing' in any form of socio-economic organization. Any *definition* of management, however, is problematic. Early theorists described and specified management as planning, organizing, and controlling (or variants thereof), whilst later workers chose to describe and explain what it is that managers actually do. Others have focused more recently on management as a political or social process, whilst 'alternative' forms of managing, such as self-management or democratic management, are examples of more contemporary definitional problems. Management is often equated with business administration, but today management is equally a concern beyond the business world as, for example, more or better management is called for in government, and other not-for-profit organizations are expected to be 'properly run'. Such definitional uncertainty, however, has not held back management education. This has grown apace at undergraduate, post-graduate, and post-experience levels, and management consultancy has become a significant business in itself. Furthermore, management has become intensely specialized so that functions, professions, education courses, research, and careers are structured around particular resource or activity areas—from financial management to personnel management.

As a subject for study, management is full of conundrums. Indeed, some would question whether it can be studied at all, for is not management a practical matter, an art not a science, the province of managers not academics? Indeed, research tends to throw up as many, if not more, questions, caveats, and controversies as it provides answers, principles, and conclusions on best practice. Moreover, management research is also beset by methodological and epistomological problems, but this is not unusual in the social sciences. More perplexingly still, some seemingly successful economies and societies underplay management as an activity in its own right, as an important technology, or as a subject for study, whilst other perhaps less successful economies appear to be possessed by management, almost to the point of reification. Furthermore, some related disciplines, for example economics, might see management as a residual, determined as much by economic context as by quality of enterprise, energy, and education. Yet in daily rhetoric and discourse, management is generally perceived to be a 'good thing', but 'good management' is perceived to be rare.

Such enigmas cannot be ignored. Yet it is not unusual in much management education, and practice, to tackle management as though it were unproblematic. The need for formal management, the benefits of managing, and even the right to manage, are either assumed without question, or only queried *en passant*. Particularly in the early years of management education and research it would seem that normative models of goal-setting and goal achievement, universal transfer of industry best practice, and static models of the environment, were dominant. Indeed, at any time, the immediate managerial pressure for answers and panaceas can squeeze out the cultivation of the ability to ask the right questions and develop frameworks for understanding and analysis.

However, there are signs that management studies is coming of age. Not content with merely teaching and advancing techniques and technologies of management, or examining current trends in management practice, 'management academics' increasingly have been concerned to examine and understand more deeply both the internal and external contexts in which managers operate. This is perhaps a recognition that the efficacy of management practices can only be evaluated in context, that today management also influences and shapes the social, economic, and political environments in which it operates, and that management studied and taught without reference to context is but an abstraction. If the spirit of management studies in Oxford University (and this volume has its heritage in Oxford) were to be analysed, such might be some of the principles that would show through.

Yet management studies is not, and has never been, the sole province of business schools, management centres, and the like. I am frequently reminded in my own particular branch of management study that many seminal researches and pieces of scholarship were done by workers in other disciplines. For example, a major contribution to management accounting was made by Joel Dean, an economist, organization theory owes much to the writings of Weber, a sociologist, and management science has been much influenced by Ashby, a cybernetician. Conversely, whilst academics with a management background have made significant contributions to the body of knowledge that makes up management studies, their contributions have not penetrated the literatures of other disciplines. Perhaps this is inevitable in what is essentially an applied subject. Other workers concerned with management, of course, have defied categorization and trod the path of interdisciplinary or multidisciplinary work in the social sciences, for example Chandler, Wildavsky, or Simon. Examples of all these three categories of scholar can be found amongst the contributors to this volume.

Indeed, such was the origin of *Perspectives on Management.* I had been impresed by the fact that workers in varying disciplines were studying topics of relevance to both managers and 'management studies' which rarely, or only belatedly, entered mainstream management literature. (Often, it might be noted, such work was almost clandestine and not admitted, for it did not bear the hallmarks of academic respectability, being seemingly 'new', 'marginal', or 'inelegant'.) Conversely, I was beginning to feel that work being done in the name of management studies might also be of interest and value to those working in parent or related disciplines. One rationale for this volume, then, is to encourage more dialogue, at least, between our various disciplines. More substantially, I hope that by bringing together different perspectives, students of management may be provided with new insights, frameworks for analysis, and ideas for research. In turn, I hope that students in other disciplines may be persuaded that management provides interesting research questions, that other disciplines and methodologies can contribute to the study of management, and that multidisciplinary and interdisciplinary research has much to offer for the understanding and solution of 'real-world problems'. I also hope that the traditional academic risks of specialists being too specialist and generalists being too general have been avoided.

The volume begins with a perspective from industrial sociology by Fox. It examines contemporary arguments about the employer--employee relationship in the light of British social history. Mathias then develops a related theme from economic history, namely the 'entrepreneurship debate', or the role of entrepreneurs in recent economic development. From the micro-economic level, Hay examines the relationship between management and economic performance, focusing particularly on the separation of ownership and control, the objectives of managements, and the internal structure of firms. By the fourth paper it would seem timely to consider what managers do, and Stewart reviews research on managerial work. One specialist function in management, accounting, is addressed in Earl's paper, in particular examining the functions of accounting information systems and the roles of accountants when accounting meets management. Tricker then takes a 'top-management' perspective, examining board-level behaviour and concepts of 'corporate governance'. An issue of considerable topical interest is tackled by Johnson, namely management in government, what it might mean and what might be expected of it. Gowler and Legge provide a perspective from social anthropology suggesting how the meaning of management is accomplished symbolically in organizations and how meaning can be managed. An editorial conclusion is then offered, suggesting implications of this volume for management research, education, and practice.

Of course, a volume such as this can only be a partial reflection on management. Readers will be able to suggest several important omissions. For example, a cross-cultural critique of management might have reduced the possible insularity of the book, and have been topical in view of widespread attention to different management styles, such as those attributed to Japan. At least three of the contributions point to the political processes inherent in management, and a perspective from a political scientist might have been valuable. Perhaps any volume on the theme of management should contain a contribution from a manager, but the design of this volume was to seek perspectives from different academic disciplines. Maybe another paper on industrial relations, examining the role and practice of management in this area, would have been of value but, curiously perhaps, management hitherto has been an under-researched topic in the system of British industrial relations.

So perhaps the reader will judge the volume on the distinctive contributions that each of the perspectives, and their background disciplines, brings to the understanding, study, and practice of management. I will conclude with an unusually subjective note. Several of the contributors found that, despite the initial appeal of their brief, the execution was much more difficult that had been anticipated. 'Management' in the large is rather a bland, amorphous concept to address with rigour, whilst production of a particular perspective tends to demand development of new frameworks and arguments and to pose problems of delineation. The contributors, in the end, feel that this challenge has been worthwhile; I hope that the readers will agree.

MICHAEL J. EARL

Oxford
November 1982

1

British Management and Industrial Relations: the social origins of a system

ALAN FOX

Clemenceau observed that war was too important to be left to the generals. In the same spirit, managers, governments, and men of affairs have long considered that work was too important to be left to the workers. Great efforts have been made, down the ages, to change their attitude towards it and towards the managers who organize and direct it. More recently some of this anxiety has even been directed upon the motivation and performance of managers themselves.

What manner of task do they take on who mount such efforts? This essay will point to, and attempt to explain, the massive and stubborn resistances that are encountered by attempts to transform basic, long-standing responses of large numbers of people in their everyday behaviour; by attempts to reverse institutional dispositions and tendencies that have been shaped over a long period; or by attempts to repudiate expectations that have likewise been gener-ated by persistent historical continuities. More specifically, it will explore the roots of the resistances offered to three major changes in behaviour that have been pursued especially urgently since the Second World War, but to some extent long before. All have an obvious and central relevance to the managerial role and how it is conducted, more especially in its relationship with employees.

The first bears upon an issue as old as paid employment itself. Some employers have always cherished the hope that their workers might be induced to enter into a fully co-operative relationship with them, accepting their leadership and initiative and seeking always to conduct with them a positive-sum game from which all interests, including those of consumers and the wider society, would benefit. Post-war governments and managements have greatly intensified such exhortations. The second change to be sought is about a century old. Informed observers, now strongly reinforced by the state, have urged employers and managers to bring to their task a keener entrepreneurial zeal; to be constantly alert to modernize, increase efficiency, explore new ventures, and resist restrictionism from wherever it comes. The third, and last, change has received particular stress since the war as a consequence of Britain's economic difficulties. The lower ranks especially must be induced to acknowledge the existence of a 'higher social good'—i.e. the 'national interest'—to which they must sometimes expect to subjugate their own perceived interests. In exploring and trying to explain the historical roots of the resistances to these attempted behavioural changes we shall also be exploring the question of how the British pattern and institutional structures of management–worker relations have come to be what they are—an issue of no small significance, perhaps, with which to begin a book about management.

The point of the exercise, however, extends beyond trying to understand how we came to be where we are. It covers also the notion that such an understanding may help each of us to make conscious and explicit judgements as to what changes we wish to see pursued, measured against whatever costs would probably be involved in attempting to break down such resistances as are likely to be offered. It encourages, in other words, the formulation of judgements as to whether pursuit of the desired changes is working with, or against, the grain of British society and, if against, what costs would be likely to result from attempts to impose them. The analysis which follows will suggest that the institutional and cultural resistances in Britain to changes in the directions specified are very considerable and that the costs—defined in the widest possible terms—of trying to impose them would be correspondingly high. Such an analysis cannot *determine* policy, for costs are worth paying if the benefits are deemed great enough. Each of us has to judge whether the benefits expected *are* great enough. The inquiry is relevant both for those who aspire to change behaviour within the existing status quo of power, function, and industrial structure, and for those from either the political Left or Right who aspire to transform the status quo itself and who assume that behavioural change would follow. Whether aware of it or not, both groups are making assumptions that call for examination and discussion.

The key propositions underlying the analysis offered here are, first, that much of our social behaviour, especially that which occurs within and around the institutional structures of work, class, and power, is profoundly shaped by the historical development of these structures and, second, that the more deeply rooted the structures in terms of unbroken historical continuity the more resistant they are to change. Both these propositions have been amply attested by historians and theorists from Marx to Schumpeter. 'Social structures, types and attitudes are coins that do not readily melt. Once they are formed they persist, possibly for centuries...' (Schumpeter 1954, p. 12). And one of Marx's formulations includes the obviously necessary point that this does not imply change is impossible, merely that it limits and shapes what change *is* possible. 'Men make their own history, but they do not make it just as they please; they do not make it under circumstances chosen by themselves, but under circumstances directly encountered, given, and transmitted from the past' (Feuer 1969, p. 360). The second proposition receives forceful expression by a leading historian. 'Political and social stability... came quickly to Britain, as they do to most countries that ever achieve them. But once established they acquire immense inertia: tradition, law, education, religion, all conspire to ensure them. It is a salutary thought that no stable society has ever yet altered the fundamentals of its social and political structure without revolution or overwhelming disaster in war...' (Plumb 1967, p. 188).

The analysis may usefully begin, therefore, in the late seventeenth and early eighteenth centuries with the movement towards a political stability that has now lasted for nearly three hundred years. There was already afoot that quickening of trade and industry which was soon to become the self-sustained growth of the industrial revolution. Its impact upon political and social structures cannot be represented, as once it was, as the very model of a bourgeois revolution in which the commercial and industrial middle classes overthrew the power, values, and ideology of a feudal landed aristocracy and substituted their own. 'England had the first, most mediated, and least pure bourgeois revolution of any major European country' (Anderson 1965, p. 13). It is of great significance for the later social shape and texture of British industrialization that certain of the key structural features and values often associated with industrialization were well in evidence in Britain long before. '...what a good deal of recent research shows is that...capitalism and capitalists developed within the rural sector... By the early sixteenth century English agriculture was largely a specialized and market-orientated agriculture...'. The English landowner and capitalist farmer 'experienced a substantial dose of embourgeoisement well before the bourgeoisie existed and before the emergence of the concept, at least as Marx envisaged it...landowners and the landed aristocracy, within a commercialized agricultural sector, led the transformation of England in the eighteenth century' (Neale 1975, pp. 92, 94). Some aspects of the law were adapted to this growing agrarian capitalism, so it was out of the needs of the landowning class, rather than those of a rising bourgeoisie, that there emerged a sophisticated and flexible legal concept of property at least as early as 1700.

Social relations on the land began to change accordingly. '...there was a massive shift away from a feudal and paternalist relationship between landlord and tenant, towards one more exclusively based on the maximization of profits in a market economy.' By the seventeenth century there was no other major country in which these relationships were 'so much governed by the laws of the market place rather than by customary relationships of service, in no other country had private property rights encroached so extensively on the commercial rights of the village...economic developments were dissolving old bonds of service and obligation' (Stone 1972, pp. 68, 71–2). It need hardly be added that these changes extended downward to the relationship between tenant farmer and worker, with the growth of a thriving market in free wage labour. Stone's formulation greatly exaggerates the speed of the change; paternalism as a technique of control remained widespread until the late nineteenth century and even beyond. Nevertheless, the beginnings were visible. They were not confined to agriculture. The emergence of the conception of labour as a commodity, though not yet elevated to the status of a formally acknowledged proposition in received economic doctrine, was already apparent in the widespread 'outworking' industries, such as cloth-making in the south-west counties. Dean Tucker, who had intimate knowledge of it, wrote in 1757 that 'the master...however well disposed himself, is continually tempted by his situation to...consider his people as the scum of the earth, whom he has a right to squeeze whenever he can.... The journeymen on the contrary are equally tempted by their situation to . . . get as much wages and do as little for it as they possibly can, to lie and cheat and do any other bad thing, provided it is only against their master and their common enemy, with whom no faith is to be kept' (George 1953, p. 49).

There had long been a strong thrust of individualism in English life which favoured these developments. Some recent historical opinion—which has not, however, gone unchallenged—traces the origins of English individualism even further back than the received view has hitherto allowed. 'Since at least the thirteenth century England has been a country where the individual has been more important than the group . . .' (Macfarlane 1978, pp. 196–7). Macfarlane uses the term 'individualism' in the sense 'that a central and basic feature of English social structure has for long been the stress on the rights and privileges of the individual as against the wider group or the state . . . . It is the view that society is constituted of autonomous, equal units, namely separate individuals, and that such individuals are more important, ultimately, than any larger constituent group. It is reflected in the concept of individual private property, in the political and legal liberty of the individual, in the idea of the individual's direct communication with God.'

These individualistic impulses not only emerged in those Puritan religious forms which fiercely rejected the notion of an authoritarian ecclesiastical hierarchy mediating between the individual and his God: they also received expression and support in two other major English institutions, Parliament and the common law. Ever since the fourteenth century, lawyers had used the common law on behalf of their well-to-do clients to support the Englishman's 'liberties' against absolutist tendencies by the Crown. Parliament likewise, also of medieval origin, had been fashioned by English country gentlemen—at a cost which included their own blood—into an institution through which they could protect themselves against arbitrary or overweening demands by the Crown. They employed for the purpose a combination of the ability to moderate royal power by keeping it short of tax revenue—English kings never having managed to construct a lasting financial independence—and the cry of 'individual liberties', here, too, supported by the common lawyers. 'Law' and 'liberty' eventually became key concepts for the landed aristocracy, who finally dismissed the Stuarts, provided for the Hanoverian succession, and laid the foundations for our long period of stability. They exploited those concepts to justify and permanently legitimize their oligarchical regime.

Individualistic impulses were emerging also, more assertively than ever before, in economics, in the form of demands that market relations between contracting individuals must be freed from all non-economic bonds, ties, obligations, traditional encumbrances, or claims based on some allegedly transcendent 'higher good'. These pressures of market individualism owed far less, of course, to the inspiration of an ideology—as yet barely formulated—than to the prospect of gain in expanding markets. Adam Smith's integration, however, in the *The Wealth of Nations* (1776) of doctrines that had been in the making for at least a hundred years did rationalize and justify a pattern of values and social relations which as a result gained strength, legitimation, and self-confidence.

Though nowadays fondly quoted by chief executives of multinational corporations whose annual turnover exceeds the gross domestic product of many nation states, Smith's grand defence of market free-enterprise individualism was designed to strengthen the relatively modest-scale entrepreneur against the monopoly privileges of favoured courtiers, chartered companies, and exclusive guilds, as well as against the restricting encumbrances of old statutes, antiquated customs, and traditional institutions. The impartial competitive market must exclude all the familiar and long standing enemies of thrusting, private-enterprise English entrepreneurship—'the whim of tyrannical lords, supersititious priests, despotic monarchs or inefficient bureaucrats...' (Reisman 1976, p. 179). If questions were asked about the implications for the commonweal of this proposed destruction of impediments to free market forces the answer given was, of course, that with certain qualifications the unrestricted pursuit by each individual of enlightened self-interest would further the best interests of all. This implied a theory of the state and of the relationship between the state and the individual. No strong central organization was necessary or desirable for any such purpose as imposing some conception of a transcendent higher good, or even government, in the supposed interests of all. Only certain minimal functions were required of the state, such as maintaining national defence, upholding order, protecting property, and enforcing contracts.

This theory of the minimal state received powerful practical reinforcement as a consequence of being highly compatible with the key preferences of the ruling landed aristocracy. This does not mean that all of Smith's doctrine was agreeable. What little there was in the way of a state apparatus in England was riddled, like the Church, with patronage, sinecures, and inefficiency, all of which Smith wanted swept away. But the concept of the minimal state was theirs also. Determined to limit—though certainly not to de-stroy—kingly power, and to be assured of maintaining ascendancy in their respective localities, they wanted no body of strong royal bureaucrats wielding royal authority up and down the country. Neither did the country gentlemen want a large and powerful standing army or centralized police force which might all too easily come under independent executive control. Some of them had been obliged to turn out and fight bloody battles for their Parliament once, and did not wish to have to do so again. An army there might have to be, but Parliament must have reserve powers of control.

These priorities suggested certain logical implications for the machinery and technique of rule. These implications were for the most part recognized and the English ruling class wielded that technique with considerable skill and finesse, subject always to local blunders and bad judgements. Sometimes they disagreed, in particular situations, about the desirable strategy or tactics, and there was no inevitability that the logical implications of their priorities would in fact be pursued. That on the whole they were so pursued says something about the pragmatic sense with which the ruling class interpreted their longer-term as well as their shorter-term interests.

The implications were of great significance for the future development of British society. If there was to be no royal bureaucracy administering law and regulation in the localities the gentry would have to do it themselves. The alliance of squire and Anglican parson, performing as justices of the peace, ruled the countryside; oligarchical corporations of merchants and other gentry ruled the towns. It was a weak civil power, supported by a relatively meagre military one, and local rule therefore had to be tempered with mercy and caution. 'Principled' agitation, crime, and the slightest whiff of conspiracy against the established order, were met with a bloody penal code and sometimes a remarkable degree of vindictive—because frightened—ferocity. But spontaneous riot-ing, casual disturbance, popular demonstrations, and a robust, unChristian popular culture might meet a surprising degree of leniency and indulgence. Magistrates must, it was felt, do their utmost to preserve order and uphold the Christian decencies, but Whitehall expected them to use their common sense and above all keep within the law. In other words, the price paid by aristocracy and gentry for a limited monarchy, a weak state, and inadequate mechanisms for enforcing order and conventional standards, was the 'licence of the crowd'. And despite the massive multiplication of capital offences there were many pardons, the prerogative of mercy being skilfully used to instil both fear of punishment and gratitude at its withholding (Hay 1977, Thompson 1974 and 1977). It was also considered judicious not to allow those incapable of supporting themselves to starve to death; the indigent were at least kept alive by a subsistence minimum administered by the parish under centuries-old poor law and financed out of a locally levied poor rate.

There was more to the technique of rule, however, than this. If rulers, national or local, felt unconfident of enforcing their will through coercion they might have to compromise, manipulate events to avoid violent confrontations, try to keep the temperature down. Stability might come to seem more important than trying to force through some otherwise desirable innovation. It came to seem important, too, to distinguish between opinion and action. Empirical common sense suggested to influential members of the ruling class that freedom of opinion for themselves could not easily be preserved unless it was also allowed to others, and that this must be endured unless and until subversive opinion resulted in subversive behaviour. The ruling-class boast of law and liberty reinforced such dispositions.

Yet opinion and action could not always be separated. Law and liberty proved to be double-edged notions with practical consequences for the ruling class which, while not necessarily subversive, could prove inconvenient and disagreeable. Precisely because in eighteenth-century England the rule of law was of massive importance as ideology and as legitimation of the regime, its principles and logic sometimes had to be upheld in ways which limited the regime's power. While in general it advanced the interests of property and the economic exploitation of the weak by the strong, there were occasions when its principles of equity and universality had to be extended to all sorts and degrees of men if the ideological appeal to the majestic impartiality of the law was to remain convincing. Not only

... were the rulers (indeed the ruling class as a whole), inhibited by their own rules of law against the exercise of direct unmediated force (arbitrary imprisonment, the employment of troops against the crowd, torture, and those other conveniences of power with which we are all conversant), but they also believed enough in those rules, and in their accompanying ideological rhetoric, to allow, in certain limited areas, the law itself to be a genuine forum within which certain kinds of class conflict were fought out. (Thompson 1977, p. 265.)

The issue of political liberty was bound up in the same argument. Many members of the gentry had assimilated lessons from their fathers, whose varied struggles during the preceding century had necessitated appeals to the ancient liberties of the 'free-born Englishman'. If such notions were to be suppressed in the interests of the regime's security against political challenge or subversion, the suppression would have to be embodied in law; a situation under which the ruling classes themselves would shift very uneasily for fear of what this might mean for them, too, at some future date. This fear, of course, faded as they settled ever more firmly in the saddle. Yet certain institutional expressions of it lingered long. The system of purchasing army commissions and promotions, for example, designed originally to retain control within the amateur hands of the aristocratic wealthy and prevent the re-emergence of an independent-spirited professional force (as in the 1640s and 50s) was not abolished until 1871. But long before that the system which the ruling class had fashioned seemed to offer great usefulness in its own right. Given the particular nature of Britain's social structure and institutions, the technique of rule that had emerged was demonstrably maintaining a degree of social cohesion that was at least adequate to protect wealth, status, and privilege, and even to accommodate marginal shifts of power within the ruling class. Resting upon this pragmatic acquiescence on the part of the interests, the system lent itself to an ideological glorification in terms of liberty which came to have a certain measure of genuine and independent force at all levels of society.

The longer the system lasted, the more nervous ruling-class leaders became of overtly disrupting it by publicly riding roughshod over principles of law and liberty. Yet these principles could be used to propagate ideas that were distinctly threatening. If the law could be stretched to ensnare the propagators the answer was obvious, but it was not always possible or even expedient. There was only one period, between 1790 and the 1820s, when the English ruling class, badly frightened by the French Revolution, came near to abandoning its own legitimations. But although law and liberty were severely dented, they held. Doctrines therefore spread which were destined to lead to marginal limitations on class power and to the extraction of concessions. Had the maintenance of due process of law and of a degree of political freedom unique in Europe really threatened to destroy the power and privilege of the ruling order they would have been sacrificed—though the decision would probably have been reluctant and anguished. But the history of political freedom in Britain is a history of the admission into the political nation of new claimant groups who showed clear signs of being prepared to operate within the existing structures in the pursuit not of revolutionary transformation but of piecemeal reform. It was a technique of rule which had its risks. A long way short of revolutionary transformation, particular groups within the ruling order might, in this open political system, have their corns trodden on—or worse. But from the point of view of the dominant groups, much was being conserved by this strategy.

The texture and temper of these English structures and dispositions were fully expressed in the dominant political and moral philosophies which emerged throughout the period. 'The individualism of all social theory between Locke and John Stuart Mill depended less on logic than on its agreement with the interests of the class that mainly produced it' (Sabine 1963, p. 531). In Locke's theory, for example, both government and society exist to preserve the individual's rights. Individual self-interest appears in his constructions as clear and compelling; the public or social interest as thin and insubstantial. Later the Utilitarianism of the early nineteenth century 'continued Locke's spirit of cautious but radical reform. Its programme continued the same idealization of individual rights, the same belief in liberalism as a panacea for political ills, the same tenderness for the rights of property, and the same conviction that public interests must be conceived in terms of private well-being' (Sabine 1963, p. 540).

Yet in describing the English governing class's technique of rule it is not enough to stress the pursuit of narrowly private interests to the total exclusion of wider perspectives. Admittedly there was little in the empirical, common-sense texture of English institutions and culture to encourage grand metaphysical theorizing about transcendent state purposes to which individuals must submit in a realization of their 'real' selves. This sort of thing, which left many English readers baffled as well as irritated, was left to the Germans. Yet the technique of rule needed some spirit of obligation if it was to work. The institutions of a limited monarchy needed aristocrats and gentry to man the Lords and the Commons, conducting the king's government but containing him at the same time. Gentry-rule in the localities needed squires and parsons to discharge the unpaid functions of the bench of magistrates. There were, of course, fat pickings for some at the higher levels of this structure, in terms of patronage, place, and sinecure. It was Walpole's skill in handling such sanctions that contributed greatly to the stability which, the longer it persisted, made men increasingly hesitant to put at risk a system which had demonstrably succeeded in preserving their property and status. Yet there were not sufficiently attractive pickings for everyone, and a significant number of the country gentlemen disdained even to pursue them (Namier 1957, pp. 4–6). Something more was needed. If aristocracy and gentry were to govern themselves and the country, they had to keep each other up to the mark in terms of active participation. Building on old traditions of service due from those holding land under the king, they sought to promote among themselves a sense of the public responsibilities bearing upon men of status and property, especially landed property. The ethic passed from existing members of the ruling class to new entrants, and from fathers to sons. Gladstone provides an example of both processes. Son of a merchant and slave-owner (who was later knighted), he married a baronet's sister, inherited a considerable estate, and later admonished his elder son as to the responsibilities which must be accepted along with it. 'Nowhere in the world is the position of the landed proprietor so high as in this country, and this in great part for the reason that nowhere else is the possession of landed property so closely associated with definite duty' (Morley 1908, p. 256).

The imputed role of the public schools was to inculcate these obligations in the young. 'It is in her public schools and universities', declared Canning in the early nineteenth century, 'that the youth of England are, by a discipline which shallow judgements have sometimes attempted to undervalue, prepared for the duties of public life' (Morley 1908, p. 20). His picture flattered the schools of the early decades, but became more appropriate after the reforms and new foundations of the mid-century.

Already, therefore, there were crystallizing out, in forms which were to prove long-lasting, certain features of central importance for the subsequent nature of British politics, industrialism, management, and industrial relations. There was widening freedom for private, individual, and competitive enterprise in commerce, finance, and industry. This, along with the movement towards free trade, represented a triumph of economic liberalism unequalled in any other country in Europe. But it was not a triumph only of the 'rising middle classes'. Some landed proprietors had long diversified into City finance, commerce, and industry. Others, of course, had not, and the 'landed interest' in its more restricted sense, with its protectionist corn laws and game laws, remained immensely powerful. But there was certainly a blurring of interests; in no other country 'were the landed classes so extensively involved in investments in overseas trade and settlement.... In few or none were the great landowners more actively engaged in exploiting the mineral resources of their land [coal and iron] or in developing their urban properties' (Stone 1972, p. 71). They, too, were interested in maximizing economic opportunities for the expanding sectors of the economy. In fact, as we have already noted, their adoption of capitalist modes and motivations long pre-dated the rise of an industrial bourgeoisie. '*There was thus from the start no fundamental, antagonistic contradiction between the old aristocracy and the new bourgeoisie.* English capitalism embraced and included both' (Anderson 1965, p. 18, his italics).

The ruling-class preference for the minimal state had now become vested with ideological legitimation by the new 'political economy', which defined it as a requisite for full economic rationality. This suited very well the employers of the growing industrialism. Obsolescent statutes upholding apprenticeship traditions and giving JPs powers to fix local wage rates had acquired nuisance value in the hands of craft groups as a basis for agitation against their employers, and were swept away. But even more significant was the enthronement by the new doctrines of a conception of labour that in practical terms had been making its way for a very long time. It was the conception of labour as a commodity to be bought and sold like any other, with no obligations attaching to the hirer other than those dictated by the strict terms of the market. As far as contractual relations in the labour market were concerned, the individual must look to himself. Duly reinforced by popularized versions of Malthus, the rising doctrine held that in market relations the rich could carry no responsibility for the poor. Few entrepreneurs read Adam Smith and Malthus. Even of those who did, some, like Robert Owen, disagreed and pursued a paternalist strategy, seeing this as a more efficient and profitable long-term system of labour control. This 'strong', as against 'weak', sense of paternalism involved a comprehensive and rigorously autocratic control over the employee's work and life, mitigated by a degree of professed concern for his welfare—which he was assumed to be incapable of judging for himself. Many employers in the expanding industries, however, found very agreeable the vulgarized versions of the new political economy that confronted them in the public prints, pamphlets, and meetings. Economically the worker was atomistically alone in the market; if he could not survive it was to the poor law of the political community that he must turn, not his employer. The new enterprise was not a politico-economic unit as the medieval guild had been; it was an economic enterprise *tout court* (Dore 1973, p. 409). Non-economic bonds, ties, and obligations were defined as irrelevant to the employment relationship. The separation of economics and ethics was doctrinally enthroned.

The nature of the predominant values and relations in the wider society was of obvious moment for the new generations of employers in the growing industrial and commercial sectors. Whether or not they were consciously aware of having to make a choice, they were being obliged to decide what the nature and texture of relations were to be between themselves and their workers. One model was especially prominent. Paternalism might still be visible in the rural economy, but the model which they observed in the great outworking industries around them; which had been increasingly propagated over a period as the proper and inevitable one; which had received theoretical justification in the widely circulated tracts of political economy; and which had been publicly supported in speech and print by prominent government leaders—Pitt, Burke, Shelburne—was that of competitive market individualism and the treatment of labour as a commodity, an ideology 'already deeply entrenched in Britain *before* industrialization began' (Dore 1973, p. 408).

But alongside the widening economic scope for this pattern of employment relations there existed a degree of opportunity for protest by those who suffered from its consequences. Half unwittingly, and with many doubts and much cruelty, Britain's ruling class stumbled towards the acceptance of movements and institutions which provided wage-earners with safety-valves that were eventually to have the effect of preserving, though with important modifications, the status quo. Protest movements, organized agitations, trade unions, and political groupings began to yield, over the decades, enough relief to give the lower orders some kind of stake in the system. It was an uneven and hazardous development. Between 1799 and 1824, for example, there existed legislation, capriciously and uncertainly applied, which tried unsuccessfully to suppress trade unionism—the 1799 Act seeking to universalize a prohibition which, by separate statutes, had been applied piecemeal over the years to about forty trades.

Yet even here an amending statute of 1800 manifested an interesting—and significant—anxiety to maintain the appearance of state impartiality by decreeing against combinations of employers as well as of workers. In practice, of course, only the latter came under attack, but eventually ruling-class leaders were brought up against the same dilemma that constantly confronted them as a consequence of their chosen technique of rule. Home Office papers reveal that many employers and magistrates, for a variety of reasons—including nervousness about reprisals or the longer-term effect on relations at the workplace—showed a marked lack of enthusiasm about initiating prosecutions and urged government ministers to take the onus upon themselves. The law officers of the Crown, invited in 1804 to comment, advised ministers that they would thereby render themselves vulnerable to pressure from workers' leaders and radicals to initiate prosecutions against combinations of *employers* also. Since this was plainly out of the question, the government would lay itself open to being publicly attacked as legally discriminating between rich and poor. Even at this early date it was a charge which British governments preferred, other things being equal, to avoid. Forced to choose between, on the one hand, drawing back from too vigorous and obvious a stance of discriminative repression against working-class movements and, on the other hand, sacrificing the legitimations and ideology of their regime, strengthening the state's coercive powers, and abandoning all pretence of being other than instruments of pure class domination, ministers chose the former course. Despite some local savagery and many other ventures into legislative repression during this period, governments could plead that these were directed only against subversion, sedition, and conspiracy, and there is indeed evidence that ministers had no interest in pulling employers' chestnuts out of the fire purely on issues of trade disputes (Aspinall 1949).

This example was no isolated one. There can be traced in all the major relevant events of the century—repeal of the Combination Acts, the 'Tolpuddle Martyrs', Chartism, the 1867 Reform Act, the trade union legislation of the 1870s—a similar state concern to mitigate a gross class bias with the outward decencies of the law, liberty, and procedural equality; to avoid bidding up the stakes in confrontations with protest movements; and to minimize by such means the need to resort to force. It would be an over-simplifying reductionism to suppose that these ruling-class predilections derived solely from calculated expediency. A class cannot continue for a century or two to voice a set of political principles without at least some of its members coming to believe in those principles for their own sake, just as many lawyers had come to believe in the rule of law for its own sake.

This was one reason why the protest movements of the first half of the nineteenth century, generated among substantial sections of the working classes in reaction to the gathering tempo of a harsh industrialism, were never goaded into large-scale violence. And after the middle of the century, craftsmen, factory operatives, and miners found that within the British social context they were increasingly securing a measure of control over their own destinies through unilateral job control or collective bargaining, and through constitutional political agitation—the latter especially after the male urban householder workman secured the vote in 1867.

There had always been, among the craft occupations, some groups which managed to maintain a relatively privileged position. Historically the crafts were linked with the pre-capitalist guilds, legalized closed shops whose most potent economic function was to control entry into the craft or 'mystery' and thereby preserve a local monopoly. Their key method was the enforcement of apprenticeship restrictions, supplemented by an array of workshop customs and practices also designed to uphold craft privileges by excluding the unapprenticed 'interloper'. Holding their charters from the Crown, guild leaders could uphold their by-laws in the courts—often their own. During the sixteenth and seventeenth centuries the gathering tempo of economic activity gradually broke down these restrictive frameworks. Given the continuing Tudor concern for social stability and regulation, however, an attempt was made in a statute of 1563 to uphold the apprenticeship regulations which the guilds themselves were less able to enforce. But the forces of economic growth and competition now developed a powerful ally in the individualistic thrust of the common law, whose practitioners, beginning in 1599, refused in a succession of cases to uphold guild and statutory restrictions on the grounds that they were 'against the liberty and freedom of the subject' and against the well-being of the commonwealth. Some of the guilds lingered long and tenaciously, but most fell into decay. Sometimes the defences of the journeymen craftsmen decayed with them, but there were many groups who managed to keep alive the traditions of pre-capitalist, medieval, corporate control. As guild and statutory supports failed them, journeymen craftsmen formed 'trade societies' to preserve and enforce the old regulations—and often to invent new ones as they went along. These eventually became the craft unions of the modern period. The very terminology of 'illegal men', i.e. interlopers who had not served the statutory apprenticeship, survived until the late nineteenth century. But what proved of immense significance was that the strategy and spirit of restrictionism, demarcations and manning levels, did not remain limited to the craft trades. They were taken up by organized workers in industries and in services, and by white-collar occupations which had never known craft organization and tradition. They remain today alive and well. Given the nature of their origins in the 'direct democracy' of local trade clubs among journeymen craftsmen, it would be a mistake to see them as trade union constructs introduced into the workplace from the outside. Union organization brought strength and confidence, but the shop-floor culture itself could often spontaneously generate a restrictionist style of rich protective ingenuity.

Kahn-Freund has two crucial things to say of this 'Bastille of customs, institutions, rules whose spirit was and is as far away from that of capitalist market economics as from that of the Marxist class struggle'. First, it is but one institutional expression of a legacy of demarcation and restrictionism that is widespread throughout the whole structure of Britain's professional and commercial activities. And second, it is 'when we come to the control and limitation of labour supply in a labour market that we are confronted with what I consider, next to direct democracy, to be the most characteristically British feature of our industrial relations . . .. The important thing is to see restrictive labour practices as part of a general pattern of attitudes especially characteristic of British society.' Here he saw 'a fundamental contrast between the historical background of trade unionism in this country and on the Continent . . .'. The 'tradition which originated in craft rules and institutions does not in Continental countries play the dominant role it does here' (Kahn-Freund 1979, pp. 32–62). These survivals of a deeply rooted pre-capitalist guild spirit were only possible in 'a society not separated from its medieval past by a social revolution . . .'. They illustrate further the central significance of peaceful historical continuities for our present institutions and their habituated modes of perception and behaviour.

They are evidence, too, of the very considerable advantages that were enjoyed by the better-placed traditional crafts. Tradition was a threefold asset: it provided defined objectives sanctified by time; it inspired the self-confidence to pursue them; and it offered practical issues on which the craftsmen could get a purchase in their resistance to the employers. But the fact that the craft tradition was strongly suffused with a determination to maintain a privileged status and assert a separateness from the rest of the working class is also important. It is one of the reasons why the pattern of their political activities never mirrored the confrontation of economic interests that often prevailed at the workplace, with its hard-edged contractualism and its culture of limited commitment on the part of both sides towards each other. Before the point is pursued, something needs to be said of this culture. It was shaping more and more of the industrial work-force, as it had been slowly doing for a long time. The trade unionism that grew out of it—and which articulated and fostered it—was forced to adopt the same stance that had long been imposed by many employers, by governments, and by established ideologies, a stance which treated the worker as a contracting agent in a purely economic relationship which involved no obligations beyond the 'cash nexus'. The result was the 'us and them' syndrome; a posture of wary mutual inspection by two parties who did not constitute a 'works community' in the sense hoped for by many employers and observers but who, rather, pursued a zero-sum game within an essentially adversary relationship.

Of course, any attempt to characterize the dominant features of a social system or subsystem must inevitably appear to overlook a host of nuances. Even in some industrialized sectors, bitter conflict over the labour contract was not incompatible with *ex gratia* gestures by employers which went beyond the contract. Workers could feel some sense of 'works community' even though it might coexist with a disposition of cynical wariness towards the employer and his managers. The general picture, nevertheless, is supported by foreign as well as domestic observers. The term 'adversary relationship' must not, however, be misunderstood. It did not necessarily imply the two parties being constantly at each other's throats. Mill characterized it in 1845 as the absence of any 'sense of co-operation and common interest'; a situation 'of hostile rivals whose gain is each other's loss'; a '*sourde* animosity which is universal in this country towards the whole class of employers, in the whole class of the employed' (Williams 1976, pp. 291–3). Its social and political implications aroused alarm in certain sections of middle- and upper-class society during the 1840s as they began to realize just how English society was developing. There were widespread lamentations at the passing of authoritarian paternalism and even some action directed towards reversing the process. But there never developed a 'critical mass' which could make any impact on the system as a whole (Dore 1973, p. 405). Of a somewhat different kind were the paternalist policies adopted after the mid-century by, for example, larger employers in some Lancashire cotton towns and by coal and iron masters in north-East England and South Wales (Joyce 1980). For the most part this represented the 'weak' sense of paternalism inasmuch as, except in South Wales, it was often accompanied by employer acceptance of trade unionism and collective bargaining. Britain's employers were pursuing a long drawn out process of submitting to the idea that, given strong traditions of spirited independent labour protest and an unfavourable social context for the strong version of paternalism, they would do better to try to work with the unions than attempt to destroy them. And given the strength in Britain of market contractualism and traditions of self-protective restrictionism by office holders, professionals, and craft groups, it is not surprising that collective bargaining and collective behaviour at the workplace took on these colorations. During the twentieth century they have been instrumental, along with other factors such as the decline of the family firm, in crowding out industrial paternalism, strong and weak, from the British scene and strengthening a pattern of arm's-length, zero-sum relations. This prevalent posture became, for all practical purposes, irreversible. It was a posture which, since it was marked on the employer's side by an assertion of his own perceived interests to the exclusion of wider obligations, was bound to evoke from the workers precisely the same dispositions. In practical terms this meant that where they perceived their best interests in terms of restrictions on the employer's freedom with respect to hiring, firing, and work organization, they mounted such obstructionism without hesitation if they could. Nothing in the culture surrounding them convinced them that there was some 'higher social good' to which they should abnegate themselves; this was not part of the English individualist tradition.

Yet the political activities of union leaders and activists did not necessarily mirror this workplace pattern of relations. Certainly there were issues which could drive as sharp a wedge between working and middle classes in the political as in the workplace arena, such as the limitation of working hours, or legal support for trade unions. And with the re-emergence of socialism in the latter decades of the century there came to be more—though not decisively more—activists who linked their experience of exploitive power relations in the workplace with a critique of exploitive power relations in society at large. But during the third quarter the most publicly assertive and influential union leadership was prepared, under the guidance of a group of Positivist intellectuals, to fight hard political battles for the legal emancipation of their unions while at the same time giving passionate support to sections of the manufacturing middle class on other political issues. These included Free Trade, Temperance Reform, extension of the franchise, the rights of Nonconformity, and resentment against aristocratic and episcopate privilege and arrogance. As this list implies, there was sometimes a religious identity between Nonconformist manufacturer and craftsman which provided a vertical bond as a basis, too, for shared social and political interests. There were echoes here of seventeenth-century alignments which could bring the smaller manufacturer and the artisan, fiercely at odds on their economic interests, into an alliance against aristocratic and episcopal domination.

Thus were forged political links between sections of the manufacturing class, led by men like John Bright, and the higher levels of the working classes, often the unionized sections, led by men like Robert Applegarth of the Amalgamated Society of Carpenters. Considerable numbers of the enfranchised working class thus became part of the uneasy coalition that was the Liberal Party, which included among its banners many of those favoured by the manufacturing and commercial middle classes. The Liberal Party was, of course, to undergo crucial changes and eventual decline, with industrialists moving over to the Conservative Party, but its commitment to constitutionalism and to a gradually widening conception of state-promoted welfare was inherited, along with some of its professional middle-class members, by the Labour Party. This transition—rendered more complex than it sounds by strong but never decisive thrusts from socialist groupings within the labour movement—was thus made possible in the first instance by a largely fortuitous combination of circumstances. A relatively favoured labour aristocracy emerging to leadership during a quarter-century of considerable but unplanned prosperity, took advantage of the governing class's technique of rule to secure certain industrial and political emancipations which have proved decisive. Because these pragmatic strategies demonstrably produced tangible results they eventually, though not without minority forays towards more turbulent strategies, drew into their ambit of ordered peaceful procedure the later unions of the semi- and unskilled, along with the political party which the unions between them created. As time wore on, the leaders of the organized working class came to feel, as had the equally pragmatic leaders of the ruling order, that they had a considerable investment in the growing system of procedures, control structures, and organizational hierarchies. Leaders, officials, and activists developed powerful vested interests in the well-being and growth of orderly bargaining systems and political constitutionalisms which afforded them not only opportunities for pursuing their principles and beliefs, but also the gratifications of power, status, and career prospects. Unless major sections of the rank and file experienced acute and prolonged frustration of their hopes and aspirations, the inertia of the system was likely to prevail.

But as already noted, the working-class acceptance of political liberalism by no means implied working-class acceptance of economic liberalism at the workplace. Acceptance of middle-class leadership or alliances in politics by no means implied acceptance of middle-class leadership and alliances in the work situation. Trade union leaders, activists, and members who adhered to a vertical class-bonding on Free Trade and Temperance Reform adhered just as tenaciously to a horizontal class-bonding on wages, working hours, and all management innovation which threatened earnings, jobs, status, and union strength. Thus developed a combination that has baffled and misled many observers of the British scene, domestic and foreign, to this day. An organized working class that was prepared to accept the leadership of the employing class in many matters political was yet capable of fighting the same class at the workplace level with remarkable solidarity and tenacity. And the restrictionist tenor of much of this resistance had been notable since the very beginnings of collective action at the workplace.

We now have some clues with which to attempt an answer to an important question. Why was it that, when Britain's industrial position began to come under threatening challenge after the 1870s, there was no concerted action by state and employers to crush these shop-floor pretensions to job control? Why was there not in Britain, once seen as the very model of bourgeois industrialism, that second bourgeois revolution which would sweep away restrictionism with a wholesale programme of modernization? Such a programme might have included official state encouragement of employers to enforce an unfettered prerogative in their pursuit of innovation and expansion, and official state support through legislation in cases where employers were obstructed by worker resistance. It might have included, too, direct state initiative in the promotion and support of new strategic industries, and in the fostering of a high-status technology-conscious education and an enterprise-conscious culture. A further feature could have been pursuit of a meritocracy by the industrial and commercial bourgeoisie, taking the form of an attack upon all the surviving traditional hierarchies and institutions which cherished privilege, conservatism, and status inequalities— long recognized as potent obstacles to enterprise, though still spared even today by Labour as well as Conservative governments.

Particular groups of employers did, of course, try their hand at subduing restrictive craft regulations—in engineering, building, printing, and footwear, for example. Only in the last-named was there any significant success. Employers soon had to learn that in this sort of struggle they were on their own. Government ministers might occasionally make encouraging noises, but there was no central state support of a practical kind. The application of Britain's class-biased law could handicap the trade union movement but it could not destroy it. Even more certainly, British governments would not go beyond the law for such a purpose; indeed, with the enlarging franchise the party competition for votes gradually brought the unions greater safety from the law, not less. Several groups of employers learned the hard way that if they engaged organized labour in a knock-down, drag-out battle, government agencies might intervene with bland offers of conciliation or arbitration, and politicians might bustle about hoping to impress the country with their capacity to promote industrial peace, but nothing more was likely to be forthcoming.

There were, of course, periods when the class nature of the state was asserted more overtly and crudely against organized labour than at others; the period 1919–22 being one such. Lloyd George and Churchill, on a number of occasions, wielded the iron fist. But this was not in pursuit of modernization, but simply to settle large-scale disputes and, it was hoped, daunt potential revolutionaries with demonstrations of the power they faced. Even then the velvet glove was not wholly absent: a recent judgement is that 'in general neither side wanted a class war' and 'conciliation and diplomatic guile were more in accord with Lloyd George's typical approach' (Morgan 1978, pp. 82–3). And among the architects of Lloyd George's downfall was Baldwin who, during the inter-war period, was *par excellence* the exponent of the technique of rule described in this essay.

Part of the explanation of this lack of support from the state for a wholesale attack on restrictionism is therefore already apparent. Ideologically, the British political system leaned heavily for legitimation upon freedom of speech and association, the rule of law, and the claim of governments to be 'national' governments ruling even-handedly between the classes. And in the practical political arena electoral considerations became increasingly important with the extension of the franchise. Even more to the point, by the end of the nineteenth century the trade union movement was sufficiently strong to ensure that it could only be decisively cowed by a massive coercive effort on the part of an authoritarian state. Such a total transformation of the British political system was now inconceivable on such an issue, there being ample evidence that major sections even of middle-class opinion would not have supported it. The liberal ethos was now too closely bound up with the beliefs of a large and articulate professional middle class which could always be relied on to criticize and moralize about the lower classes, but not to smash their organizations.

In any case, opinion within other sections of the ruling classes on the subject of trade unionism was itself far from unanimous. For all the club and dinner-table talk of 'union agitators' there were many influential voices which, given the inevitable restiveness of labour in an industrial Britain with its variable fortunes, cyclical fluctuations, and independent shop-floor spirit, saw the unions as useful instruments of labour regulation and control. At any given time there were always important groups of employers prepared to agree.

But in explaining the absence of any sustained ruling-class thrust to destroy restrictionism and promote dynamic enterprise there must also be some attention given both to entrepreneurial motivation and to dominant British conceptions of the role of the state. Judgements have been offered on the former issue which seek to explain past and present managerial dispositions by reference to their position within the whole development of British capitalism and the impact on its nature of the Victorian and Edwardian public schools. For present purposes the key feature of that context was the way in which British capitalism embraced both aristocracy and middle class. Partly as a consequence, the new public schools reared successive generations of the middle and upper classes in a code which represented a blend of values from both. 'They took the fees of the textile magnate and the lawyer, and in return they exposed their sons to the full public service traditions of the aristocrat and the country squire... the public school bias that preferred government service to private profit-making was all part and parcel of a gentleman ideal.' This meant, not that no public school men went into industry, but that those who went took with them values and behaviour habits which stressed 'moderation, compromise, and self-restraint'; which 'seemed best suited to a minimal concept of government'; which 'saw the ruler as guardian rather than innovator'; and which encouraged the need 'to keep order rather than initiate major new schemes'. When 'new forces arose to threaten the old order ... the prevailing instinct of British leadership was to accommodate and contain rather than suppress' (Wilkinson 1964, pp. 4, 62). The same theme and its consequences have been pursued by many; there is only space here to quote Plumb on the eighteenth century. 'The power of the land and of commerce fused to create a paradise for gentlemen, for the aristocracy of birth; it thus became much easier for England to adopt an imperial authority, to rule alien peoples, and to train its ruling class for that purpose, rather than to adjust its institutions and its social system to the needs of an industrial society' (Plumb 1967, p. 187). The imprint, it is claimed, has persisted, with implications for the low value placed on scientific and technical training; on the businessman's status; on the organizational exploitation of innovation—and on the kind of entrepreneurial ruthlessness that would have been necessary for a sustained attack on shop-floor restrictionism. The argument assumes, of course, a process far more complex and subtle than direct influence within industry by those who applied the traditional ruling-class technique of rule. It assumes a thousand-and-one external influences, cues, pressures, and constraints bearing upon industry from the surrounding traditions, culture, and institutions, including those of government. The whole discussion has recently been located within a comprehensive survey of Britain's strong and pervasive 'anti-enterprise' culture which is said to derive from the rural aristocratic imprint and which is seen as blunting the energetic pursuit of industrial innovation, expansion, and profit (Wiener 1981).

The nature of the British political system and dominant conceptions of the role of the state did nothing to counteract these tendencies; indeed they afforded them free rein. British governments and state agencies worked to no model of a strong active state stimulating and mobilizing industrial strength for the enhancement of national power and glory. They moved mostly in response to pressures from organized interests, reformist groups, and opinion lobbies. Attempts at masterful, dynamic state leadership in a society where individualism and instrumental collectivism were rife, and where cultures and sub-cultures gave little support to conceptions of a 'higher national good', were more likely to split parties than rally a mass following. Britain had a long way to go to universal suffrage, but by the mid-1880s both the urban and the rural householder had the vote.

Organized interests mattered, and governments which preferred on the whole to conserve by concession rather than by overt coercion might well choose to heed them. In the late nineteenth century, governments provided the unions with legal status and protections, while a state agency encouraged employers to partici-pate in the conciliatory compromise procedures of collective bargaining. There is a connection here with the idea of service. The late nineteenth-century products of the public schools and Oxford —especially Jowett's Balliol—included some who were fired to dedicate themselves to service in a wider sense than hitherto. Whether at home or overseas—where it fostered a certain style of imperialist rule—it could be expressed in something more than a concern for the Queen's government, national security, law and order, and the public weal. It could include acceptance of responsibility for improving the condition of the lower orders. There was a marked streak of paternalism in such a stance. But infused with the more expansive definition of liberalism now developing it could also include the strong encouragement of collective efforts by working men to improve their lot by 'sober' and 'responsible' self-help within the framework of a humane constitutionalism. Toynbee Hall; Oxford House; the London Ethical Society; the Fabian Society—these were elements in a reformer's universe which had influential links with Westmin-ster and Whitehall and which helped to shape state policy towards trade unionism and collective bargaining. Men like Llewellyn Smith went from this background into the Labour Department of the Board of Trade—perhaps the only government office before 1914 to have 'a departmental opinion' (Middlemas 1979, p. 31)—where they worked quietly but consistently to encourage employers to enter into collective bargaining and to accept conciliatory and arbitrationist intervention by respected public persons manifestly anxious, according to their lights, 'to do justice to both sides'. By virtue of its accumulating expertise and collectivist momentum the department came to outweigh both the Home Office and the Local Government Board as the source of official industrial relations policy (Middlemas 1979, p. 59).

There was, accordingly, no state support for authoritarian rule and unqualified managerial prerogative in industry. There was even to appear soon a statutory acknowledgement that labour had a *right* to the restrictive practices that often extended far back in industrial history. Yielded up during the First World War to facilitate speedier armaments production, they were duly restored by legislation when fighting ended, with financial penalties for employers who resisted. It was an indication that there was no stomach for what would have been a massive battle had the government attempted to maintain a restriction-free industry.

Through the great expansion of collective bargaining and the unions' penetration into an elaborate network of administrative, welfare, and cultural activities—greatly reinforced by war—the movement gradually became intertwined with a multiplicity of institutions, national and local. Unions and employers' associations became elevated to 'a new sort of status; from interest groups they became "governing institutions"'. The state, increasingly drawn to intervene in industrial and commercial affairs, was only too ready 'to admit representative bodies to its orbit rather than face a free-for-all with a host of individual claimants'. Britain developed 'its own distinctive form of triangular collaboration in the industrial sphere between government, trade unions and the business class . . .'. Earlier hopes, however, that this could be taken to the lengths of corporatist deals conveniently arranged at top level were soon disappointed; neither the unions nor the employers' associations were in a position to whip their members into line if a sufficient number objected. Nevertheless a subtle and flexible form of corporate interchange continued to develop (Middlemas 1979, pp. 20, 123, 209).

The process of assimilation was fostered by the unions' commitment to a rigorously constitutional reformist Labour Party trading on the proven fact that constitutionalism could secure genuine, if limited, gains. The total effect, duly given the necessary encouragements by predominant groups within the old ruling order, was to encapsulate unions and party within the framework that had been fashioned piecemeal, through trial and error, by that same ruling order—a framework of peaceful procedure, compromise, and flexible adjustment to marginal shifts in the power structure. This process was perfectly acceptable to most of the leaders of both industrial and political wings of the labour movement. As we have seen, besides offering real, if limited, practical achievement, it also offered organizational power, careers, and status for those in the numerous trade union and political hierarchies that grew in this context of official acceptance, legal security, and institutional opportunity.

For those concerned with the interests of property, status, and power among the upper classes there were enormous benefits from these developments. With some luck but also good judgement, the old ruling order had contained the rising forces of industrialism and democracy and brought them into systems of conflict resolution which, at the expense of some concessions, left the fundamentals of the social order in recognizable shape. This was for them a remarkable achievement, but it was not an achievement without cost. Among the costs was the fact that the encapsulation of the unions was an encapsulation of the unions as they were, not as the ruling order would have liked them to be. And it had long been apparent that the unions had been shaped by the interaction between, on the one hand, the impersonal contractualism, market individualism, and *laissez-faire* conceptions fostered by the ruling order itself and, on the other hand, the direct democracy and restrictionist strategies of a craft tradition with deep roots in a pre-capitalist self-governing past—strategies that were already spreading far beyond their points of origin. They were the response of a working class within which there existed, alongside the unconfident and in some respects deferential dispositions of a subordinated class, a robust class culture, a certain class pride, and a certain capacity for spirited independence and solidary action. Brought to bear upon the industrial order imposed on them, these class characteristics had resulted, as we have seen, in the widespread incidence at the workplace of adversary relationships marked by a restrictionist spirit, rejection of management leadership, and the zero-sum game of arm's-length bargaining. As against the conception of a 'works community' towards whose total product all constituent groups were supposed to contribute freely and constructively in order that all might derive increasing benefit, there was more likely to be the conception—varyingly diluted by less-abrasive sentiments—that what benefited management must be the workers' loss, and vice versa.

These were the long-habituated, deeply rooted dispositions that gradually became built into the social order. They could be destroyed, if at all, only at the cost of destroying the whole political and constitutional settlement painfully and slowly worked out and built up since the 1870s—indeed, in one sense, since the late seventeenth century. The implications are obvious for a managerial class that could hardly avoid being influenced by a centuries-old technique and culture of rule which emphasized stability at the expense of innovation, and compromise at the expense of confrontation. Those implications have their place among the diverse causes of Britain's relative economic decline over the past century. They are expressed by a familiar set of terms frequently invoked to describe the British condition. These terms include: 'inefficient', 'backward looking', 'class-ridden', 'complacent', and 'insular'. But if the preceding analysis is sound it could support an argument that these are the 'defects' of British society's 'qualities'. For there is another set of terms that appears almost as often. It includes: 'moderate', 'orderly', 'decent', peaceful and tolerant', and 'constitutional' (Nairn 1977, pp. 44–5). The British have to brace themselves for the probability that these two sets of terms are opposite sides of the same coin.

Whatever these characteristics of Britain's political and industrial relations systems may have contributed to the creation of her present economic predicament, it can hardly be denied that they have significantly handicapped extrication from it. Responses to the first of the hoped-for changes itemized at an early stage of this essay have not been encouraging to those seeking them. The hope of seeing organized labour enter into co-operation with management in pursuit of greater efficiency, innovation, and output can hardly be said to have been realized. When every allowance has been made for the Establishment itch to cast organized labour as the scapegoat, as well as for Fleet Street's relentless trivialization and peddling of popular clichés, a clear and academically verified picture remains of many managers who venture innovations and improvements being frustrated by 'restrictive practices, frequent strikes, and obstruction to change' (Pratten 1976, p. 57). And there seems no reason to doubt that others have been daunted even from venturing. An appraisal of this effect is inseparable, however, from an appraisal of managerial motivations and priorities. Here, too, on our second issue, change is not conspicuous. British management does not appear to have raised the general level of its entrepreneurial dynamic. The consensus appears to remain what it has long been: that while there is a managerial vanguard which compares, in entrepreneurial zeal and thrust, with the vanguard anywhere, there is a long and undistinguished tail. The complaint persists that not enough of

Britain's best talent goes into business management, preferring the Civil Service, academic life, and the other professions, or banking and the City. Recent opinion has it that despite the resources directed to management education and training since the war 'there is no recognizable evidence of an improvement in standards of management in the UK; indeed the evidence is mainly of deterioration (Snaith 1981).

The relevance of management priorities goes beyond the importance of innovative thrust and organizational flair. A greater intensity of entrepreneurial drive would certainly have produced more strikes and here, too, a certain stance persists. We have noted the wariness of the British state and its agencies towards giving overt practical support to employers in their labour conflicts, fearing to give political enemies too obvious a chance to charge them with blatant class rule. The preference has been to urge conciliation, 'sensible' compromise, and judicious restraint. This had long been the ruling class's technique of rule: they could see no reason why it should not be industry's. Managers may have many reasons, of course, for being anxious to avoid strikes. But there is reason for believing that outside the sectors totally habituated to them, many British managers respond to the prospect of strikes with some shock as a failure of rule. It is hard to believe that this does not owe something to the political culture, implicit in state policy, which surrounds them.

The political culture expresses itself also in responses to the third of our issues. Have the British people, more especially the lower ranks, come to acknowledge the existence of a higher social good than their own immediate perceived interests? The question has a bearing on the earlier two. Successive governments of both major parties since the war have hoped to urge managements into greater dynamism; unions into greater pay restraint; and workers into greater acceptance of managerial leadership and initiative, by appealing with wearisome reiteration to the concept of a 'higher good'; the 'national interest'; the 'wider community'. For the most part these exhortations have fallen upon deaf ears. The springs of managerial motivation lie too deep to be touched by verbal appeals. The trade unions, in their turn, understand and respond to the language of negotiation, but there is little in Britain's political and industrial history, culture and traditions, which renders the organized employee class—or for that matter the employer class—notably sensitive to conceptions of a higher social good. The argument is not that there is no sphere in which the British citizen is prepared to serve a higher end than his own perceived interests. This perplexing people could not have survived two total wars without some measure of this capacity. It is rather that, by the very nature of the nation's political development, patriotism attaches to the concept of 'Britishness' rather than to the 'state' or other specific institutions. Although great skill has gone into the cultivation of popular monarchy as a symbol of Britishness and national unity, this symbol is projected, with a good deal of success, as being 'above party'. For that reason, unyoked as it is to the *overt* party power structure, it cannot be exploited for *overt* party political ends. Its very potency, in fact, as a force for social cohesion resides in the assumption that it transcends class conflict and political controversy. Beneath this benign royal umbrella, individualism and sectional interest wax as briskly as ever they did—indeed, even more so as more and more groups learn the name of the game.

The emphasis on British individualism may seem refuted by the collectivism of the labour movement. There are, however, very different kinds of collectivism. At one extreme lies the 'organic' collectivism whose members stand prepared to sacrifice themselves, if necessary, for some transcendent purpose; at the other, a purely 'instrumental' kind which survives only so long as enough individual members remain convinced that they can do better for themselves combined than standing alone. It would be a travesty to describe Britain's trade unions as wholly occupying the latter position. Such a description would be inadequate to explain fully either the origins of unions, or their survival in bad times, or the devotion of many unpaid activists, or the persistent consciousness, still vaguely haunting the British movement, that it entertains the larger hope for a qualitatively better society. But equally there are prominent features which cannot be explained except in terms of strongly instrumental, pragmatic, and individualistic perspectives—the readiness of favoured workers, for example, in a tight labour market to push forward in small workplace groups if higher leadership seems unable or unwilling to seize the advantage on their behalf; the widespread scepticism shared by many rank-and-file members towards national officers, and the intensity of the struggles waged to uphold traditional group differentials against policies designed to raise the relative position of the low-paid.

For all the crocodile tears of Establishment figures who mourn the supposed degeneration of the union movement's once noble humanitarian purpose into mere sectional selfishness, such characteristics have always been apparent. They were, after all, the protective responses of particular groups of workers to the more blatantly selfish and *sauve qui peut* characteristics of the social order imposed on them. Like other features examined in this essay, they demonstrate as remarkable a persistence as many of the other structural aspects with which they interact in a circular process of mutual perpetuation.

It would be a major task, requiring space far beyond that available here, to apply this analysis to the economic strategies currently pressed by the reformist and radical wings of both political Left and political Right. The purpose of this essay has been limited to suggesting an analysis of how Britain's pattern of management–worker relations came to be what it is. Some indication must be offered, however, of certain immediate conclusions. The first relates to those who speak and act as if they believe that fundamental changes in economic behaviour can be achieved without fundamental changes in economic and social structures. For them, no doubt, the propositions with which this essay began concerning the persistence of long-standing values and institutions will appear, when viewed against the background of the subsequent analysis, to carry deeply pessimistic overtones. And it is true that, by comparison with the historical development of some other countries such as Germany and Japan, that of Britain may seem to leave small room for manoeuvre to those who seek, whether from the political Left or Right, to intensify the economic dynamic among her citizens. When it is suggested that they have to work with the grain if they are to achieve anything but disruption and confusion, they may reply that the grain lies the wrong way for their purposes. And from their point of view progress has, admittedly, to be disappointingly small.

But there are equally germane implications for those who see all too clearly that a necessary condition of transformed behaviour is transformed structures. Among these are some at the furthermost extremes of both Left and Right who seem prepared to level to the ground and start again. At what cost? It is relevant here to recall that the coin on which is displayed Britain's inefficiency has another face. Those furthermost figures of the Left and Right are apt, however, to convey a certain indifference and disparagement towards such qualities and towards the deeply ingrained ideologies and practices of law and liberty which support and are supported by them. For reasons easily understandable within the British context, neither extreme receives a good press. We hear little of the far Right but it is an obvious ploy for opponents of socialism, within the media and elsewhere, to identify *all* its adherents with the readiness to destroy such shackles on power as have been painfully and precariously constructed over the centuries. We have witnessed for a long time attempts by the Press and the Conservative Party, joined now by some on the centre and right of the Labour Party and by the Social Democrats, to convince us that *all* those seeking radical changes in society are destroyers of the valued political freedoms. Yet few have written more brilliantly about the importance of preserving institutional and ideological limits to power than E. P. Thompson, a figure of the libertarian Left who is deeply suspicious of the authoritarian Left. He is rightly insistent that it is not difficult to present a picture of Britain's past in terms of a class domination which, behind a humbug façade of law and liberty, exploited the weak as busily as any other ruling class. Much of this humbug is still with us today. Yet he is also insistent that this is not, and never was, the whole picture. Still less can we conclude that the very concept of the rule of law is humbug. '... the rule of law itself, the imposing of effective inhibitions upon power and the defence of the citizen from power's all-intrusive claims, seems ... to be an unqualified human good. To deny or belittle this good is, in this dangerous century when the resources and pretensions of power continue to enlarge, a desperate error of intellectual abstraction' (Thompson 1977, p. 266). Those who, in making their judgements about the political scene, wish to see it clear and see it whole as far as they can, must therefore beware of attempts by interested politicians and publicists to conjure out of sight the firm British tradition of a socialistically transformed society which yet preserves these defences against power.

We need all the clarity and wholeness we can muster if we are each to make considered judgements on the questions which this essay has sought to identify. What are our economic and social priorities, and what changes in institutions and behaviour are required to pursue them affectively? Would they work with or against the grain of British society? If they work against the grain, what would be the probable costs of trying to impose them? Are the costs worth paying? Such questions are too important to be discussed with the brevity that would be unavoidable at the close of a brief essay. In any case the intention here is not to offer conclusions but to suggest a framework for individual judgement—a framework which alerts us to the extent to which we are the product of our past.

REFERENCES

Anderson, P. (1965), 'Origins of the Present Crisis' in *Towards Socialism* (eds. P. Anderson and R. Blackburn), London, Fontana.

Aspinall, A. (1949), *The Early English Trade Unions: Documents from the Home Office Papers in the Public Record Office,* London, The Batchworth Press.

Dore, R. (1973), *British Factory–Japanese Factory,* London, George Allen & Unwin.

Feuer, L.S. (ed.) (1969), 'The Eighteenth Brumaire of Louis Bonaparte' in *Marx and Engels: Basic Writings on Politics and Philosophy,* London, Collins, The Fontana Library.

George, D. (1953), *England in Transition,* Harmondsworth, Penguin.

Hay, D. (1977), 'Property, Authority and the Criminal Law' in *Albion's Fatal Tree: Crime and Society in Eighteenth-Century England* (D. Hay, P. Linebaugh, J. G. Rule, E.P. Thompson, C. Winslow), Harmondsworth, Penguin.

Joyce, P. (1980), *Work, Society and Politics: The Culture of the Factory in Later Victorian England,* Brighton, Harvester Press.

Kahn-Freund, Sir O. (1979), *Labour Relations: Heritage and Adjustment,* Oxford University Press, for the British Academy.

Macfarlane, A. (1978), *The Origins of English Individualism: The Family, Property and Social Transition,* Oxford, Blackwell.

Middlemas, K. (1979) *Politics in Industrial Society: The Experience of the British System since 1911,* London, André Deutsch.

Morgan, K.O. (1978), *The Age of Lloyd George: The Liberal Party and British Politics 1890–1929,* London, George Allen & Unwin.

Morley, J. (1908), *The Life of William Ewart Gladstone,* Vol. 1, London, Edward Lloyd.

Nairn, T. (1977), *The Break-up of Britain: Crisis and Neo-Nationalism,* London, NLB.

Namier, L. (1957), *The Structure of Politics at the Accession of George III* (2nd edn.), London, Macmillan.

Neale, R.S. (1975), *Feudalism, Capitalism and Beyond* (eds. E. Kamenka and R.S. Neale), London, Edward Arnold.

Plumb, J.H. (1967), *The Growth of Political Stability in England 1675-1725*, London, Macmillan.

Pratten, C.F. (1976), *Labour Productivity Differentials within International Companies*, Cambridge University Press.

Reisman, D.A. (1976), *Adam Smith's Sociological Economics*, London, Croom Helm.

Sabine, G.H. (1963), *A History of Political Theory* (3rd edn.), London, George G. Harrap.

Schumpeter, J.A. (1954), *Capitalism, Socialism and Democracy* (4th edn.), London, George Allen & Unwin.

Snaith, J. (1981), The Guardian (10 June).

Stone, L. (1972), *The Causes of the English Revolution 1529-1642*, London, Routledge & Kegan Paul.

Thompson, E.P. (1974), 'Patrician Society, Plebeian Culture', *Journal of Social History*, 7/4.

Thompson, E.P. (1977), *Whigs and Hunters: The Origin of the Black Act*, Harmondsworth, Penguin.

Wiener, M. (1981), *English Culture and the Decline of the Industrial Spirit, 1850-1980*, Cambridge University Press.

Wilkinson, R. (1964), *The Prefects: British Leadership and the Public School Tradition*, London, Oxford University Press.

Williams, G.L. (1976), *John Stuart Mill on Politics and Society*, London, Fontana/Collins.

2

Entrepreneurship and Economic History: the state of the debate

PETER MATHIAS

An important intellectual and methodological mutation occurs—not always fully appreciated by instinctively empirical, conceptually innocent Englishmen—between talking of entrepreneurs and 'entrepreneurship' in history, or even between entrepreneurs and 'the entrepreneur'. The former are creatures of flesh and blood, living with ulcers and the fear of Carey Street, hoping to make a fortune or reach the House of Lords; the latter remains a Platonic ideal, archetype, ideal type, model, or paradigm, given significance by the theoretical schema which embraces it. To study entrepreneurs is to be concerned with empirical questions—who they were, what social groups they sprang from, how they were educated and recruited. Equivalent empirical questions govern enquiries about the historical practices of management, the organization of enterprise, and the like. With most productive assets in the British economy during the eighteenth- and nineteenth-centuries being in the hands of the single-owner firm or the small partnership, and most technical changes, investment decisions, labour recruitment, and the like being taken by such men of business, such empirical investigations are clearly important—whether as studies of individuals, families, firms, industries, or wider groupings. The more we know about the structure and function of business in the eighteenth-century, the greater our understanding of the processes of economic change and industrialization being generated within the economy. Even if the prime sources of impetus did not lie in the voluntaristic mechanisms of businessmen, who were responding to opportunities evolving in their habitat, they were the executants of change in these relationships, part of an institutional structure which profoundly influenced the nature of economic change.

But entrepreneurship is a more conceptualized, disembodied entity, and the descriptive entity has significance, as so often, in relation to the analytical concept, the theoretical framework within which interest in the entrepreneurs has been cast. The questions are posed, the problems are isolated, the argument about variables pursued, and the causes identified in the light of the hypotheses derived from a model. In less formal terms, ideas, perceptions, even hunches, pre-condition the questions which are asked and suggest answers, even if subsequent empirical investigation shows that the facts will not sustain them. Entrepreneurship is now often, if loosely, invoked as a factor of production with labour, capital, and resources, even if not fitted into a traditional classical analysis of explaining increases in output in the light of changing inputs and prices of traditional factors. In the analysis of increases in output relative to inputs in all advanced countries, the high 'residual' exposed in the sources of economic growth through a rise in total factor productivity, provides a potential slot for entrepreneurship.[1] Where growth is not accountable in terms of extra inputs of traditional resources at static levels of productivity, the residual (not precisely allocatable, by definition, because it is calculated as the residual difference between measured output translated against measured inputs) is a catch-all containing such ingredients as technical change, improvements in organization, higher quality of labour through education and investment in human capital—and entrepreneurship. The latter can be regarded as a variable in its own right and also as an ingredient required to valorize many of these constituents of improved efficiency in the deployment of productive assets. Insofar as the gains of entrepreneurship or better management are reflected in the enhanced efficiency deployed in other factors of production, and technical change, it can never be wholly measured as an autonomous variable.

The pre-history of the concept of the entrepreneur (and its linguistic identification) in terms of a conceptual entity, as well as identifiable human beings responsible for the functions of risk-bearing and the co-ordination of factors of production in the operation of an economic system, belongs to Richard Cantillon and J. B. Say, who have been much neglected in the debate.[2] For them profit was the reward for fulfilling these functions and to be distinguished from interest payments, as the yield on capital employed. However, operationally, present-day theory springs from

Joseph Schumpeter, who deployed entrepreneurship as a leading
concept and the organizing principle of his *Theory of Economic
Development* (published first in his native German in 1911;
translated into English in 1934).[3] This set up a conceptual schema in
which the entrepreneur was the leading source of impetus, as the
unmoved mover, in the process of economic development. Schumpeter's thesis proposed a sort of entrepreneurial Darwinism. The
model posited that the normative state of an economy was one of
circular flow, a 'steady-state' equilibrium, with traditional technology, 'normal' profits, and imitative responses by decision takers in
business adopting and generalizing the technology and business
techniques that existed and were on offer for adoption. Such a
steady-state economy was characterized by 'managerial' decision-
taking rather than 'entrepreneurial' decisions.

By definition the entrepreneurial function was that of discovering, or implementing, new combinations of factors which set
business on a new course and broke out of the circular flow. 'New
combinations' embraced many developments—promoting new
products, discerning new markets, mobilizing new sources of
finance, improving the organization of the business unit, and
lowering costs in the production of existing products. The process
was 'creative–destructive'—or daemonic—as the improved efficiency in existing patterns of production and distribution, or the
higher attractiveness of new products, drove the imitative, traditional businesses to the wall, or into adopting the innovations.
The entrepreneur could capture monopoly profits—'entrepreneurial
profit'—between the introduction of the innovations and their
adoption by others, but this was an inherently temporary phenomenon, 'the competitive mechanism tolerating no permanent
surplus values, but rather annihilating them by means of just this
stimulus of the striving for profit which is the mechanism's driving
force' (ibid. (1934), p. 156). This was the central impetus behind the
process of growth in a competitive context and the entrepreneur,
and his skills and his motivations, were thus placed at the centre of
the development process.

Schumpeterian analysis has remained apart from the mainstream
of theorizing in economics and very difficult to absorb within the
general corpus of development theory, or indeed of neo-classical
economics more widely. In economic history it was not very well
known or influential until the Research Center in Entrepreneurial

History, inspired by Schumpeter, was set up at Harvard in 1948 and its journal, *Explorations in Entrepreneurial History,* and various other publications, spread the message and institutionalized this body of theoretical ideas very effectively.[4] Schumpeterian theory has thrown a very long shadow over business history in particular, which has put a gloss of conceptual sophistication over a much more long-standing, empirical, and naïve historiography (flourishing in Victorian England under Samuel Smiles and his predecessors, such as Andrew Ure), which saw the businessman as hero, the saviour of the poor, and the creator of the wealth of nations.[5] This was sycophantic upon, or at the least a sympathetic buttress for, the role of the businessman in a free-entreprise economy. Schumpeterian theory assumed a context of a market economy, with effective comeptitive forces (monopoly profits being won only in the interval between the introduction and diffusion of new combinations by innovating entrepreneurs) and individual businessmen being the critical decision makers. It has not been very adaptable to a world of oligopoly or the dynamic of socialist economies—or even to subsequent theories of the firm. Business history has also, not accidentally, failed to provide an empirical base for any significant trends in theoretical economies.

In the wake of Schumpeter, 'entrepreneurship' has been argued over as a separate and significant variable in the historical process of economic growth. The Industrial Revolution occurring first in England has been explained, in whole or in part, by the plenitude, or vigour, of her entrepreneurs, compared with lesser breeds elsewhere, and new life has been breathed into the old Weberian model of the protestant/puritan ethic. Protestant non-conformity provided the *fons et origo* of the entrepreneurs and their motivations, although in the present debate not coming on stage with capitalism, Calvinism, and the Reformation in the sixteenth-century, but remaining in the wings of European history until the Industrial Revolution in the eighteenth-century, when the cast was composed anew with Quaker merchants and iron-masters, bankers and brewers, and Unitarian cotton spinners *et al.* Equally, a long debate took place in the 1950s between John Sawyer, David Landes, Rondo Cameron, and Alexander Gershenkron about the role of weak entrepreneurship limiting the speed of industrialization and growth rates in nineteenth-century France.[6] An equivalent debate is now in progress about the responsibility of entrepreneurship as an independent variable for the relative failings of the British economy between 1870 and 1914, compared with the US and Germany.[7] A continuing theme of explanations for all subsequent sequences of slower growth, stagnation, and decline, whether in absolute terms or relative to the performance of other economies, has been 'failure of management'. In present circumstances, for these reasons, entrepreneurship has become a word in common currency, escaping from the technical language of the economist and economic historian into the City pages of newspapers and the public pronouncements of politicians, doubtless innocent of any direct acquaintance with the writings of Schumpeter.

The extension of entrepreneurial theory beyond Schumpeter does not seem to me to have changed the fundamentals of his assumptions, but rather to have explored further dimensions within the canon. As a psychologist concerned with the expertise and techniques of the behavioural sciences, David McLelland in *The Achieving Society* sought to identify the motivational structure of entrepreneurs—in particular the strength of their motivations for achievement—thus giving a psychological and cultural dimension to entrepreneurship and economic growth and providing a more general conceptual basis to previous theorizing about protestantism.[8] However McLelland assumed that all this was to be poured into a Schumpeterian mould and that actors would be participating in a Schumpeterian way in the economic arena. He was concerned to understand their motivations in the past with a view to promoting higher 'N' achievement levels in the present. It was essentially meant as a contribution to the debate on present-day development theory rather than to economic history.

Whereas McLelland was a psychologist turned theorist of economic growth, Everett E. Hagen became economist turned psychologist.[9] He also was concerned to integrate personality theory with sociological theory to explain 'how economic growth begins', the subtitle of his book *On the Theory of Social Change*. This analysis concerned particularly the withdrawal of status respect from particular individuals and minority groups, which could encourage the energizing of minority groups into enterprise roles in society. He conducted brief surveys into the proportions of entrepreneurs in eighteenth-century England who were nonconformists or Scotsmen, and enquired into the socio-economic status of their fathers. This enquiry, again, was essentially exploring the motivational structure of individuals and social groups: asking why particular groups had greater propensities for entrepreneurial roles than others, rather than in modifying the Schumpeterian analysis of what the entrepreneurial roles were, or how those roles were related to the process of economic change. McLelland and Hagen absorbed much of the Weberian analysis, although presenting it in a new guise and generalizing it to embrace minority groups other than those professing particular sub-tenets of a Christian theology.[10] For example, Parsees and Gujeratis within the wider groupings of Hindu culture in India; Indian minority groups in East Africa; Chinese minorities in South-East Asia; and the Jewish communities world-wide, were potentially analysable in these terms, without benefit of a single specific Calvinist or nonconformist Christian theology. These authors also depend heavily on Parsonian sociological theory, with its dichotomy between status and satisfactions derived from ascription and achievement in society.

More recent economic theory, particularly theories of the firm, also do not seem to me to have extended Schumpeterian concepts of entrepreneurship so much as to have grown out of a quite independent theoretical context. The unit being considered is the firm, rather than the individual entrepreneur, particularly the firm run by professional, salaried managers in an oligopolistic context, and the discussion, following the theories and evident existence of imperfect competition, has been particularly concerned to establish the motivations and objectives of firms, where earlier simpler assumptions of profit maximization were not tenable in circumstances of oligopoly, anti-monopoly legislation, and decision-taking by managers whose income was not primarily determined by profit levels, unlike the classical entrepreneurs as owner-managers of their businesses.

Hence, such theories as that of Baumol that the objective of the firm was to maximize sales rather than profits; or of Mrs Penrose that the path of growth of a firm was conditioned by the pool of existing resources within it.[11] In addition, of course, there is a vast body of literature emerging from the business schools and from business consultancies about how best to organize activities, how best to structure organizations, or how to choose and train managers in order to enhance performance. But this mass of expertise does not appear to me to be of much operational value for economic historians concerned to understand processes of change in historical periods where the institutional structure, the mode of operations, and the whole context of the economy was so very different from that which this corpus of 'business management' literature necessarily assumes. And even within this field of expertise, it seems to me, drive and business creativity, the Schumpeterian entrepreneurial virtues, are acknowledged to remain amongst the higher mysteries. Theorizing about entrepreneurship, particularly that which is relevant for economic historians interested in the eighteenth- and nineteenth-centuries, is still thus very much within the Schumpeterian heritage.

Theories invoke counter-theories, and counter-theorizing has not been lacking in the debate on entrepreneurship. Indeed anti-theorizing is currently in the ascendant, not so much with a view to denying the significance of studying businessmen and firms as the main actors and primary institutions of industrial and commercial change in the past, as in the present, but more conceptually, challenging the assumption that entrepreneurship is significant as a variable in the analysis of economic performance. The claim is that it must be relegated to the role of a subordinate, if not completely dependent, variable, or seen as the sum of the influence upon it; and that other hypotheses give necessary and sufficient explanations for trends of business growth, stability or decline, without invoking entrepreneurship. Thus entrepreneurship is taken to be one of those useful, even necessary, myths of economic history that flourish only in the absence of data which allows analysis in measurable terms—a shibboleth or prayer-wheel, along with the rise of the middle classes or the growth of a money economy, incanted or twirled by historians as a convenient rationalization to calm unease in the presence of the unexplained mysteries of economic growth and decline. The banner for this thesis is Sir John Habakkuk's sentence 'Great generals are not made in time of peace; great entrepreneurs are not made in non-expanding industries', deployed when arguing one side of the case that entrepreneurship was not an important independent causal variable in explaining the greater vigour for technical change in the American economy than in Britain between 1870 and 1914.[12] The entrepreneur thus becomes a response to context; supply is created by opportunities. Failure to adopt new technology is to be explained by a difference in relative factor prices (particularly labour being cheaper relative to capital than in the innovating country), different cost structures applying to different technologies, the lack of a market, etc.—in short because it would have been less economic to adopt the new technology, given the context immediately facing entrepreneurs, rather than because there was a lack of rationality or lack of enterprise by decision takers in business. In this tradition of analysis basic decisions were for the best even if the British economy was not the best of all possible worlds for entrepreneurial decisions in the late nineteenth-century.[13] Thus Professor Sandberg has sought to demonstrate the rationality of British entrepreneurs in cotton-spinning in the late nineteenth-century in not foregoing traditional mule-spinning for ring-frames, given the structure of costs, product mix, and particular markets which they faced. Professor McCloskey has sought to do a similar exercise for iron and steel. Other studies have concerned alkali manufacture, machine tools, and sectors of engineering.

Another mode of argument supports this attack. In certain sectors of the British economy in the last quarter of the nineteenth-century—in retailing, food-processing, building contractors in international business, and some consumer goods industries such as soap, brewing, and pharmaceuticals—archetypal entrepreneurs appear and preside over the transformation of these activities: William Lever, Jesse Boot, Cadbury, Bass, Lipton, the Wills brothers, and their fellows.[14] The same was true in certain branches of heavy engineering such as shipbuilding and marine engines, in some branches of heavy armaments, and in special steels in Sheffield.[15] If expanding sectors of the economy could throw up entrepreneurs in such a context no failure of the national genius or any other nationally diffused institutional weakness is needed to evoke a 'failure' in entrepreneurship in order to explain relatively weak performance in other sectors.

Within this general context one set of arguments can be made to apply to the experience of existing large staple industries—textiles, iron and steel, etc.—which also concerns their performance in terms relative to their past record and in comparison with the newer industries of other countries; and another set of arguments can be made which applies to the failure of certain indigenous new industries to develop equivalently to their progress elsewhere—fine chemicals and electrical engineering, for example. Even if the failure to innovate by the former group may be explained by particular combinations of factor prices in relation to products and markets, the failure of 'new' industries to develop may be responsive to a different set of constraints, including a failure of enterprise. Of course, this can track back to underlying explanations of 'rational' responses by businessmen taking decisions within the particular context facing them, which for reasons beyond their control was a context marked by an absence of cadres of requisite skilled chemists and applied scientists, which is to be explained in terms of public educational priorities. Most of the debate at present has been concerned with the issue of entrepreneurial failings as a variable in the relative decline in the performance of the British economy, in levels of investment, innovation, and rates of growth, compared with the US and Germany in the period 1870–1914: but the mirror image of this analysis will doubtless be projected onto entrepreneurship as a variable in the relative precocity of the British economy compared to others, in these same respects, in the eighteenth-century.

In this sense economic historians still stand at the beginning of the debate rather than at its end. Certain general analytical points can still be made, however. One specific issue concerns the time-scale over which assertions about rationality in decision-making and maximization are being made. Short-run maximizing, in the face of actually existing production functions, relative factor costs, technology currently on offer, and other aspects of the contemporary situation, may invoke a very different allocation of resources compared with longer-term maximization. Projecting forwards in anticipation of future gains will require considerable research costs, jettisoning of sunk costs in existing, but not worn-out plant and buildings, the anticipation of an ultimate pay-off from improved new technology, and the like. In the face of uncertainty and risk, the qualities needed for acting on such a forward view add faith and conviction to the normal determinants of effective administration. Doubtless, during the proving stages of any innovation it is less economic than the technology which its eventual success will replace; and strict rationality in the very short term would also preclude the acceptance of high research costs. Neo-classical assumptions used to justify the path actually taken by British manufacturing business during the late nineteenth-century, in comparison with emerging industrial rivals, depend upon such a static analysis. All these positions have been sharply challenged, in different ways, but with the common accusation that they ignore the dynamic possibilities in the longer run, which could have changed the course of Britain's industry, With the longer run in view, research and development *could* have produced new, relevant technology, *could* have adapted products and markets, *could* have evolved cost structures and profit opportunities of greater long-term advantage than those actually adopted. Thus the issue of a failing in entrepreneurship, as one relevant variable, still remains open.

More generally, the criteria of rationality itself have to be specified. We may agree, as any anthropologist or psychologist would assert, that all societies (like all individuals), however 'primitive', are strictly rational within their total value systems, in terms of the assumptions they make for themselves and in terms of their own consciousness when interpreting 'external' events. But this is not necessarily to assert rationality within terms of purely economic imperatives, still less in terms of profit-maximizing in the short run, or in maximizing the rate of expansion or the speed of innovation. This does not necessarily eliminate entrepreneurship as a potentially significant variable, but it means that entrepreneurial responses always have to be analysed within a particular context. Local insecurity and conditions of high risk, for example, often endow kinship links with a much higher premium in organizing business than a purely meritocratic process of selection, or encourage the diversification of assets within an extended family. Family businesses have interests in preserving the continuity of succession, and in maintaining and enhancing the status of the family in their locality or region, where the firm is identified both with the local community and with the family, in ways other than just short-term financial maximization. It has been argued that, in order not to threaten family control, French family firms were loath to seek long-term equity external finance. The point is that the satisfactions which are being maximized, and which establish the rationale of decisions, are not *just* profit or income-maximizing or growth in the short run. In the wider context, the institutionalization of interest groups of all kinds, with their resultant political influences, shows a diversity of objective and motivation ranging far beyond perceived national economic efficiency.

Arguments about the rationality of entrepreneurial decision-making focus upon the individual firm and the range of decisions available to the individual actor in the market. Much which is of relevance to economic performance lies outside this range and in the wider context—international and market factors, such as tariffs, and pre-existing efficient and low-cost provisions in earlier technologies that reduce the initial market for innovations, as the extensive provision of gas did for electricity generation in late nineteenth-century Britain, and which efficient local urban public transport did for the initial market for private motor cars. The institutional pattern within which individual businesses have to operate has to be considered as largely a datum for individual firms, whether in relation to the existing structure of banking and the capital market, to government policy, or to trade unions. Doubtless all such relationships are subject to influence, and are not entirely unresponsive to pressures for change. But in the short view, and for the single decision-making unit, the assertion is broadly correct. It is thus perfectly possible to recognize a 'failure' of Victorian Britain (relative to German or American industrialization or innovative capacity), and yet to acknowledge the existence of 'rational' entrepreneurship in these narrow terms—because the explanations for 'failure' lie beyond the terms of decision-making by individual entrepreneurs in 'institutional' variables, sunk costs, markets, etc.

It is easy to assert that any single factor can be wished away from the analysis of a dependent variable, by the argument that the supply would have been responsive if all other necessary and sufficient factors had been present. This is particularly facile in the case of a variable such as entrepreneurship whose impact is, of its nature, unquantifiable (or constituting an unquantified fraction of the residual) and mediated through the performance of other factors. By this argument all rigidities can be dismissed—imperfections in the capital market will be eliminated when new needs are formulated (offering new gains to be captured); government will respond to pressure from the organized business community to provide appropriate policies and educational resources (resolving imperfections in the external matrix of business operations); and an economy will have the trade union system which is appropriate to its needs . . . In short, there is an exact fit (time-lags apart) between structure and function, between the institutional matrix in its multitudinous forms, and functional efficiency in economic terms.

This is clearly to describe a mythical country. Institutions follow many imperatives other than the promotion of national economic efficiency, although a degree of such allegiance is probably necessary for their existence. Even if structure and function are in close alliance when an institutional form first develops, changing circumstances can widen the gap, and institutional inertia prevent an accommodation with the new circumstances. A long literature about such institutional sclerosis exists (much organizational theory is designed to counteract it in business structures) and one recent thesis maintains that some great national crisis (such as defeat in war) is necessary to break such institutional rigidities and release national energies once more through new, more appropriate, structures.[17] Other theses maintain the view that the impress of cultural values, associated with educational institutions, career choices, aspiring assimilation to traditional élites, and similar expressions of cultural priorities, exerts an influence upon business culture, and hence affects business performance. Indeed, Dr Wiener's *English Culture and the Decline of the Industrial Spirit, 1850-1950* reads like the analogue of various older studies which once explained the absence of an industrial revolution in eighteenth-century France in similar cultural terms.

Arguments derived from the assumptions of neo-classical economics discounting entrepreneurial failure also rest heavily upon the assumption that prices accurately measured factor costs, and that firms were operating under effectively competitive conditions. The implications are that if entrepreneurial failure could explain the fate of a single firm (as it clearly can), it could not explain the sluggishness of an industry or a wider sector of economic activity. A sluggish firm would pay the penalty by going bankrupt. New, more thrusting, newcomers would prosper. But this makes big assumptions about the ease of entry, perfect information, the availability of external finance, the absence of collective agreements or defensive arrangements which preserved extensive quasi-rents and monopolistic positions more widely, and made the general context of enterprise such that the pattern of costs and prices enabled the sluggish to survive. The very wide spread between the best-practice and average firms in many industries, between the most efficient and profitable and the marginal firms that contrived to survive, puts a big question mark against this assumption of competitiveness and the effectiveness of 'entrepreneurial Darwinism' by which only the fittest survive.

It is intellectually simplistic to see entrepreneurship as an autonomous factor of production, and comparable in some disembodied way between contexts widely differing in time and society. We are accustomed to analyse capital as embodied in technology and in assets. Behind a factor price there is a pyramid of explanatory relationships, and equally so behind the level of effective demand for any product. Extrepreneurship also requires to be analysed in relation to real factors and within specific institutional contexts. It operates not independently but conjoined to other factors, and to deny this range of relationships' significance in the past is, by implication, to deny the significance of great resources being invested in the attempts to improve the level of managerial efficiency in the present. But this is to escape from the precise methodological assumptions of the Schumpeterian schema which presumed a particular context, and to return to the analysis of entrepreneurial role and functions in real terms—education, recruitment, social origins, motivational structure (itself integral with a cultural complex with real institutional roots in church, family, and education), organizational context, and the like. If economic historians took some ideas about structural analysis from anthropologists, seeing functions integrally related with institutional structures and value systems, as well as with narrowly economic relationships, they would find the problems more interesting but the discovery of conventional 'answers' doubtless more difficult.

NOTES

1 E.g. M. Abramovitz, 'Resource and Output Trends in the United States since 1870', *American Economic Review* (1956). The debate on the residual is admirably convered in N. Rosenberg (ed.), *The Economics of Technological Change*, Harmondsworth, Penguin Books (1971).
2 R. Cantillon, *Essai sur la Nature du Commerce en Général, (Amsterdam (1756); Cantillon, The Analyses of Trade, Commerce, etc.* London (1759); J. B. Say, *Traité d'Economie Politique,* Paris (1803); Say, *Cours Complet d'Economie Politique,* Paris (1828–9).
3 J. A. Schumpeter, *The Theory of Economic Development* translated from

the German by R. Opie), Cambridge, Mass., Harvard University Ress (1934).
4 For the main claims made for the subject see A. H. Cole (ed.), *Change and the Entrepreneur: Postulates and Patterns for Entrepreneurial History*, Cambridge Mass., *Harvard University Press (1949); and H. G. J. Aiken (ed.), Explorations in Enterprise*, Cambridge, Mass., Harvard University Press (1965); F. C. Lane and J. C. Reimersa (eds.), *Enterprise and Secular Change*, London, Allen and Unwin (1953), especially the article by A. H. Cole, the director of the centre.
5 See praise of canal builders in J. Phillips, *A General History of Inland Navigation*, London, printed for S. Hooper (1972), Ch. 7; industrialists in e.g. A. Ure, *The Philosophy of Manufactures*, London, Charles Knight (1835), especially Chs. 1 and 3; J. Aiken, *A Description of the County from Thirty to Forty Miles around Manchester*, London, printed for J. Stockdale (1795); Samuel Smiles main biographies of investors and businessmen are S. Smiles, *Lives of the Engineers*, London, John Murray (1861–2); Smiles, *Industrial Biography, London, John Murray (1886). His attitudes are most clearly expressed in a series of general homilies, which sold in great numbers, especially Self-Help*, London, John Murray (1859); *Character*, London, John Murray (1871); *Thrift*, London, John Murray (1875), *Duty*, London, John Murray (1900).
6 D. Landes, 'French Business and the Businessman' in Aiken (ed.) op. cit. in note 4; B. F. Hoselitz, 'Entrepreneurship and Capital Formation in France and Britain since 1700' in *Capital Formation and Economic Growth*, ed. M. Abramovitz (N.B.E.R., Princeton, N.J. (1956); Hoselitz, *Sociological Aspects of Economic Growth*, Glencoe, Free Press (1960); D. Landes, 'French Entrepreneurship and Industrial Growth in the 19th Century', *Journal of Economic History*, IX (1951), Landes, 'Social Attitudes, Entrepreneurship and Economic Development', *Exploration in Entrepreneurial History*, VI (1954); A. Gerschenkron, 'Social Attitudes, Entrepreneurship and Economic Development', ibid; Gerschenkron, 'Further Notes . . .', ibid., VII (1955).
7 C. H. Wilson, 'The Entrepreneur in the Industrial Revolution', *History*, LXII (1957). E.g. D. H. Aldcroft, 'The Entrepreneur and the British Economy 1870–1914', *Economic History Review*, XVII (1964); D. L. Landes in *Cambridge Economic History of Europe* (eds. M. M. Postan and H. J. Habakkuk), vol. VI no. 1, Cambridge University Press (1965). For the iron and steel industry see D. L. Burn, *The Economic History of Steel-Making, 1869-1939*, Cambridge University Press (1940). D. C. Coleman, 'Gentlemen and Players', *Economic History Review*, XXVI (1973), and P. L. Payne, *British Entrepreneurship in the Nineteenth Century*, London, Macmillan (1974), offer a balanced assessment of the role of entrepreneurship. For recent general surveys of British economic history over this period see P. Mathias, *The First Industrial Nation* (revised edn.), London, Methuen (1983); F. Crouzet, *The Victorian Economy*, London, Methuen (1982); M. W. Kirby, *The Decline of British Economic Power since 1870*, London, Allen and Unwin (1981).

8 D. C. McClelland, *The Achieving Society,* Princeton, N.J., Van Nostrand (1961).

9 E. E. Hagen, *On the Theory of Social Change,* Homewood, Ill., Dorsey Press (1964).

10 On the debate more generally see T. Burns and S. B. Saul (eds.), *Social Theory and Economic Change,* London, Tavistock, 1967; K. Samuelsson, *Religion and Economic Action,* New York, Basic Books (1962).

11 E. Penrose, *The Theory of the Growth of the Firm,* Oxford University Press (1959).

12 H. J. Habakkuk, *American and British Technology in the 19th Century,* Cambridge University Press (1962), p. 165.

13 D. N. McCloskey and L. Sandberg, 'From Damnation to Redemption: Judgements on the Late Victorian Entrepreneur', *Explorations in Economic History,* IX (1971); D. N. McCloskey, *Economic Maturity and Entrepreneurial Decline: British Iron and Steel, 1870-1913,* Cambridge, Mass., Harvard University Press (1973); McCloskey, *Enterprise and Trade in Victorian Britain,* Part II, London, Allen and Unwin (1981), pp. 55-135; L. Sandberg, *Lancashire in Decline,* Columbus, Ohio, State University Press (1974); W. Lazonick, 'Factor Costs and the Diffusion of Ring-Spinning in Britain prior to World War I', *Quarterly Journal of Economics,* XCV (1981); P. A. David, 'Mechanisation of Harvesting', in *Essays on a Mature Economy: Britain after 1840* (ed. D. N. McCloskey), Section III, London (1971); P. H. Lindert and K. Trace, 'Solvay and Leblanc Processes in Alkali Manufacture' in McCloskey (ed.), op. cit. above.

14 C. H. Wilson, *The History of Unilever,* London, Cassell (1954); Wilson, 'Economy and Society in Late Victorian England', *Economic History Review* (1965); P. Mathias, *Retailing Revolution,* London, Longman (1967); D. Davis, *A History of Shopping,* London, Routledge and Kegan Paul (1966); J. B. Jeffreys, *Retail Trading in Britain 1850-1950,* Cambridge University Ress (1954); B. W. E. Alford, *W.D. and H.O. Wills and the Development of the UK Tobacco Industry, 1786-1965,* London, Methuen (1973); S. D. Chapman, *Jesse Boot of Boots the Chemists,* London, Hodder and Stoughton (1974).

15 R. C. Trebilcok, *The Vickers Brothers,* London, Europa (1978); M. Sanderson, 'The Professor as Consultant: Oliver Arnold and the British Steel Industry, 1900-1914', *Economic History Review,* XXXI (1978). Arnold is not mentioned in the standard monograph on the British steel industry by D. L. Burn, *The Economic History of Steel-Making, 1869-1939,* Cambridge University Press (1940); T. C. Bridges and H. H. Tiltman, *Kings of Commerce,* London, Harrap (19298), pp. 90-8.

16 M. Olson, *The Rise and Decline of Nations,* Newhaven, Conn., Yale University Press (1982).

17 M. J. Wiener, *English Culture and the Decline of the Industrial Spirit 1850-1950,* Cambridge University Press (1981). See also J. McVeagh, *Tradefull Merchants: the Portrayal of the Capitalist in Literature,* London, Routledge and Kegan Paul (1981).

3

Management and Economic Performance

DONALD HAY

1. Introduction

In 1967 the Brookings Institution of the US produced a survey of the British economy entitled *Britain's Economic Prospects.*[1] It was written by a team of economists under the direction of Professor Richard Caves of Harvard University. A detailed survey of macro-economic factors and policies produced no decisive set of reasons for the rather weak growth performance of the British economy in the post-war period, when compared with its OECD competitors. Indeed, detailed growth performance comparisons were left with an unexplained residual which was small in the British case and large for other countries. This is the residual left when differences in accumulation of capital stock, and growth in the size and skill composition of the labour force, have been accounted for. Some economists attribute this to technical progress: others prefer to refer to it as the 'coefficient of ignorance'. In an attempt to unravel this factor, Caves himself undertook a survey of micro-economic aspects of British Industry. A number of possible explanations were adduced, researched, and then rejected. For example, he found no particular evidence to suggest that British factories were smaller or less modern than those of Britain's competitors. Nor was there conclusive evidence of inefficiency arising from uncompetitive market structures, though there was some suggestion that British manufacturing had been shielded from international competition in the home market by an overvalued exchange rate. Caves' conclusion was that British industry simply was not achieving as much output from the same resources as its international competitors. This was attributed to two factors: restrictive labour practices and poor management. The American team were inclined to blame the latter for the former.

The Brookings study's conclusions have been subjected to a good deal of critical scrutiny, and there have been a number of very detailed studies of international differences in productivity. Pratten[2] compared the performance of identical plants (technologically speaking) in the UK and Sweden. He found that the Swedish plants were operated with a greater degree of efficiency that was simply startling: differences of 30–100 per cent were common. Bacon and Eltis[3] confirmed what Caves *et al.* had suggested: that UK industry did not have on average an older, and thus less efficient, stock of machine tools than its European competitors. More recently, in a study of trade performance, NEDO (Stout)[4] showed that the UK had the same overall industrial composition of exports, but that within sectors the UK specialized in low value-added products. This suggests a lack of dynamism on the product development side, matching the low productivity performance. Finally, a number of studies have shown that UK industry lags behind in the resources that it devotes to research and development.[5]

The responsibility for these failures has generally been laid at the door of British management, though it is not denied that trade union intransigence cannot be entirely excluded from blame. The irony of this conclusion is that management and managers have been almost entirely omitted from mainstream economic analysis as a purposive element in the allocation of resources and their efficiency in use. The exception is industrial economics, which has always retained a strong interest in the activities of real firms in real markets. Unfortunately, this preoccupation has not penetrated economic analysis as a whole.

The traditional concept of 'the manager' in economic analysis is that of an *organizer* and *administrator*. Perceiving the opportunities afforded by the market, he brings together the resources of labour, capital, and inputs in the desired combinations, and seeks to maximize the profits of the firm by keeping costs down, and by ensuring that at the margin additional orders will generate sufficient revenue to cover the costs of supply. It is this concept that economic analysis derived from Marshall,[6] though Marshall himself was fully aware of a much richer variety of managerial activity. We may note that this concept was particularly suited to the small, owner-managed firm. The owner-manager, *qua* owner, defined the objectives of the firm and took the risks (and the profits) and, *qua* manager, organized the production to meet those objectives.

Because the firm was small, it was necessarily passive in its stance *vis-à-vis* the market. It took opportunities, rather than created them.

The inadequacy of this model as a complete description of modern industry is evident from consideration of the following facts:

1. The existence of very large industrial firms. The facts have been conveniently summarized in recent work by Prais.[7] He showed that in 1970, the 100 largest firms in UK manufacturing accounted for 41 per cent of the net output of the manufacturing sector, a proportion which had nearly doubled in the post-war period. The same 100 firms accounted for 60 per cent of the net assets of the sector. In 1972 no fewer than 30 UK firms had work-forces exceeding 40,000. The growth of large firms is associated with multi-plant operations. Prais showed that the average number of plants controlled by each of the 100 largest UK firms had risen from 27 in 1958 to 72 in 1972. This is also associated with diversification of the activities of these firms. Utton[8] provided an analysis of the 200 largest UK companies in 1974. On average the five primary activities of each firm accounted for some 89 per cent of their employment, and the most important activity for 57 per cent. Activity here is defined by the three-digit Standard Industrial Classification. Prais showed that the degree of diversification has been steadily increasing. The administration and direction of such large enterprises are likely to be a quite different proposition from the tasks confronting the owner-manager of a small firm. This is not to suggest that the small firm is unimportant in the economy, though Prais showed that their numbers have been rapidly diminishing in the UK.

2. The pattern of share ownership. It is evident that a dispersed pattern of shareholding is common to most large firms. The seminal work in this area was that of Berle and Means[9] for the 200 largest US corporations in 1929. They found that in only 22 of these did any one individual or family group own more than 50 per cent of the shares, and thus have formal control of the business. A comparative study by Larner showed that by 1963 only 5 of these firms had a single majority shareholder and in only 30 was there a single individual or family group with more than 10 per cent of the shareholding. Similar figures for the UK were presented by Sargent Florence.[10]

Furthermore, it is uncommon for the directors and managers of

the firm to have large shareholdings in the firm they run. Prais
found that in 1972, in the 100 top UK companies, directors owned
more than 10 per cent of the equity in only 11 cases, and in 73 cases
they held less than 2 per cent. On the other hand, Marris[11] pointed
out that director's shareholdings in large firms were rarely
negligible. In part, small percentage shareholdings are simply
explained by the limited wealth of the average manager or director,
compared to the very large total value of the company.

The conclusion is that there is rarely a correspondence between
ownership and managerial control in the largest UK companies.
However Beed[12] has argued that a shareholding in the range 1 per
cent to 5 per cent is sufficient to give actual control of a company in
a situation where shareholdings are widely dispersed. Using a
similar argument, Marris argued that this effectively delivered
control to the managers. The directors' shareholdings gave them a
basis for control, to which could be added two major advantages.
First, they were able to act as a group in proposing policies for the
firm. Second, they were able to count on the proxy votes of a large
number of shareholders who took no particular interest in the
detailed operations of the company. Only another individual or
group with a substantial shareholding, and a definite alternative
programme for the company, would be able to dislodge the
managerial group by attracting proxy votes. This was most likely in
cases where the performances of the existing management had been
poor, and the company was affected by some sort of crisis.

A possible objection to this argument is that there has been a
considerable increase in institutional shareholders since the 1950s,
and that such shareholders are more likely to dispose of sufficient
shares, and take an active interest in the affairs of the firms. Moyle[13]
has shown that institutional shareholdings in the UK rose from 28
per cent in 1957 to 41 per cent in 1970. Dobbins and Greenwood[14]
have extrapolated this trend to predict a 70 per cent share by 1990.
However, it is doubtful whether this increased institutional shareholding has in fact led to more effective control over managers, in
the UK at least. The situation is quite different in Germany and the
US where there is more of a tradition of having active representatives of institutional shareholders on the boards of companies. UK
institutions appear to prefer to hold only a small holding in any one
company, and simply sell out if they are unhappy about performance.

The fact of dispersion of share ownership has prompted the conclusion that ownership and control are likely to be divorced in the large quoted company, with effective power over the firm being exercised by the managers. A theoretical understanding of this development is the subject of Section 2 which follows.

Management control of the firm has been the starting point for the analysis of management in recent work in industrial economics. We may conveniently divide the literature into two parts. The first part is surveyed in Section 3 and deals with managerial objectives. Given that the manager has considerable discretion, for reasons which will be more fully discussed below, how is he likely to exercise his discretion in the setting of objectives for the firm? The second part concerns itself with the management task in the internal organization of large firms, and is the subject of Section 4. How can the top management communicate its objectives to the constituent parts of the large firm? And how can it ensure that such objectives are achieved with a modicum of efficiency? In discussing each part we will begin with theoretical considerations, look at some of the relevant evidence, and indicate the implications for efficiency.

2. The Divorce of Ownership and Control

The introduction has already given the empirical reason for supposing that managers may have a good deal of discretion in setting the objectives of the firm. The dispersion of shareholding makes it difficult for the owners to act as a group to monitor the activities of the managers. So disaffected shareholders 'vote' by selling their shares, rather than incur the costs of organizing opposition to the board. However, such supine behaviour on the part of shareholders seems unlikely, especially in the case of institutional shareholders. One might expect at least some attempt at legal or institutional reform in order to circumvent the present high costs of exercising owners' rights of control. Hence it is worth enquiring whether there is not some deeper reason for leaving things to managerial discretion.

An important insight into the problem has been given by the theoretical analysis of the principal–agent relationship (Ross,[15] Shavell,[16] Harris and Raviv[17]). The principal in this case is the body of shareholders. The agent is the managerial team. The question at issue is the exact form of the relationship between the agent and the principal. This involves the type of instructions given to the agent, the degree of monitoring required, and the incentives held out to the agent to encourage him to pursue the objectives of the principal. Three different methods of control can be envisaged. The first is that the agent is given, by the principal, precise instructions as to what he is to do. The agent is not a decision taker, only an administrator or executive. The second method requires the principal to specify the decision rules to be used by the agent, but leaves the agent to take the appropriate decisions. The third is that the principal designs a set of incentives, based on the measured performance of the enterprise, which encourages the agent to seek the objectives of the principal. But the decision rules, and the actual decisions themselves, are taken by the agent.

A number of factors enter the choice between these three possibilities. First, the possibilities represent a diminishing degree of involvement in the work of the agent on the part of the principal. In the first method the principal requires detailed information about the enterprise as a basis for the detailed instructions that he will give. He will also have to accompany the work of the agent to monitor his compliance with the instructions. The second method requires less information about the detailed workings of the enterprise, but the principal must be able to formulate precise decision rules and be able to monitor the use of these rules by the agent. The last method appears most promising from this point of view, so long as the performance criteria are clear, and the incentive payment formula is not too complex. The principal need know little about the actual enterprise or the decisions of the agent. However, a second consideration enters at this point. A fundamental difference between the agent and the principal is that the agent has to exert himself, while the principal does not. Suppose, for simplicity, that both the principal and the agent concur in the objective set for the enterprise: let us suppose that it is maximization of profits. Then the agent will take into account the disutility of his own effort in increasing profits (more time spent, more worry about the decisions, etc.), while this will be of no consequence to the principal. Thus, in general, the greater the scope given to the agent, as in the third method of control, the more likely it is that his decisions will differ from those desired by the principal. Only in the first method is this difficulty avoided, though at some cost to the principal, as we have seen.

But there is yet a third consideration to be taken into account. This is the existence of uncertainty affecting enterprises in the real world. The performance of the enterprise is then a result of factors over which it has control—i.e. in the decisions that it takes—and of exogenous factors which it can only estimate or forecast, and which are thus subject to uncertainty. Unfortunately it is very difficult, *ex post*, to unravel the contributions of these two sets of factors to performance. The consequence of this difficulty is most apparent in those cases where the principal takes a major part in deciding what should be done. If the results are unsatisfactory, they may be attributed either to exogenous factors or to lack of effort on the part of the agent in execution of the policy set out by the principal. But it is difficult to attribute the blame. Hence the phenomenon of 'moral hazard'*: there is no incentive for the agent to exert himself to attain a good performance. The only counter to moral hazard, in a situation where the principal makes the decisions, is a greater degree of monitoring of the agent as he carries out his task. This may be compared to a situation in which the rewards to the agent are related to performance only, so that he has every incentive to put effort into his work. To put it simply, he is given responsibility, and thus bears the blame for failures and reaps the reward of success.

The balance of all these considerations is that principal–agent arrangements that give decision scope and responsibility to the agent are preferable, despite the intrusion of the agent's personal objectives into the decisions that he takes. The literature on incentive contracts (Shavell, Harris and Raviv[18]) then deals with optimal contracts that minimize the adverse effects, to the principal, of the scope that the agent has for taking decisions. The basic idea is to relate the rewards to performance in such a way that the agent has an incentive to pursue the principal's objectives. The analysis becomes particularly interesting when risk is introduced into the picture. Outcomes are affected by random factors exogenous to the enterprise, as well as factors over which the agent has control. Suppose, now, that the principal has a low relative risk aversion in respect of this one enterprise, since he disposes of interest in a portfolio of enterprises, thus reducing the variance of his overall

---

*'Moral hazard': e.g. full cover for accidental damage to cars is an invitation to drive carelessly—there is no incentive for the motorist to take care to avoid accidents.

returns. But the agent, the manager of the enterprise, has his whole livelihood tied up in it. Hence he is likely to have high relative risk aversion. It follows that any incentive contract to encourage him to take risks must contain a fixed component to ensure his security, but a relatively small incentive bonus. On the other hand, if the performance is strongly related to managerial effort, then the greater should be the incentive bonus. We return to the question of managerial remuneration below, but it is worth noting here that a mixture of salary and performance-related bonuses is common in managerial contracts. The bonuses may either be offered directly, or may be provided by a small shareholding in the company itself.

Uncertainty about the future is another fundamental reason for believing that the separation of ownership and managerial control in a mature capitalist economy is due to more than the wide spread of shareholding. The technical analysis is abstract and complex,[19,20] but the main issues can be described here. We have already seen that the performance of a firm depends on a combination of factors which are under the control of the firm, and exogenous factors, which are not. The random nature of the latter is captured by the concept of the 'state of the world'. The state of the world will vary unpredictably, and in each state the performance of the firm will be different, likewise the profits that it can pay out to shareholders. Hence the present market value of the share reflects the sum of the returns expected in every conceivable state of the world. Now, if the number of different shares was greater than the number of states of the world, and if any given state of the world affected the performance of a large number of firms, it would be possible to deduce from the share prices 'a market price' for returns in any given state of the world. Given these market prices, the task of the manager would be to seek that set of investment and production projects which would maximize the value of the firm in the market. Thus any plan will have associated with it different returns in different states of the world. Each of these can be valued appropriately, and summed to arrive at the value of the firm should that plan be adopted. Shareholders, given the market prices of returns in various states of the world, arrange their portfolios to maximize their utility. They set the ratio of their personal marginal expected utilities (marginal utility of return in a particular state of the world multiplied by their subjective probability estimate of that state) equal to the ratio of market prices for these states.

Now there are a number of reasons why this harmonious picture does not correspond with reality. The first is the empirical fact that the number of states of the world is infinite, and the number of shares is limited. Hence the markets can be neither complete nor perfect. Second, even if they were, the situation would not be ideal. The system outlined would meet precisely the problem of 'moral hazard' described before. All risk would be transferred to the shareholders, and there would be no incentive for the managers to exert themselves. Unfavourable outcomes could simply be attributed to unfavourable states of the world.

The impact of this market failure is considerable. Notably, it precludes the possibility of defining an unambiguous objective which reflects completely the interests of the shareholders.[21,22] There is no presumption that a share price-maximizing strategy is in the interests of the current shareholders, indeed a majority might vote against such a policy. The specific probability assessments of shareholders over different states of the world have to be taken into account. Because there is no single competitive market for return in a given state of the world, the firm will need to know these assessments. In addition, one firm may have monopoly power in particular states, so that the actual returns will be dependent on the policy the firm adopts.

King[23] has suggested two institutional arrangements which may solve this theoretical impasse. One is the institution of majority-voting rules among the shareholders, to arrive at decisions about the firm's activities. The other is the idea of different management teams proposing policies for a firm, and the shareholders then voting as to which team (and set of proposals) to accept. The mechanism would be take-over offers. Because of the lack of detailed information available to shareholders about markets, and the consequences of different policies in different states of the world, this latter perspective appears to be closer to reality. The important point to note is that the manager, or managerial team, has once again taken an important role in deciding what the firm should do. The manager or team decides objectives, takes risks, and maintains a flow of information to the owners. The limitation on what the manager or team can do is the possible arrival of a new management team with a take-over proposal acceptable to shareholders. But given the privileged access of existing managers to information about the firm, they are clearly at an advantage in such competition. Hence they have considerable scope for action.

3. Managerial Objectives in the Theory of the Firm

Having established the reasons for expecting managers to have considerable scope for individual action, we now need to consider what use they make of their freedom.

In seeking information about the motives and objectives of managers, the economics literature has tended to look to psychological and sociological studies for new ideas. We will not summarize these studies here, restricting ourselves to the use economists have made of them. The most detailed consideration of the subject is that of Marris.[24] He drew on psychological studies which concluded that executives have strong drives towards achievement, identifying their ego with the success of the firm. Sociological studies suggested that managers were motivated by a degree of conscience concerning the interest of shareholders. This was not primarily due to fear of dismissal or take-over. Rather, it was based on the idea of a norm of professional competence. Managers showed a distinct preference for difficult tasks. They were not content to be mere administrators of a going concern, however large it might be. The organization of new ventures, and the development of new executive teams, were regarded as *the* test of a businessman's ability. Marris summed up his approach, and gave it content in terms of economic models, by classifying objectives under two headings. The first consisted of broad economic objectives: power, status, scope for creativity, and security within the organization. These he translated into a simple trade-off between growth of the firm on the one hand, and security (not taking too many risks in order to grow) on the other. The second heading was more narrowly economic: the financial elements of salary, bonus, and stock options accruing to the manager. Later writers have concurred with this classification in its broad outlines, though emphases have been different, or more detailed. For example, Williamson[25] translated the broad economic motives into 'expense preference'. He suggested that within the costs of the enterprise, managers may derive utility from particular expenditures, especially those on staff and administration and on managerial 'perks'. But there is much less agreement about the appropriate variables to account for broader economic motives, and the twin objectives of growth and security have come to be generally accepted, if only because they are amenable to economic analysis.

Managerial remuneration, and its relation to the performance of the firm, has attracted a great deal of attention. It seems likely that the principal–agent literature will generate more detailed studies of this aspect. Marris[26] identified three elements. The first was bonus schemes which, in a sample of US firms studied by him, amounted to about 30 per cent of all remuneration. Two types were found. There were those which were dependent on the size of the enterprise, which were more common, and clearly favour growth policies on the part of the manager. Other types were dependent on scale independent-performance variables, such as the rate of return on capital. Second, about 75 per cent of Marris's sample also had stock option schemes, brought in since 1950 in response to favourable tax legislation affecting capital gains. The attractiveness of such stock to the manager depends on the conditions under which he may sell. Obviously, there are insider gains available if sale is unrestricted. As we have seen already, such shareholdings usually constitute only a very small part of the total equity of the firm. The suggestion is that they encourage the managers to avoid risk, e.g. high gearing ratios. The third element was that of salary.

The empirical relationship between managerial remuneration and firm performance has attracted a lively debate in the literature. The seminal contribution was that of Roberts,[27] in a study of executive compensation in large US corporations in the period 1945–50. He reported that the most important determinant of salary was the sales revenue of the firm, profitability and the sector in which the firm operated not being significant. This result was confirmed by later studies, e.g. McGuire, Chiu, and Ebling.[28] However Lewellen[29] cast doubt on the accepted wisdom by showing that salary was only a small part of the total compensation of the top five executives in fifty of the 500 largest US corporations. Only about one-sixth of the *top* executives' rewards came from salary, and only about one-fifth for the top five executives as a group. With Huntsman, Lewellen[30] then examined the relationship of the total remuneration to profits and sales, and found that the part of salary and bonuses was correlated strongly with profits, but not at all with sales. Cosh[31] drew attention to econometric difficulties in the work of Lewellen and Huntsman, and in a study of 1,600 quoted and unquoted large UK companies reaffirmed the predominant role of size in the determination of the remuneration of chief executives. However, profitability was also significant for some industry groups, and for smaller companies in the sample. To complete the picture, Meeks and Whittington[32] argue that managerial remuneration is linked both to profit and to size. The empirical evidence that size is more important is misleading, because the size range itself is so great. It is simply not an option for a small firm to increase its size substantially in a short period, so as to increase the remuneration attributable to its manager. But it *is* possible for a firm to raise its profitability substantially through managerial effort. So in terms of the options open to the manager, profitability is a more effective tool than growth for increasing his remuneration. Evidence on changes in managerial remuneration recorded over a two-year period confirmed this hypothesis.

There is another serious difficulty with these studies, which bears on the question of managerial ability. The studies are not able to adjust for differences in managerial *abilities,* which must account for a substantial part of the observed differences in remuneration. The neo-classical theory of executive remuneration is addressed to this question.[33,34] It assumes that different individual managers have different amounts of a homogeneous quality, 'executive ability'. The maximum a firm will pay for an executive is his marginal contribution, defined as the additional profit he can earn over the profit brought in by the next best executive, plus what it would have to pay for the latter. The minimum the firm will pay is what the executive can gain in the next-best occupation. A number of conclusions follow. First, the most able executives are likely to end up in control of the largest firms, where their abilities can have most scope for making profits. Second, if executives succeed in extracting the maximum pay—the whole rent of their efficiency—then profit rates, net of management compensation, should be the same for all firms. Hence no relation between profit rates and remuneration is to be expected. But third, if executives extract only a proportion of their whole rent then one would expect profit rates and remuneration to be related in cross-section, since the manager has an incentive to increase the profits.

The alternative theories of managerial remuneration criticize the neo-classical theory for its postulate that salaries are determined by the market. They point to the very low mobility of executives between firms, and the evidence that many management skills are firm-specific (for example, executives displaced by a take-over often have to accept inferior positions in other companies). A specific theory was proposed by Simon.[35] He pointed to the bureaucratic nature of the management hierarchy in a large company. Assuming a given span of control and given salary differentials between levels of the hierarchy, it is easy to arrive at the conclusions that top-executive remuneration will be a function of the size of the firm.

No study of managerial remuneration has yet managed to distinguish satisfactorily between these theories of executive compensation. So the effect on managerial motivation is still not resolved. Nor has there been much systematic study of the relation between the precise form of the remuneration (salary bonus, stock option) and the performance of the firm.[36]

The conventional wisdom of industrial economics is to accept the thesis that managers have strong incentives to increase the size of their firms, incentives related both to the compensation they receive and to personal motives of power, status, and prestige. This growth objective is subject to a security constraint. The manager is unwilling to pursue the development of the firm in such a way that his security is threatened, either by financial failure, or more likely, by take-over. These ideas have been most effectively expressed by Marris, in various versions of his growth model of the firm.[37,*]

Marris's model has as its central hypothesis an inverse relationship between the growth and profitability of the firm. The reasons why fast growth should encounter diminishing returns are various. First, growth within existing markets can only be achieved by expanding market shares by price-cutting, thus reducing profit margins. Second, growth in new markets, by diversification of activities, brings diminishing returns as the firm moves into the production and marketing of products less closely related to its existing activities, and costs are higher and success rates lower. Third, rapid growth will require the recruitment of new managers, who will require training in tasks specific to the firm. This is called the 'Penrose effect'.[42,43] If the rate of growth is too fast either the new

---

*We will not consider the extensive literature which deals with the effects of alternative objectives of the firm in static models. The important contributions are those of Baumol,[38] Yarrow,[39] and Williamson.[40] The literature is reviewed in Hay and Morris.[41] It is our view that managerial objectives are more plausibly expressed in a dynamic theory of the firm, and that this literature has been, or should be, superseded by the theory of the growth of the firm discussed in the text.

managers will not be fully integrated, or the rest of the work of the firm will suffer. Either way, costs will rise and profit rates fall. It is important to note that the theory depends critically on the idea that the firm is a unique bundle of resources, and that some of the efficiency of the resources is specific to it.

The managers then make a choice of growth rate and profit rate along this trade-off, a higher profit rate being understood to afford more security. In more elaborate versions of the model the combination of profit rate and growth rate at each point is used to derive a market valuation of the shares of the firm. The assumption is made that the returns, which are growing over time, can be discounted at a given market rate of interest appropriate to the riskiness of the firm.* Marris identified the valuation ratio—the ratio of the market value to the book value of the assets of the firm—as the key variable. In his model, too low a value of this ratio would precipitate a take-over. In one version, faster growth and lower valuation ratios increase the probability of a take-over. In another, there is a minimum valuation ratio to avert take-over, determined by the costs of a take-over, given that the maximum gain of the take-over raider is the maximum possible valuation of the firm, minus the costs of the operation. It has been suggested by Yarrow[44] that these costs should be related to the shareholding distribution, as an index of the difficulty of arranging a successful take-over bid.

This model has attracted a number of empirical contributions seeking to establish the validity of its central precepts as a theory of the firm. An early paper by Richardson,[45] based on interviews with managers, confirmed the supposition that the Penrose effect was the most important constraint on firms' growth. Physical and financial problems were not felt to be serious obstacles. A second test of the theory arises from the prediction that one would expect differences in performance where otherwise-similar firms have different patterns of control. The most popular distinction in the literature is between owner-controlled, and manager-controlled firms. The simplest hypothesis is that owner-managed firms will maximize valuation to increase the owners' wealth, while managerial firms are more willing to sacrifice profit to growth. Kamerschen[46] tried to

---

*There are plenty of theoretical objections to this procedure, but discussion of these is not appropriate in this paper.

verify the prediction concerning profit rates in a study of 200 of the largest non-financial US corporations in the period 1959–64. He regressed profit rates on variables for control type (managerial or non-managerial), change in control type (where a company had changed in the relevant period), and a large number of other variables to control for industry structure and firm size. He concluded that control type was significant, and that the change in control type from owner-controlled to manager-controlled was generally associated with a *rise* in profits, which appears to be inconsistent with the managerial hypothesis. Similar contradictory results were reported by Radice[47] for a sample of 86 firms from the UK food, electrical engineering, and textile industries. On average he found that owner-controlled firms had high profit rates, *and* higher growth rates, than managerial firms. The same pattern held for each sector except food, where it was the *owner*-controlled firms that had higher growth rates and lower profit rates than their managerial counterparts. Various other studies have been contradictory or inconclusive.[48]

A number of reasons can be adduced for this lack of clear differences between the two control types. First, theory is greatly complicated by the introduction of personal taxation. For example, if capital gains are taxed at a lower rate than income at the margin, then an owner-manager may maximize his wealth by retaining and reinvesting profits in the company, thus generating a faster growth rate. Second, the distinction between owner-controlled and management-controlled firms may not be given. For example, it may be only the most efficient owner-controlled firms that can continue in being as such, less-efficient firms falling victim to financial difficulties, or to the peculiar taxation problems of such firms, and thus being taken over. Third, the comparison depends critically on identifying firms that are identical in all respects except for control, or in being able to control statistically for other sources of difference. Unfortunately, this is not always easy—for example, owner-controlled firms are by and large smaller than managerial (quoted) firms. Fourth, it is not always clear how we may distinguish the two types of firm. For example, we have already seen that control may be effectively exercised with a very small shareholding. So the distinction may require a very careful analysis of the precise pattern of control within the firm.

Another type of evidence concerns the take-over constraint. Is there any evidence that the threat of take-over circumscribes the liberty of managers to pursue growth goals? The Marris model would predict that firms which were victims of merger for managerial reasons would have lower profit rates and valuation ratios, and higher growth rates, than those firms that have survived. Presumably the theoretical reason for take-over is that the victims have misjudged the strength of the take-over constraint on their behaviour. This hypothesis has been exhaustively studied by Singh[49] and by Kuehn[50] for UK manufacturing sectors. Their conclusion is that while performance differences between victims and survivors do exist on average, they are too small to discriminate effectively between the two groups. The strongest discriminant is *size*, which is not a performance indicator at all. This last result gives support to another aspect of the managerial theory. If the probability of take-over diminishes with size, then there is yet another reason for a long-run growth objective—to increase managerial security.

The inconclusiveness of empirical study of the take-over mechanism can be traced to a number of sources. First, the more-theoretical work on the valuation of the firm by its shareholders suggests that market valuation alone is not a valid indicator of what they think of the firm. In particular, take-over bids are generally well above the previous market valuation, indicating that intra-marginal shareholders are inclined to place a much higher valuation on the firm.[51] Second, if the take-over mechanism were reasonably effective in disciplining firms, as Manne[52] and Hindley[53] have suggested, then the efficacy of the mechanism could be evident from the *absence* of take-over activity. Third, there are other reasons for merger which complicate the empirical analysis. For example, Kuehn has argued for a theory of merger in which managerial firms grow by take-over as a more rapid route to achieving large size (and, incidentally, security due to reduced probability of take-over).

The lack of empirical confirmation of the managerial theory of the firm is disconcerting. There are two possible responses to this failure. One is to try to devise more appropriate empirical tests: we have already seen that there are serious weaknesses in the empirical work to date. The other is to modify the theory, while remaining within the managerial framework, for which reasons were adduced in Section 2. We deal with these in turn.

A major difficulty with the theory of the growth of the firm, from the empirical standpoint, is that it is a summary model: too many of the underlying decisions and mechanisms are hidden from view. So a good place to start is with a process of dismembering the model into its constituent parts: an investment function, a 'growth expenditure' function, a dividend function, and a 'supply of funds' function, which might itself distinguish between different sources of funds. The Penrose effect could either be incorporated in the investment function, or modelled separately. What links all these elements together is the managerial requirement to balance the flow of funds through the enterprise. Shareholders' interests are expressed in the dividend function, and by the costs to the firm of raising funds in capital markets. A little empirical work has been done with such models,[55,56,57] but the results are not sufficiently established to decide the question of managerial models in general. The great benefit of such models is that they emphasize the kind of financial management which is a major part of the managerial task. An alternative type of model, which emphasizes balance sheets rather than flow of funds, has also been developed recently,[58] and should eventually shed light on the attitudes of managers to risky financial portfolios.

Modifications of the managerial theory are rather few. The work of Williamson[59] on 'expense preference' has already been mentioned. It is a notable omission in the literature that so little has been done to follow up his work. For example, it needs to be reconsidered in the context of a growing firm. The difficulty is that once multiple managerial objectives are introduced (growth, managerial remuneration, size of staff, etc.) it becomes very hard to make any very definite predictions about the behaviour of the firm. Too much depends on the utility weights attached to different goals, and the precise trade-offs between them. So empirical verification becomes essential. Herein lies the problem: detailed information about company activity, especially that relating to different costs, is generally confidential to the firm and simply not available to the researcher.

Recently Aoki[60] has proposed a slightly different managerial paradigm. The manager is viewed as acting as arbiter between the shareholders and workers in the matter of division of the income of the firm between the two groups. His task is to propose solutions to the bargaining game, such that the two groups will accept and combine for the continuation of the firm. His particular interest is that the game should be solved without conflict, as his continuing managerial position will depend on successful resolution of the question.

In conclusion, we note what managerial theories of the firm have achieved. They have successfully isolated broad objectives for managers that are plausible and consistent with a range of literature on managerial motivation. They have distinguished objectives which are related to the performance of the firm (growth and security), and those which are more narrowly tied to questions of managerial remuneration. The precise links between these two elements have also been the subject of scrutiny. Furthermore, the theory of the growth of the firm has incorporated these objectives in a coherent economic model which yields at least some predictions about the behaviour of different kinds of firms. But the theory has not been successful empirically, and a reassessment is therefore required. The most likely direction this reassessment will take is a disaggregation of the model into its main components, each of which will be subject to more detailed scrutiny. It seems unlikely that the managerial paradigm for the analysis of firms will be easily discarded.

There is, however, an alternative aspect of management, which relates not to the overall objectives of the firm, but to the control that management exercises over what goes on *within* the firm. This aspect is the subject of the next section.

4. Management and the Internal Structure of Firms

Economics has for the most part regarded the firm as a 'black box'. The behaviour of the firm is determined by the external conditions it faces in markets for products, inputs, and finance, and by the objectives of the managers. The actual process of decision-taking, and the execution of decisions within the firm, are presumed to have no effect on the outcomes. This analytically convenient presupposition has attracted considerable criticism, mainly from the behavioural school.

The most important contribution of the behavioural school is the work of March and Simon,[61] and of Cyert and March.[62] They argue that the managerial team does not act as a unified group. Rather, it is a coalition of individuals, with different responsibilities within the firm, and hence with different objectives. Cyert and March identify five organizational goals:

1. Production goal. There is a distinct preference on the production side for growth of production, without fluctuations.

2. Inventory goal. The sales staff have a preference for larger inventories, so that they can respond to customer pressure for prompt deliveries.

3. Sales goal. The performance of the sales staff is judged by their capacity to maintain and expand the sales of the company. This goal will be shared to a certain extent by all members of the managerial team, but is a particular concern of the sales staff.

4. Market share goal. This may be an alternative to the sales goal, or complementary to it. The comparative performance of the company relative to its competitors may be particularly important to the top management.

5. Profit goal. Profits are essential for investment, dividends, and growth expenditures. The profit rate is regarded by top management as an important comparative indicator of performance.

That these goals may involve conflicts is obvious. Sales goals may involve lower prices, thus conflicting with the profit goal, and demand more rapid growth of production than is comfortable for the production team. Sales and production goals may favour higher inventories, which will reduce profits. To resolve these conflicts, Cyert and March postulate four features of the decision-taking process within the firm. The first is that goals are stated in terms of 'aspiration levels'. The managers do not maximize. They 'satisfice' by seeking satisfactory levels of performance. Second, decision-taking is directed towards problems in the form of unfulfilled aspirations. These problems will frequently arise one at a time, and thus the managerial task is to solve difficulties sequentially. This reduces markedly the degree to which conflicts are felt within the organization. Third, standard operating procedures are derived for taking decisions within different parts of the firm. Once these procedures or rules are accepted, they can be applied without reconsideration of basic conflicts. Fourth, every business organization operates with a degree of 'slack'. Thus solutions to the problem of unsatisfactory performance in one part of the firm do not necessarily involve sacrifice of some other objective.

The description of the decision-taking process provided by Cyert and March is clearly apt. The difficulty arises in translating it into an operational model which can actually predict the behaviour of the firm. For example, what are the determinants of aspiration levels relative to each goal? How precisely are decisions affected? Morris[63] has drawn attention to the fact that decisions are taken at different levels within the firm, depending on their importance. Thus decisions about finance, investment, and research and development are taken at a very high level. Lower levels in the management hierarchy can only influence these decisions by control over information flow to the top. Effectively, then, conflicts are reduced, and it may be possible to continue to model firms' behaviour 'as if' decisions were the decisions of a single executive with particular goals.

This approach is strengthened by consideration of organizational form. Williamson[62] has distinguished two major organizational forms in business enterprises. The traditional form is a U-form enterprise, with a chief executive and functional divisions—sales, production, finance. Each functional division has a manager who reports to the chief executive. This form is common in small and medium-sized firms. The disadvantage, especially as the firm expands, is that all decisions have to be taken by the chief executive at the peak of the pyramid. These decisions are then transmitted down the organization, with consequent likelihood of 'control loss' (i.e. dilution or errors in transmission of information, either by omission or by deliberation). Williamson showed[65] that the effects of such control loss on the cost efficiency of the organization could be considerable. A further disadvantage is that the U form encourages precisely the kind of conflict of objectives identified by Cyert and March. Each manager of the functional divisions is identified with the goals of that particular division. Hence the chief executive will find that much of his time is taken up with the resolution of conflicts between the divisional managers.

The alternative form of organization, the M form or multidivisional organization, was a response to these difficulties in U-form organization, and is now widely adopted in large business firms.[66] The divisions are organized on the basis of product or geographical markets. Each division becomes a quasi-firm with its own function divisions of production, sales, and finance. But each is kept sufficiently small to avoid the problems of U-form firms. In addition, the manager of each division has his performance measured in terms of profit, growth of sales, and return on resources used. So he has every incentive to ensure that his goals are imposed on his part of the enterprise. The top management is now freed from the need to resolve conflicts between different operating divisions. It can devote its attention to the overall strategy of the firm, including the creation of new operating divisions as the firm diversifies. Its involvement with the operating divisions is limited to the scrutiny of requests for financial resources for investment, and to evaluation of performance. This gives it sufficient power and information to ensure that the activities of the operating divisions are in line with the overall objectives of the firm. Once again, it would seem that the particular difficulties described by Cyert and March have been circumvented, and we are able to analyse firms 'as if' they had unified objectives.

Another important element in the internal organization of firms, identified by Cyert and March, is 'organizational slack'. Typically, economic theory has assumed that firms are internally cost efficient in their operations. This is consistent with survival if the firm is operating in perfect markets for capital or goods. It is consistent with profit maximization if the firm is operating in imperfect markets. This assumption has been challenged by Leibenstein,[67] who coined the term 'X-efficiency'. His starting point was evidence from a number of sources that industrial plants could be operated much more productively without changes in inputs. The discrepancy between actual productivity, and potential productivity, needs an explanation. Leibenstein suggested that the efficiency of the firm was dependent on the internal and external motivations to efficiency.

Analysis of the internal motivation to efficiency begins with the fact that contracts for labour supply within the firm are incomplete. They do not generally include a specification of the job, so effectiveness of labour depends on motivation and on monitoring. One way of looking at this is to derive a relationship between the effort a particular worker puts in and his personal utility. There is an increasing range, since he prefers doing something to doing nothing; there is a wide range of efforts which do not affect his utility very much, as he feels reasonably comfortable; and then there is a range of efforts where he begins to feel under pressure. Now it is probable that, for the firm, the returns to his effort are increasing over the whole range. They therefore wish him to exert himself. But the individual will be satisfied with a much lower effort, and can only be kept at a higher level with constant monitoring. The second element in the analysis is the concept of 'inert areas'. The individual develops work routines to which he becomes accustomed. To move from those routines involves a degree of discomfort, so he is resistant to change. Hence pressure to effect small changes in effort will fall into an inert area, i.e. the individual will find it easier to resist the pressure than to change his output. Only major initiatives by the management to achieve higher output per man are likely to have any effect. The conclusion is that firms are very unlikely to be cost efficient in the sense required by traditional theory, partly because of worker resistance to small changes in working methods, partly because labour contracts are incomplete in their specification of what each worker is to do.

A rather different perspective of this problem is offered by Alchian and Demsetz,[68] and by Williamson.[69] The essential feature of production in firms is that it is done in teams. Team production brings together different resources, the product is not the sum of the separable outputs of each contributing resource, and not all resources are contributed by one person. The jointness of resources in production immediately leads to a problem. There is always an incentive for one member of the team to shirk, since the consequent reduction in output will be a loss which falls on the whole team and not just on himself. Williamson links this particularly to the problem of moral hazard and information. A member of the team may misrepresent his abilities, and ask for a higher reward than his productivity warrants. Poor performance can be excused in terms of some difficulty in the work, rather than attributed to his own inferior qualities. The particular managerial requirement then is for monitoring of each individual's performance. More monitoring (i.e. managerial effort) can increase performance in terms of output.

The immediate question, then, is what determines the degree of managerial activity to overcome organizational slack, and X-efficiency. Leibenstein argued that it was market or other pressures in the firm that generated managerial activity. Specifically, he suggested that managers were motivated by the knowledge that their cost performance was inferior to that of their competitors. The evidence on this point is not systematic, though some dramatic examples of cost-cutting in the face of business difficulties lend it some support.[70]

5. Conclusions

Managerial models of the firm have not yet won wide acceptance in the economics literature, even within industrial economics. Yet the reasons for thinking that managerial objectives are important get stronger. The evidence for the separation of ownership and control in the large industrial firm is stronger than ever. Firms are now larger, shareholdings tend to be more dispersed, and those institutions (in the UK) which could exert more pressure on the firms in which they have shareholdings do not appear to want to do so. From a theoretical point of view, advances in our understanding of the role of securities in risk-bearing and the application of the moral hazard argument both suggest a much greater role for management than textbook theory would suggest.

But having accepted all these points, one is bound also to note that the existing managerial theories have not been particularly successful from an empirical point of view. The simple predictions of the theory appear to get little support. The reason is that the theory is too simple to incorporate the complexity of real firms. At present it is more a paradigm—a framework which needs to be given detailed context—than a properly articulated theory. The question is what detailed context is appropriate. One area which needs more consideration is the effect of detailed arrangements for managerial remuneration on the objectives and performance of managers. The principal–agent framework would appear to be appropriate. The major decision areas of the firm also need individual study—investment, growth expenditures, development of managerial teams, dividends, and finance. Some work in these areas has already been done. For example, there is already a sophisticated literature on investment[71] and finance.[72] But it needs to be placed in the context of the 'growth of the firm' paradigm. In particular, the standard models are based on the neo-classical presumption that capital markets are sufficiently perfect for investment, finance, and dividend decisions to be independent. This scarcely accords with the experience of most firms.

None of this gives us very much in the way of leads on the efficiency question raised in the introduction. It is clear that a firm which pursued managerial growth objectives would be inefficient in the sense that returns would be lower than is desirable. Also, expense preference models of the Williamson type predict that costs may be excessive in a managerial firm. But it is doubtful whether this helps explain the more generalized inefficiency uncovered by the Brooking study. Almost certainly what is required is a more detailed study of what goes on *inside* firms. Economists have been generally reluctant to do this. In part it reflects the presupposition of much of economics that the firm is a 'black box' which should not be opened up. Certainly the work of the behavioural school, and of Leibenstein on X-efficiency, is not a great encouragement to probe the 'black box'. Everything becomes very complicated, and terminology foreign to economics is introduced. Economic models based on optimizing behaviour seem to be inadequate to describe the full range of behaviour observed within firms, even when these models explicitly introduce uncertainty and the costs of obtaining information, and even when new elements are introduced into the individual's utility function. So there is a very real doubt as to whether such models are appropriate, and the economist finds himself increasingly turning to other disciplines to provide him with the analytic tools he needs. In this situation, the box is perhaps best left unopened by economists, and remitted for the attention of some other branch of management studies. Economists, of all people, should be the first to acknowledge the gains from a division of labour.

NOTES

1 R.E. Caves (ed.), *Britain's Economic Prospects,* Washington, George, Allen and Unwin (1968).
2 C.F. Pratten, *Labour Productivity Differentials within International Companies,* Cambridge University Press (1976).
Pratten, *A Comparison of the Performance of UK and Swedish Companies,* Cambridge University Press (1976).
3 R.W. Bacon and W. Eltis, *The Age of UK Machinery,* London, National Economic Development Office (1975).
4 D.K. Stout, *International Price Competitiveness, Non-Price Factors and Export Performance,* London, National Economic Development Office (1977).
5 C. Freeman, 'Technical Innovation and British Trade Performance' in *De-industrialisation* (ed. F. Blackaby), London, Heinemann (1980).
6 A. Marshall, *Principles of Economics,* London, Macmillan (1890); Marshall, *Industry and Trade,* London, Macmillan (1919).

7 S. Prais, *The Evolution of Giant Firms in Britain,* Cambridge University Press (1976).

8 M.A. Utton, 'Large-Firm Diversification in British Manufacturing Industry', *Economic Journal,* 87(1977), pp. 96–113.

9 A. Berle and B.C. Means, *The Modern Corporation and Private Property,* New York, Macmillan (1932).

10 P. Sargent Florence, *Ownership, Control and Success of Large Companies,* London, Sweet and Maxwell (1961).

11 R. Marris, *Economic Theory of Managerial Capitalism,* London, Macmillan (1964).

12 C. Beed, 'The Separation of Ownership from Control', *Journal of Economic Studies* (1966), pp. 29–46.

13 J. Moyle, 'The Pattern of Ordinary Share Ownership 1957–70' (DAE Occasional Paper 31, Cambridge (1971).

14 R. Dobbins and M.J. Greenwood, 'The Future Pattern of UK Share Ownership', *Long-Range Planning* 8/4(1975).

15 S.A. Ross, 'the Economic Theory of Agency: The Principals' Problem', *American Economic Review Papers and Proceedings,* 63(1973), pp. 134–9.

16 S. Shavell, 'Risk-Sharing and Incentives in the Principal and Agent Relationship', *Bell Journal,* 10(1979), pp. 55–73.

17 M. Harris and A. Raviv, 'Incentive Contracts', *American Economic Review,* 68(1978), pp. 20–30.

18 Shavell, op.cit. in note 16; Harris and Raviv, op.cit. in note 17.

19 K. Arrow, 'The Role of Securities, Markets in the Optimal Allocation of Risk-Bearing', *Review of Economic Studies,* 31(1964), pp. 91–6.

20 M.A. King, *Public Policy and the Corporation,* London, Chapman and Hall (1977), Ch. 5,

21 S. Ekern and R. Wilson, 'On the Theory of the Firm in an Economy with Incomplete Markets', *Bell Journal, 5/1(1974), pp. 171–80.*

22 S.J. Grossman and J.E. Stiglitz, 'On Value Maximization and Alternative Objectives of the Firm', *Journal of Finance,* 32(1977), pp. 389–402.

23 King, op.cit. in note 20, Ch. 5.

24 Marris, op.cit. in note 11, Ch. 2.

25 O.E. Williamson, *The Economics of Discretionary Behaviour: Management Objectives in a Theory of the Firm,* Englewood Cliffs, Prentice-Hall (1964).

26 Marris, op.cit. in note 11.

27 D. Roberts, *Executive Compensation,* Glencoe, Illinois, Free Press (1959).

28 J. McGuire, J. Chiu and A. Ebling, 'Executive Income, Sales and Profits', *American Economic Review,* 52(1962), pp. 753–61.

29 W. Lewellen, 'Management and Ownership in the Large Firm', *Journal of Finance,* 24(1969), pp. 299–322.

30 W. Lewellen and B. Huntsman, 'Managerial Pay and Corporate Performance', *American Economic Review,* 60(1970), pp. 710–20.

31 A. Cosh, 'The Remuneration of Chief Executives in the UK', *Economical Journal,* 85(1975), pp. 75–94.

32 G. Meeks and G. Whittington, 'Directors' Pay, Growth and Profitability', *Journal of Industrial Economics*, 24(1975), pp. 1–14.
33 Cosh, op.cit. in note 31.
34 G. Yarrow, 'Executive Compensation and the Theory of the Firm' in *Market Structure and Corporate Behaviour* (ed. K. Cowling), London, Gray-Mills Publish Ltd (1973).
35 H. Simon, 'The Corporation of Executives' in *Sociometry* (1957).
36 R.T. Masson, 'Executive Motivations, Earnings and Consequent Equity Performance', *Journal of Political Economy*, 79(1971), pp. 1278–92.
37 R. Marris, 'A Model of the Managerial Enterprise', *Quarterly Journal of Economics*, 77(1963), pp. 185–209.
Marris, *The Economic Theory of Managerial Capitalism*, London, Macmillan (1966), pp. 249–65.
R. Marris and A. Wood (eds.), *The Corporate Economy*, London, Macmillan (1971).
38 W. Baumol, 'On the Theory of Oligopoly', *Economica* N.S., 25(1958), pp. 187–98.
39 G. Yarrow, 'On the Predictions of the Managerial Theory of the Firm', *Journal of Industrial Economics*, 24(1976), pp. 267–79.
40 Williamson, op.cit. in note 25.
41 D.A. Hay and D.J. Morris, *Industrial Economics: Theory and Evidence*, Oxford, Oxford University Press (1979), pp. 266–76.
E. Penrose, *The Theory of the Growth of the Firm* (revised edn. with introduction by M. Slater), Oxford, Basil Blackwell (1980).
43 M. Slater, 'The Managerial Limit to the Growth of Firms', *Economic Journal*, 90(1980), pp. 520–8.
44 Yarrow, op.cit. in note 39.
45 G.B. Richardson, 'The Limits to a Firm's Rate of Growth', *Oxford Economic Papers*, 16(1964), pp. 9–23.
46 D.R. Kamerschen, 'Influence of Ownership and Control on Profit Rates', *American Economic Review*, 58(1968), pp. 432–47.
47 H. Radice, 'Control Type, Profitability and Growth in Large Firms', *Economic Journal*, 81(1971), pp. 547–62.
48 Hay and Morris, op.cit. in note 41, pp. 312–19.
49 A. Singh, *Takeovers*, Cambridge University Press (1971).
Singh, 'Takeovers, Economic Natural Selection, and the Theory of the Firm', *Economic Journal*, 85(1975), pp. 497–515.
50 D.A. Kuehn, *Takeovers and the Theory of the Firm*, London, Macmillan (1975).
51 M.A. Firth, 'The Profitability of Takeovers and Mergers', *Economic Journal*, 89(1979), pp. 316–28.
52 H. Manne, 'Mergers and the Market for Corporate Control', *Journal of Political Economy*, 73(1965), pp. 110–20.
53 B. Hindley, 'Separation of Ownership and Control in the Modern Corporation', *Journal of Law and Economics*, 13(1970), pp. 185–222.
54 Kuehn, op.cit. in note 50.
55 P. Dhrymes and M. Kurz, 'Investment, Dividends and External Finance

Behaviour of the Firm' in *The Determinants of Investment Behaviour* (ed. R. Ferber), New York, Columbia University Press (1967).

56 E.F. Fama, 'The Empirical Relations between the Dividend and Investment Decisions of Firms', *American Economic Review*, 64(1974), pp. 304–18.

57 H. Grabowski and D. Mueller, 'Stockholder and Managerial Welfare Models of Firm Expenditures', *Review of Economics and Statistics*, 54(1972), pp. 9–24.

58 R.A. Taggart, 'A Model of Corporate Financing Decisions', *Journal of Finance*, 32(1977), pp. 1467–84.

59 Williamson, op.cit. in note 25.

60 M. Aoki, 'A Model of the Firm as a Stockholder—Employee Cooperative Game', *American Economic Review*, 70(1980), pp. 600–10.

61 J. March and H.A. Simon, *Organizations*, New York, Wiley (1958).

62 R. Cyert and J. March, *Behavioural Theory of the Firm*, Englewood Cliffs, Prentice-Hall (1963).

D. Morris, 'The Structure of Investment Decisions' (unpublished D. Phil. thesis), Oxford (1964).

64 O.E. Williamson, 'Managerial Discretion Organization Form and the Multidivision Hypothesis' in *The Corporate Economy* (eds. R. Marris and A. Wood), London, Macmillan 1971).

65 Williamson, 'Hierarchical Control and Optimum Firm Size', *Journal of Political Economy*, 75(1967), pp. 123–38.

66 D. Channon, *The Strategy and Structure of British Industry*, Boston, Mass., Graduate School of Business Administration, Havard University (1973).

67 H. Leibenstein, 'Allocative Efficiency v. X-Efficiency', *American Economic Review*, 56(1966), pp. 392–415.

Leibenstein, 'Organizational or Frictional Equilibria, X-Efficiency and the Rate of Innovation', *Quarterly Journal of Economics*, 83(1969), pp. 600–23.

68 A. Alchian and H. Demsetz, 'Production, Information Costs and Economic Organization', *American Economic Review*, 62(1972), pp. 777–95.

69 O.E. Williamson, *Markets and Hierarchies*, Glencoe, Illinois, The Free Press (1975).

70 M. Reder, 'A Reconsideration of Marginal Productivity Theory', *Journal of Political Economy*, 55(1947), pp. 450–8.

71 S.J. Nickell, *The Investment Decisions of Firms*, Cambridge, James Nisbet and Co. and Cambridge University Press (1978).

72 S.H. Archer and C.A. D'Ambrosio (eds.), *The Theory of Business Finance: A Book of Readings*, New York, Macmillan (1976).

4

Managerial Behaviour:
how research has changed the
traditional picture

ROSEMARY STEWART

Management theories rest on assumptions about managerial behaviour. These assumptions may be explicit or they may be implicit, even quite unrecognized. Whichever they are, they should be identified and then checked against what research has taught us about how managers behave. The aim of this chapter is to show the changes in our understanding of managerial behaviour that come from studies of what managers do.

Traditional, and many of the current, writings on management theorize about the nature of managerial work and assume that that is what managers do. The researchers have taken a different approach: that of trying to understand the nature of managerial work by studying managerial behaviour.

The traditional picture of managerial work, and one that underlies many management theories, is of rationality, planning, and pursuit of organizational goals. These characteristics have been seen as applying to all managers. The studies of managerial behaviour suggest a different picture.

Pattern of Managerial Work

The best-documented finding in the studies of managerial behaviour is that the work of many managers consists of short episodes, so that the manager's attention is frequently shifting from one subject or person to another. This was first remarked by Sune Carlson (1951) in his pioneering study of nine Swedish managing directors, when he expressed concern at how short were the periods that they had alone and uninterrupted. They had, he complained, little time

for reading and thinking. Later studies have reported upon the
number of such episodes in a day, showing that their duration
averaged seconds for foremen and minutes for managers. Mintzberg
(1973, pp. 31–5) summarized the relevant studies, and described the
pattern of the manager's day as characterized by brevity, variety,
and fragmentation. Stewart's (1967) study of specially designed
diaries kept by 160 middle and senior managers for four weeks
found that they averaged nine uninterrupted periods of half an hour
or longer during that period. This average included managers in
some accounting and administrative jobs who would be likely to
have more such periods than those in production and sales.

Is such fragmentation of the working day a necessary feature of
managerial work or rather is it the way that managers choose to
work? There is some evidence that the latter is at least partly true.
Mintzberg (1973) in his observation of five chief executives in
different types of organization concluded that they chose their work
pattern. They could have freed themselves more from interruptions
and given themselves more time alone. Further, they frequently
interrupted what they were doing to make telephone calls or to ask a
subordinate to come in. Similar self-imposed fragmentation was
also found in the observational studies reported in Stewart (1976).

The reasons for this fragmentation, whether self-imposed or not,
could be important for our understanding of managerial behaviour
and, therefore, for the assumptions that we may make about it in
our management theories. Mintzberg (1973) suggested that it was
partly due to the manager not wanting to discourage the flow of
current information, but he thought that a more significant
explanation might be that 'the manager becomes conditioned by his
workload' (Mintzberg 1973, p. 35). He saw the manager as
necessarily overworked and conscious of the opportunity cost of his
time, so that whatever he is doing he is aware of what he is not
doing. Mintzberg seems to be arguing that even self-imposed
fragmentation is not really a choice, but a necessary condition of
managerial work.

There are other possible explanations for the fragmented pattern
of many managers' work. One that is frequently put forward by UK
managers is that they need to be available. They give various
reasons for this: the expectations of those they work with, whether
boss, subordinates, colleagues, or customers, that they will be
available when required to answer queries and to help with

problems; the fear that they would not get co-operation unless they were available; the belief that it is their job to be available; and the worry that they would get cut off from what was going on and what they needed to know if people did not think they could go to them freely. Such reasons do not explain the self-imposed fragmentation. One possible explanation is that managers get into the habit of working in a fragmented way and so feel uncomfortable when there are no interruptions. A related explanation is that they get used to operating by their stream of consciousness so that they switch their attention as soon as they think of something else, rather than trying to concentrate on one subject at a time. The development of this habit of working may be due to the fragmented character of operational work in junior management, where there may be little or no opportunity to work in any other way. Such habits may continue into more senior posts despite the choice that may then exist to work in a different and less fragmented way. Whatever the explanations, self-imposed fragmentation poses some interesting questions for effectiveness: are managers who work on the basis of their stream of consciousness any more or less effective than those who try to minimize interruptions and attempt to organize their time into longer periods? Does the answer vary with the type of personality or with the kind of job?

The episodic character of the way managers work is, it was suggested above, one of the more securely based generalizations that can be made about managerial behaviour. Even so, there is evidence that there are differences both between jobs and in individual behaviour in similar jobs. Some jobs are necessarily more fragmented than others: those in operational management, for example, compared with those in some staff jobs (Stewart 1976). Individuals in similar jobs can also behave very differently. The main evidence for this statement is a comparative observational study of eleven senior administrators in the National Health Service in the UK (Stewart et al. 1980). This showed very marked variations in the pattern of the administrator's day. Some worked in a very fragmented manner. They tended to be the ones who focused their attention on operational issues and worked with their subordinates on the resolution of the problems that arose. At the opposite extreme were administrators who attached considerable importance to their contribution to planning and policy-making, and protected themselves from interruptions so that they could work on policy papers. They mainly saw their subordinates at meetings and were rarely interrupted by them at other times. They delegated the operational management to one or more senior colleagues. The administrators whom we studied may have had more opportunity for choice in how they organized their time than senior managers in some companies, but the evidence of such wide variations in the patterns of their day suggests that individuals, particularly at the more senior levels, can and will vary in the extent to which their work is characterized by brevity, variety, and fragmentation. There are probably also variations stemming from organizational and national cultures, but we do not have comparative studies that document these. The expectations of personal availability may vary between organizations and between countries, and so may the importance attached to verbal or written communication, and to the use of the telephone. The latter can contribute a lot to the frequency of interruptions.

The common pattern of the day that has been observed for many different kinds of managers, despite the above account of job and individual variations, has potential implications for how managers do their work, indeed *can* do their work. An individual who for much of the day is switching his or her attention every few minutes from one person and subject to another has little opportunity, while that is happening, to reflect on what should be done, or to plan what ought to be done. The pattern of the day is one reason for questioning the model of the manager as a reflective planner.

Managing as a Reactive, Instinctive Activity

The traditional description of managerial functions includes planning, organizing, and controlling. The emphasis in that description, and in much writing on decision-making, is on a logical, sequential process. The pattern of the day that we have just described presents a different kind of picture; not of ordered and controlled sequences, but of a rapid change of subject matter, requiring the manager to adapt and respond to a wide variety of problems. This fragmented pattern may require, at least for some, perhaps even much, of the time, an ability to respond, to react instinctively to problems and people as they appear. Is such responding compatible with the concept of the manager as a planner, a concept which suggests a need for longish periods for thinking about and planning what to do? Does a plan, or at least conscious thought about what should be done, underlie the rapid responses shown in studies of managerial behaviour?

There is no definite answer to the questions that have just been posed because there has been very little research into how managers think about their work and whether, and when, they consciously think about what they should do. Recently a number of different methods have been used to try and discover how managers think about managing. Burgoyne and Hodgson (1982) asked managers to articulate what they were doing shortly before the interview. Valerie and Andrew Stewart (1981) and others have used repertory grid* as a way of identifying managers' conceptual thinking.

A study by Marshall and Stewart (1981) of middle managers from different educational backgrounds in three manufacturing companies showed wide variations in whether the managers said that they were trying to plan their activities. Many of those interviewed said thay they mainly worked instinctively, being carried along by the momentum of events. It was only occasionally that they had to think what they should do. However, a minority of them did say that they had plans for what they were aiming to do and tried to direct their activities to accomplish them.

Marshall and Stewart's (1981) study suggests that there are differences in the extent to which managers seek to plan their work or manage instinctively. Such differences probably have a variety of explanations such as: the kind of job, including the level of management; the time that the manager has been in the job; the novelty or familiarity of the problems that arise; as well as individual differences. We do not know how representative were the managers in this study, but it seems likely that many managers, particularly at the junior and middle-management levels, spend much of their time reacting instinctively, or perhaps more correctly, habitually, to problems that arise.

We can think in terms of opposites, of managers who try to plan and direct their activities, and of those who primarily respond. This may be too simple a dichotomy: a more useful way of thinking about how the manager who seeks to pursue particular goals goes

---

*Repertory grid is a particular form of structured interview. It seeks to elicit the relationships for a person between sets of constructs and assigns mathematical values to them.

about achieving them is that, suggested by Mintzberg (1973) and Kotter (1982), of the opportunistic manager. This kind of manager has thought through his or her own objectives in the job and uses opportunities as they arise to try and forward them, in addition to more planned attempts to do so. Kotter describes such opportunism as the 'efficiency of seemingly inefficient behaviour', showing how brief conversations even on chance meetings can be used to forward a manager's aims.

A change in our conception of managerial activity, from emphasizing planning to recognizing that behaviour is frequently responding and opportunistic, poses interesting questions for research and for management training. Research topics include the following: how and when are a manager's ways of responding learnt? how enduring are these and what changes them? in what situations is a more calculated approach to managing more or less efficient? Some of the possible training implications are: should training take account of the pattern of much managerial work? Does the use of habitual methods of response mean that training in the first managerial job is particularly important? Can, and should, managers be taught to think opportunistically?

Managers Talk and Listen Most of the Time

Managers work with, and by means of, other people. This generally accepted description of management says nothing about how they do this. Studies of managerial behaviour show that the large majority of managers' time is spent in conversations with other people. They are rarely alone and, when they are, rarely for more than a few minutes without a telephone call or a brief contact. The range of time managers' spent with others, as shown in studies of British and American managers, is from about half (for the more back-room desk jobs) to over 90 per cent, with an average (excluding the back-room jobs) of at least two-thirds of their time and probably more. A rather curious fact reported in Stewart (1976) is that nine of the sixteen managers who were intensively studied underestimated the amount of time that they spent with other people by 10 per cent or more, and three of them by 25 per cent or more. This may be because paperwork bulked larger in their minds, and that they tended to overlook their many short conversations.

There are some differences in the amount of time that managers in different types of job spend with other people. Production managers, for example, spend more time than do managers in accounting (Stewart 1967). There are also individual differences for which the best-documented evidence is the observational comparisons of senior administrators in the National Health Service cited earlier. The differences in the administrators' contact time were, like those in the pattern of their day, related to the kind of work that they concentrated upon. Those who spent a higher proportion of their time talking with others were likely to attach more importance to operational management than those who spent less time doing so.

Verbal contact with others takes various forms: telephoning, brief informal conversations, longer discussions, and formal meetings. Again, the form that is used varies with organizational practice; some organizations make much more use of formal meetings than others. Even in organizations that do much of their work through formal meetings there may be scope for some individual variation in attendance at meetings. This is shown by comparisons of the time spent in meetings by the forty-one senior administrators studied in the National Health Service. (The observational study of eleven of them mentioned earlier was part of this larger study.) The administrator who spent most time in meetings in the previous five weeks attended twenty-four regular meetings and twenty *ad hoc* ones. The one who spent least time attended five regular meetings and one *ad hoc* meeting. Situational differences, particularly size of district, can explain some of the variations, but there remains an element of individual choice. Another opportunity for choice in the method of verbal communication is in the use of the telephone compared with face-to-face contact, though the geographical location of the main contacts will affect this. There is often a choice, too, in whether the manager talks to people individually, particularly subordinates, or whether he favours group discussions.

Mintzberg (1973) stressed the preference for verbal communication shown by the chief executives whom he observed. He attributed this to their wish for live data, for their need to use informal and speculative information that could best be obtained in conversations. Another reason that managers themselves sometimes give for talking rather than writing is that it helps them to judge the value of the information that they are being given. Yet another is that it is easier to influence and motivate other people face to face than in writing.

One of the reasons, given above, for managers' frequent use of verbal rather than written communication is important for understanding other aspects of managerial work and behaviour. It is the need for informal information, including gossip and speculation. It was Mintzberg (1973) who drew attention to this, but it seems to be more generally true, as in my discussions with many different kinds of managers in Britain all have agreed that informal information is important. This means that the manager needs to supplement the formal system of management information, even if it is partially self-designed, by an informal network of contacts. The formal management information systems will not, and cannot, contain much of the information that a manager may need, or wish to know. The truth of this statement will vary with the nature of the job, the nature of the organization in terms of methods used to obtain and disseminate information, and the kind of information. In many jobs managers' access to information will be partially dependent upon their contacts and the supportiveness of the relationships.

Managing as an Informal Network of Reciprocal Relationships

Three American research workers, especially, have contributed to the picture of managers as dependent upon a network of useful contacts, which they establish and seek to maintain. Sayles (1964) stressed the extent and importance of a manager's peer relation ships. This was in marked contrast to American social scientists' interest in leadership studies seen primarily as leader–follower relations. Sayles also emphasized the manager's dependence upon others. He summed this up as follows: 'The one enduring objective is the effort to build and maintain a predictable, reciprocating system of relationships...' (Sayles 1964, p. 258).

Mintzberg (1973) described a liaison role in which the manager exchanged favours and information with peers and people outside the organization. Kotter and Lawrence (1974) analysed the network of relationships of American mayors in terms of the different interest groups in the city who could have an influence upon what the mayor was able to do. They illustrated the positive or negative nature of the relationship that different mayors had with each group. They argued that for mayors to be able to carry out their agendas they must have developed a supportive network of contacts. In a later study of fifteen general managers Kotter (1982) used the idea of a network of relationships as a way of analysing what they did. One of the things that struck him in his study of these general managers was the trouble that they took to keep their relationships in good state. He comments:

... the GMs all allocated significant time and effort early in their jobs to developing a network of cooperative relationships to and among those people they felt were actually needed to accomplish their emerging agendas. Even after the first six months, this activity still took up considerable time (Kotter 1982, p. 67).

This network-building activity, as I observed it and as it was described to me, was aimed at much more than direct subordinates. The GMs developed cooperative relationships to and among peers, outsiders, their bosses' bosses, and their subordiates' subordinates. Indeed, they developed relationships with (and sometimes among) any and all people upon whom they felt dependent because of their jobs (ibid.).

This activity of general managers has parallels with that of journalists who depend upon 'reliable sources' of information, and so take care to warm up their relationships at intervals even though they may have no immediate need for information.

The word 'dependent' in the last quotation from Kotter is important because it points to a major aspect of the manager's situation. Managers are dependent upon many other people to get their work done. This is true of subordinates, which is often a hard lesson for the new manager to learn. It is true, too, of the manager's boss and colleagues, and usually of more junior and senior people in other departments. Many managers will also be directly dependent upon people outside the organization. It is this dependence that makes it important for the manager to develop what Sayles called 'reciprocating relationships'. Such relationships may also have a political character. Thus a brief discussion of management as a political activity is appropriate as part of the account of studies of managerial behaviour.

Managing as a Political Activity

The flavour of what is meant by political activity is caught in a definition given in *Chambers Dictionary* (1952): 'manoeuvring and intriguing'. A more thorough and academic definition is given by Mayes and Allen (1977): 'Organizational politics is the management of influence to obtain ends not sanctioned by the organization or to obtain sanctioned ends through non-sanctioned influence means' (p. 675).

Dalton's (1959) participant observation study of the behaviour of middle managers is the most famous account of managers pursuing their own interests, both individually and as a local group, against head office. It showed that managers may not necessarily pursue the interests of the organization, or formal organizational goals. The fact that workers may not do so had been highlighted by the Hawthorne Studies (Roethlisberger and Dickson 1939) and by many subsequent ones, but managers were expected to be different. The traditional picture of the manager was, and often still is, of someone who helps to set organizational goals, or even if not involved in doing so, is committed to them. This conflicts with Dalton's and others' descriptions of the manager as someone who has individual and sectional interests which may conflict with organizational goals and policies, and who may pursue them by lobbying, concealment, or misrepresentation of information.

The attitude to Dalton's work shows a gap between academic and managerial thinking. His study has been treated as a major contribution to our understanding of managerial behaviour. It is, and should be, an important book on academic reading lists. However, managers, at least in my experience, dismiss it as old hat: 'Of course we all know that goes on!' Their interest is, rather, in learning how to play the political game more skillfully.

One of the reasons for political activity is that there are so many uncertainties in management that even an objective examination of the facts may often lead to different possible conclusions. This uncertainty and its results have been well described by Sayles (1964):

Trading, compromise, give and take are the order of the day. Many, if not most, of the subjects dealt with have no fixed objective answer even in a technical environment. Interpolation and judgment mean differences of opinion, and the manager must expect to engage in extended bargaining ... The manager who believes that the facts speak for themselves and that he can be passive after presenting them is self-deluded (pp. 130–1)

It is surprising that management writers have not paid more attention to politics in organizations, even though social researchers working in them rapidly discover examples of the political activity that exists if their subject of investigation is one that touches upon current political interests. Over the years a few social scientists have pointed to the significance of political activity in business organizations. Bacharach and Lawler (1980) suggest that organizations are politically negotiated orders in which survival is a political act. An even smaller number of social scientists have sought to explore political activity in organizations—see Madison et al. (1979).

What interest there has been amongst social scientists in understanding political activity in organizations has had little impact on management writers from other disciplines. They have not been concerned with the effects that political activity may have on managerial behaviour. This omission is probably most important in writings on decision-making, where the decision process is often discussed without regard for the distortions that participants' individual and group interests and rivalries can introduce into the logical processes that are advocated in the textbooks. The assumption is often that managers will seek to assess information objectively and try to arrive at the best decisions for the organization. Yet studies have shown the extent to which considerations other than an objective assessment of the facts or concern for organizational goals can form an important part of the decision process—see Strauss (1962–3) and Pettigrew (1973).

Differences in Managerial Behaviour

Progress in our understanding of managerial behaviour is likely to come both from having a better picture of what are the common characteristics, and from knowing more about the differences. So far most attention has been given to generalizing about management behaviour. This has been true of theoretical writers, most notably Fayol (1949) and his followers, and of researchers, particularly Mintzberg (1973). In this chapter we have so far been presenting research-based generalizations about managerial behaviour that contrast with the generalizations of traditional theories. They are generalizations that apply to many managers in the US and the UK, upon whom most of the research is based, but not to all managers in these countries. The existence of individual, job, and organizational differences has also been noted. We now need to look briefly at the research evidence for these differences and to consider its implications for our understanding of managerial behaviour. We will discuss differences in behaviour that are attributable to the individual, and those that stem from the nature of the job and its setting.

Individual variations The existence, and if so the extent, of individual variations in behaviour in managerial jobs can best be examined by comparing the behaviour of managers in similar jobs in the same organization. Mintzberg's (1973) study was of heads of very different kinds of organizations, and he was interested in trying to identify the similarities in what they did rather than in considering the differences. Kotter's (1982) study of fifteen general managers was also of people in different organizations, although he was interested in individual as well as in common behaviour.

The main study, cited earlier (Stewart *et al.* 1980), of behaviour of managers in similar jobs is that of district administrators, a senior post in the National Health Service in the UK. This study compared the behaviour of forty-one administrators by asking them in detail about their activities during the previous month, by collecting a record of the meetings attended, and by observation of eleven of them for from three days to a week. There were, of course, differences in their situations, in the size and character of the districts in which they worked, in the abilities and characters of the other members of the management team, and in the identity of their subordinates. No managerial job is exactly like another, and these had more variations than the jobs of, say, more junior personnel reporting to the same boss. Yet these variations in their situation could not adequately explain the very great differences in how the administrators did their jobs. Differences both in what was done and in how it was done; in content and in methods of work. Differences so great that comparisons showed that these administrators could spend much of their time doing different kinds of work.

Such marked differences are not peculiar to the particular administrators who were studied. A parallel observational study of six pairs of middle managers in similar jobs in the same organization also found considerable differences in the way that they did their jobs (Stewart 1982). These jobs were more formalized than those of the district administrators and so allowed less opportunity for the individual job-holder to do the job in a distinctive way, but the differences were still sufficiently marked to show the potential inaccuracies of generalizing about a job, or about managerial behaviour, by observing or questioning a particular job-holder.

There are many ways, as the observations and interviews showed, in which managers can do jobs differently, both in the content of their work and in its methods. One of the more common differences is in the attention that is given to subordinates and the time that is spent with them compared with other contacts within the organization or outside it. This may reflect a judgement by the administrator or manager of the relative importance of either monitoring, coaching, or working with subordinates compared to working with colleagues in other departments. Another common difference is in the emphasis that is given to the more technical aspects of the job. There are also differences in the subjects discussed earlier in this chapter: in the pattern of work, including whether the manager attempts to plan his or her day and to keep to the plan at least some of the time; in the methods of communication; in the attention given to developing a network of useful contacts; in the awareness and use of political activity; and in whether the individual manages in a mainly reactive way, or has a well-developed set of objectives and priorities which he or she seeks to further.

The existence of such marked differences in individual behaviour even in similar situations suggests that any theorizing about the nature of managerial work needs to allow for the flexibility, that is the choice, that exists in all managerial jobs. It also means that assumptions about managerial behaviour should take account both of the generalizations that can be made and of the wide variations that can exist in individual behaviour, particularly in the more flexible jobs.

Job differences The commonly recognized distinctions between managerial jobs are those of function and level, though the nature of these distinctions has never been adequately explored. Martin's (1956) small-scale study of differences in decision-making at four levels of management is a rare attempt to explore one of the accepted differences between managerial jobs. The study of district administrators shows that any realistic description of a job will also need to take account of the different work that can be done in it, which can be called the choices in a job. One of the differences between jobs is in the amount and nature of the choices that the job offers, although all managerial jobs do offer choices (Stewart 1982).

These differences in choice are not identical with the usual distinctions between functions and levels.

An earlier study (Stewart 1976) showed other kinds of differences between managerial jobs that also cut across functions and levels. Jobs in the same function, such as accounting, and at the same level in the hierarchy, may yet differ in ways that are relevant to the kind of person suitable for the job, the training that may be needed, and the experience that the job can provide. One of the differences shown in the earlier study was in managers' contacts. In some jobs, for example, managers will only work with people within the organization, while in others they will have to spend time with people outside the organization. There are jobs where managers only work with their subordinates and boss, while in others they will have to have a wide range of contacts in other departments. There are also major differences between jobs in the relative difficulty of the relationships they involve, a difficulty that comes from the work relationships and not from the particular personalities (Stewart 1976). Another of the distinctions between jobs shown by the 1976 study was in the pattern of the day. Some jobs, for example, are necessarily far more fragmented than others and have more unexpected work and trouble-shooting. Yet another difference shown by that study was whether a job was one where the job-holder was exposed, in the sense that mistakes and poor performance could be individually identifiable.

The differences between managerial jobs, other than those of function and level, that have been briefly summarized above, suggest the need for us to develop a wider range of concepts for thinking about differences in managerial work than those that are traditionally used. Researchers from outside management studies may more easily bring a fresh approach to developing concepts than those who have been brought up with traditional concepts and may find it harder to look at managerial work and behaviour afresh. Concepts are important because they will affect how the tasks of selection, appraisal, and training are considered. They are important, too, for management development and for understanding the kinds of experience that different jobs can provide. They affect other subjects as well: the design of management information systems, the transferability of managerial skills, and the implications for acquisitions.

TABLE 4.1

Summary of the Changes in Our Understanding of Managerial Work and Behaviour

From viewing managerial behaviour as primarily:

Orderly	*to* Disjointed, characterized by 'Brevity, variety and fragmentation'.
Planned	*to* Reactive and instinctive.
Working with subordinates and boss	*to* Recognizing importance of lateral relationships.
Having established relationships	*to* Developing and maintaining reciprocal relationships.
Using formal information	*to* Also using informal, speculative information.
Non-political: focused on organizational objectives	*to* Political, pursing own and own group's objectives.

From emphasizing:

The managerial job	*to* Recognizing differences between managerial jobs.
Common behaviour	*to* Recognizing wide differences in behaviour.

Conclusion

The picture that has been built up from studies of how managers behave gives a very different impression from the traditional one that underlies much of the writings on management. The common description of a manager as one who plans, organizes, co-ordinates, motivates, and controls suggests a logical, ordered process where these different activities can be distinguished by the individual, or by an observer, and where the manager has time to devote to planning. The picture that emerges from studies of what managers do is of someone who lives in a whirl of activity, in which attention must be switched every few minutes from one subject, problem, and person to another; of an uncertain world where relevant information includes gossip and speculation about how other people are thinking and what they are likely to do; and where it is necessary, particularly in the more senior posts, to develop a network of people who can fill one in on what is going on and what is likely to happen. It is a picture, too, not of a manager who sits quietly controlling but who is dependent upon many people, other than subordinates, with whom reciprocating relationships should be created; who needs to learn how to trade, bargain, and compromise; and a picture of managers who, increasingly as they ascend the management ladder, live in a political world where they must learn how to influence people other than subordinates, how to manœuvre, and how to enlist support for what they want to do. In short, it is a much more human activity than that commonly suggested in management textbooks.

These, then, are the new generalizations than can be made from studies of managerial behaviour. They are summarized in Table 4.1. They do not negate the traditional concepts but they do represent a major shift in emphasis. It is hoped that this account of the findings of studies of managerial work and behaviour will help all those who have to think about the nature of management to have more appropriate concepts of the activity of managing.

REFERENCES

Bacharach, S.B. and Lawler, E.J. (1980), *Power and Politics in Organizations: the Social Psychology of Conflict, Coalitions and Bargaining*, San Francisco, Jossey Bass.

Burgoyne, J.G. and Hodgson, V.E. (1982), 'An Experiential Approach to Understanding Managerial Action' (paper given in July at the International Symposium on Managerial Behaviour and Leadership Research, Oxford).

Carlson, S. (1951), *Executive Behaviour: A Study of the Work Load and the Working Methods of Managing Directors*, Stockholm, Strömbergs.

Dalton, M. (1959), *Men Who Manage: Fusions of Feeling and Theory in Administration*, New York, Wiley.

Fayol, H. (1949), *General and Industrial Management*, London, Pitman.

Kotter, J. (1982), *The General Manager*, New York, The Free Press.

Kotter, J.P. and Lawrence, P. (1974), *Mayors in Action: Five Studies in Urban Governance*, New York, Wiley.

Madison, D.L., Allen, R.W., Porter, L.W., Renwick, P.A. and Mayes, B.T. (1979) 'Organizational Politics—Tactics and Characteristics of Its Actors', *California Management Review*, XXII/1 (Fall).

Marshall, J. and Stewart, R. (1981), 'Managers' Job Perceptions' (Part 2), *Journal of Management Studies*, 18/3.

Martin, N.H. (1956), 'Differential Decisions in the Management of an Industrial Plant', *Journal of Business*, 29.

Mayes, B.T. and Allen, R.W. (1977), 'Toward a Definition of Organizational Politics', *Academy of Management Review*, October.

Mintzberg, H. (1973), *The Nature of Managerial Work*, New York, Harper and Row.

Pettigrew, A.M. (1973), *The Politics of Organizational Decision-Making,* London, Tavistock.

Roethlisberger, F.J. and Dickson, W.J. (1939), *Management of the Worker,* Cambridge, Mass., Harvard University Press.

Sayles, L.R. (1964), *Managerial Behaviour: Administration in Complex Organizations,* New York, McGraw-Hill.

Stewart, R. (1967), *Managers and Their Jobs: A Study of the Similarities and Differences in the Ways Managers Spend Their Time,* London, Macmillan.

Stewart, R. (1976), *Contrasts in Management: A Study of the Different Types of Managers' Jobs: Their Demands and Choices,* Maidenhead, McGraw-Hill.

Stewart, R. (1982), *Choices for the Manager: A Guide to Managerial Work and Behaviour,* Maidenhead, McGraw-Hill; Englewood Cliffs, New Jersey, Prentice-Hall.

Stewart, R. with Blake, J., Smith, P. and Wingate, P. (1980), *The District Administrator in the National Health Service,* London, King Edward's Hospital Fund for London.

Stewart, V. and Stewart A. (1981), *Business Applications of the Repertory Grid, Maidenhead, McGraw-Hill.*

Strauss, G. (1962), 'Tactics of Lateral Relationship: The Purchasing Agents', Administrative Science Quarterly, September, pp. 161–86.

5

Accounting and Management

MICHAEL J. EARL

Accounting has become a significant activity in the functioning of modern industrial societies (Birchell *et al.* 1980), an influential component of economic management at the levels both of the firm and of society. In turn, accountancy as a profession has grown prodigiously so that in the UK and Eire in 1982 there were approximately 110,000 qualified accountants, of whom about 81,500 were employed outside professional accounting firms in administration and business. In 1981 10 per cent of UK university graduates joined their ranks. The accountant in practice combines auditing, taxation and investment advice, liquidations, and consultancy with the task of bookkeeping. The accountant in business has added financial planning and control, information-processing, funds management, and internal audit to the task of financial reporting to outsiders. Industrial accountants increasingly are moving into related, but non-accounting, functions and sometimes take on general-management positions; conversely non-accountants sometimes take on finance and accounting responsibilities. Accountants are called upon to revive flagging businesses and to introduce efficiency and accountability into government, and conversely are accused of stifling investment and growth in industry and of emphasizing costs and failures in management.

The history of accounting has been one of continuous responses to the needs of society, of evolutionary adaptations and modifications to meet additional demands rather than of any blueprint design (Macve 1981). It has developed largely out of practice and pragmatism, so that accounting research and theory are still regarded circumspectly by many accountants in practice and only called upon in periods of crisis and controversy. Accounting has a long heritage from record-keeping in ancient times, through charge and discharge stewardship accounting on feudal estates; double-entry bookkeeping for the cash, credit, and stocks of medieval merchants and traders; accounting for decision and control as the industrial revolution and factory system brought new problems of scale, technology, complexity, and market competition; accountability reporting to accompany the Joint-Stock Companies Act, limited liability legislation, and separation of ownership and control; disclosure to investors and capital markets through the legislation and regulation of the financially distressed 1930s; to the multi-purpose internal and external accountings of the modern industrial (or post-industrial) state which have responded to new notions of accountability, periodic financial failures and crises, increased management sophistication, occasional government pressures, and the emergence of accounting research and theory (Parker 1981, Freear 1977, and Solomons 1968).

Thus accounting numbers have come to influence economic policy formulation through national income accounting, economic management through measurement procedures in income and prices policies or public-utility regulation, military and defence management through costing procedures and performance standards, government and business functioning through tax and credit accounting, and resource allocation through reporting to capital markets and investment appraisal methods. Likewise, at the microeconomic level of the firm, accounting numbers influence policy and operating decisions through cost analysis techniques, are central to planning and control in performance measurement and evaluation systems, and are the stuff of accountability reporting through record-keeping and calculation of costs and surplus. This pervasiveness of accounting numbers, together with some notorious failures of accounting, has emphasized just how accounting practices can affect a nation's economic and social welfare. For this reason, accounting is not only the concern of accountants, but also of government and the public (Metcalfe 1976). Accounting is clearly a tool, a social and organizational artefact, which can serve a variety of purposes and interests. For example, concepts of accountability, as expressed by external financial reporting, today extend from traditional economic democracy to latter-day social responsibility, and the calculus of accounting can span different balances of labour and capital.

Three topical issues demonstrate some of these claims. First, information disclosure to employees is almost the norm for large UK companies and can be justified on several grounds (Maunders

1981). For example, employees are stakeholders of the corporation as much as shareholders, information disclosure is a prerequisite for political shifts in bargaining power or moves towards co-determination, and reporting performance to employees might facilitate efficient allocation of the nation's labour resources or improve wage-bargaining by inducing rational expectations—or even benefit investor reporting by simplifying accounting language. Accounting thus can serve a variety of ends and means. Second, it is also a complex, dynamic socio-economic phenomenon, as the current inflation accounting debate demonstrates. Inflation accounting is a response to an economic pressure, lack of it seems to have economic consequences for managers, employees, investors, and government, disagreement on how to proceed has raised the visibility of accounting theory, alternative measurement bases have highlighted different concepts of accountability and of the role of the enterprise, government has felt the need to intervene, the accounting profession has been prompted into greater regulatory responsbilities, the roles of accounting and accountants are becoming better understood —and yet the inflation accounting problem was being discussed sixty years ago (Zeff 1974). Third, in response to seemingly rapid social and economic change, new and distinct forms of accounting and corporate reporting have emerged, satisfying a wide variety of user needs. Human resource accounting and social accounting are examples and, curiously perhaps, they often have neither been planned nor subsequently governed by accountants (Lee 1981).

Within organizations, accounting has served and facilitated certain management structures, practices, and ideologies. Cost accounting has been central to the pursuit of efficiency, integration of tasks, stabilization of capacity, co-ordination of operations, rationalization of production, and allocation of resources—in short to the development of managerial hierarchies, internalizing activities and transactions previously assigned to markets (Chandler and Daems 1979). As a technology in support of functional forms of organization (Litterer 1961), then of divisionalized structures (Johnson 1978), followed by project (Sayles and Chandler 1971), and matrix organizational designs (Knight 1977), internal accounting has supported and maintained the growth of managerial capitalism (Chandler 1967, Galbraith 1966) and thereby created enlarged opportunities for its own application. It is interesting to note again that these technologies have not always been invented by accountants, although the profession may claim and protect them today. Control accounting has been much influenced by general managers, for example by Sloan and Cordiner, and decision accounting by engineering and production specialists, for example Emerson, whilst corporate planners, management scientists, and computer specialists have developed and tailored accounting technologies to meet modern business needs. These uses of accounting by managers may also be more subtle than they first seem, creating particular patterns of visibility or consciousness (Becker and Newhauser 1975), perpetuating distributions of power and influence (Bariff and Galbraith 1978), and using the symbolic value of accounting information to legitimize actions past and present (Smith 1982).

Inevitably, with such a managerial heritage, accounting has been implicated in particular forms of social and economic behaviour. Its use in motivation, centralization, and standardization is interpreted to have been supportive of Weber's formal rationality (Birchell *et al.* 1980); the development of standard costing and variance analysis parallel the age of scientific management (Solomons 1968); the focus on implementation aspects of control systems accompanied the human-relations school (Cooper 1981); most decision accounting techniques have been founded on neo-classical economics (Scapens 1980) and, with control accounting's role in managerial hierarchies, have been, for Marxists, instrumental in capitalist organisation of production and in capital's reaping of labour's surplus (Chandler and Daems 1979); whilst, in contrast, alternative accountings have been designated to promote new forms of work organization or to further the interests of organized labour (Hopwood 1978). More pragmatically, management accounting often has been charged with being bureaucratic, mechanistic, economistic, cybernetic, simplistic, and rationalistic, both in design and use (Hofstede 1978, Banbury and Nahapiet 1979).

However, accounting in organizations and society is far from uniform. Financial accounting is likely to reflect both its economic, legal, political, social, and business context, and the stage of evolution of different societal institutions (Choi and Mueller 1978). Management accounting is probably contingent upon both internal and external environmental factors (Otley 1980). And, within each set of these variables, there are several accountings available to suit the purpose or the capabilities—financial or social, decision or control, prospective or retrospective, flows or balances, and subjective or objective (Birnberg 1980). Nor is the evolution of these accountings entirely reactive or deterministic, for the accountancy profession exercises some autonomy (Hopwood *et al.* 1979) through its educational processes, its regulatory functions, and its specialist activities. Indeed, the customary professional claims of competence, altruism, special skills and knowledge, and codes of conduct, sustained by training, barriers to entry, organization and mystical language, and strengthened by the power inherent in financial responsibility, all help to foster this autonomy, for better or for worse.

Finally, accounting is now an important academic pursuit. Education has been a professional concern for over a century, but in universities, in the UK and US at least, the rapid growth in degree courses, departments, chairs, and research bodies in accountancy is relatively recent. Accounting is a new and nascent subject suffering all the traditional problems of legitimacy, status, methodology, and delineation, and there is as yet little established theoretical structure (Carsberg 1977). Nevertheless, a substantive literature and robust research are developing and have been influenced by related disciplines such as economics and sociology, and more recently by computer science and management science. Thus the accounting problematic, our understanding of accounting and of the roles assumed by or attributed to it, may well reflect these influences. Whatever the theoretical heritage, it is often suggested that accounting practice lags its theory (Scapens 1980). Yet business practice, forced to experiment in the face of change, equally may be in advance of more academic research (Earl 1978). Indeed, it has been suggested that accounting is a world of two cultures (McCosh *et al.* 1981), not only of the 'profession' and business, but of theory and practice.

This 'positioning' of accounting may seem excessive, but when accounting information systems and accountants meet management, as this paper goes on to suggest, they serve particular functions and take on particular roles, which are not only significant to management but also to accounting in its broader societal context.

Accounting and Management

Accountants in business and administration are engaged in both financial accounting (reporting to outsiders) and management accounting (reporting to managers). Accountants in professional practice interact with management in bookkeeping (for small firms), auditing, and advisory and consultancy services. There is considerable accounting research on these areas.

Research into *financial accounting* has, of course, often focused on issues of measurement and presentation at a technical rather than managerial level, for example accounting for goodwill or depreciation, and on the development of theory of income and value measurement. However, as the social economic, and political context of accounting has been better understood, the *management* implications of these apparently technical or theoretical questions have been studied and discussed. Two related issues, to be referenced again later, are illustrative. Accounting numbers can affect society's allocation of resources and distribution of income (Selto and Neumann 1981) both directly, through taxation, regulatory rates of return, and the like, and indirectly, by influencing decisions, say in capital markets or government policy units, and by changing individuals' attitudes and thus perhaps their behaviour. Such 'economic consequences' of accounting include the actions of managers: for example, the inclusion of accounting numbers in management compensation schemes, or the fear of market misinterpretation of accounting reports, may influence a manager's operating or financial decisions (Benston and Krasney 1978). The rise of economic consequences in accounting has become a controversial and complex issue (Zeff 1978). Not unrelated has been the surge of interest and research in the process of accounting policy formation or standard-setting. There is strong evidence and argument that various self-interests are pursued in this process (Watts and Zimmerman 1978 and 1979, Benston 1980), and that in particular the interests of management are far from insignificant. In many senses, then, the politization of accounting is clear (Solomons 1978).

Research into *management accounting* has taken three paths (Scapens 1980). There has been the normative work of developing and refining techniques for optimal decision-making, for example, using constructs from micro-economics in costing and cost analysis

(Coase 1968) and applying mathematics and statistics to them (Hertz 1964, Samuels 1965). In contrast, there has been the descriptive work, behavioural and organizational studies of the role, impact, and efficacy of management accounting in organization functioning—for example, of budgeting (Argyris 1952, Hopwood 1973). In between, there have been empirical studies, often functionalist and multidisciplinary work, of management accounting technologies and how to make them work, for example management planning and control systems (Anthony 1964, Solomons 1968). Two sets of management accounting research are illustrative. Budgetary planning and control have been studied along many dimensions, for example their impact in terms of stress and pressure on people, and their responses (Argyris 1952), the psychology of target-setting and motivation (Stedry 1962), the benefits of participation in making budgets (Coch and French 1948), style of budgetary information use (Hopwood 1973, Otley 1978), the conducive social and technical factors (Hofstede 1967), budget-smoothing and bias (Lowe and Shaw 1968), and the politics of the budgetary process (Wildavsky 1964). The second example is the development of a contingency theory of management accounting, based on the premise that there is no universally appropriate accounting system which applies to all organizations in all circumstances. Research is beginning to suggest that a management accounting system should be designed to fit, or tends to reflect, the particular organizational context, for example environmental uncertainty (Khandwalla 1972, Otley 1978), organizational structure (Bruns and Waterhouse 1975, Hayes 1977), technology (Daft and MacIntosh 1978, Waterhouse and Tiessen 1978), task (Piper 1980, Daft and MacIntosh 1978) and decision-making style (Gordon and Miller 1976).

These research examples demonstrate the behavioural nature of both financial and management accounting and emphasize the necessity to understand the organizational and social roles of accounting, especially the relationships between accounting and management. However, most of the research evidence on these relationships is either fragmented, arising from the customary needs to narrow the focus of research questions and adopt a particular perspective, or it is suggestive, based on more integrated studies of information-processing and decision-making in organization (Cyert and March 1963, Pettigrew 1973, March and Olsen 1976) or on studies of accounting and economic behaviour at large (Chambers 1966).

An exception to this trend was the Simon *et al.* (1954) seminal study of internal accounting in management. They identified three quite different accounting activities: score-card, answering questions of how well management is doing, attention-directing, highlighting issues that managers should be examining, and problem-solving, suggesting the best way to proceed. These activities were found to be so different in purpose, execution, and data that Simon and his colleagues recommended that they be organized separately to ensure that each activity was afforded the appropriate time, effort, and expertise. Their study further suggested what roles might be realistically expected of both accounting and accountants in business administration, and emphasized that the organization of the relationship between internal accounting and management, whilst being far from easy, was crucial to organizational performance. There were also recommendations on the development of accountants and their profession to meet these challenges. Curiously, however, accountants in management have remained under-researched, notable exceptions being studies of accountants' management style (McKenna 1978) and of their possible role conflicts (Hopper 1980) plus a prescriptive polemic on their changing responsibilities (Tricker 1967). In contrast, managers often are acutely conscious of the importance of the accounting and management relationship, particularly when they describe how organizational results are achieved and how organizational decision-making actually works.

The remainder of this paper therefore attempts to provide an integrated understanding of the relationship between accounting and management, in the hope that it may provide accountants with insights into what is demanded of them and how to react, that it may be of value to managers in understanding how and when to use accounting and accountants, that it may remind researchers of the complex context in which accounting and accountants operate, and that it may be of use to all who are interested in accounting and are faced with evaluating existing, evolving, and future forms of accounting and accounting institutions, particularly those with either a management purpose or a management connection. The paper examines the roles of accountants in management, the roles that are formed by the expectations and behaviours of managers, the aspirations, heritage, and actions of accountants and their profession, and the structural, processual, and symbolic characteristics of the relationship between the two. The functions of accounting information systems are examined in the same way, describing what seems to be their purpose in practice. These roles and functions are given metaphors as descriptive shorthand, and are fused together to suggest four different relationships between accounting and management (Figure 5.1). The resultant 'model' is descriptive, being derived from research and observation, but some prescriptive implications are suggested.

Relationship between accounting and management	Role of accountant	Function of accounting information system
Accounting *for* management	Protector	Self-interest
Accounting *to* management	Prefect	Surveillance
Accounting *in* management	Pivot	Support
Accounting *as* management	Priest	Stability

FIG. 5.1 Accounting and Management

Accounting For Management

This 'accounting' describes the relationship between managers and financial reporting to outsiders. The thesis is that financial accounting has evolved to serve managers' interests first and owners' interests second. The financial accountant therefore acts as a *protector* of managers and owners against other potential stakeholders in the firm, and thereby is accounting *for* management, in their *self-interest*.

The argument opens with the standard-setting process. Accounting standards are uniform rules for dealing with financial accounting problems (Bromwich 1981), their purpose being to narrow choices in the interests of reporting comparability (Watts 1981). They supplement the minimal accounting framework contained in company law, and in both the UK and US were belated responses to public accounting crises or scandals (Zeff 1972) and thereby to the profession's wider responsibilities. In the UK, the accounting institutes formed the Accounting Standards Committee, or ASC, answerable to themselves and composed of their members. This aspect of accounting regulation, therefore, was kept within 'the private sector' and within 'the profession'. The American equivalent, the FASB, eventually became an independent body in structure and constitution, and thus quasi-public. The ASC has consulted with accounts users, and now has user representation, but hitherto it has served to protect the providers of accounting information in that the principal actors can only truly represent accountants and their managements. The same bias has been attributed to the outputs, if not the members, of the FASB (Moonitz 1974, Chatov 1975).

Indeed, Dupoch and Sunder (1980) remark that US standards have been compromises and reflections of interested parties, and not reflections of official statements of accounting objectives. In particular, intense pressure is sometimes exerted on standard-setting bodies by corporate managements (Moonitz 1974, Horngren 1973, Zeff 1972) and is likely to continue if accounting standards have potential effects on a firm's future cash flows, according to Watts and Zimmerman (1978). They argue that managements lobby on accounting standards out of self-interest: for example, protecting their compensation, status, and security. In regulated environments, managers will choose accounting standards which report lower earnings, thereby protecting their own and their shareholders' welfare from potential wealth transfers, rather than choose standards which report higher earnings and thereby increase their own incentive compensation. In unregulated firms, managers will select standards which report higher earnings, if the expected compensation gain exceeds the foregone expected tax consequences. Managers will also consider the impact of information production costs on their welfare. Thus Watts and Zimmerman (1978), and similarly Moonitz (1974), consider that management's role is central in standard-setting and in any discussion of financial reporting.

My own enquiries in UK firms (Earl 1983) suggest that accountants lobby the ASC for four reasons: to protect their results, to protect their accounting systems from 'inappropriate' or costly changes, to ensure that operating and financial decisions taken for 'sound economic' reasons are fairly reflected, and to prevent 'inappropriate' accounting treatments which they fear may be misinterpreted by capital markets. Both management and ownership interests can explain these stances.

Standard-setting thus has become political through pursuit of self-interest and also because the ASC and FASB have to sell their standards to the producers (Horngren 1973, Watts 1981) and because they need allies to support standard-setting in principle and practice (Moonitz 1974). Furthermore, it is inherently political in seeking to resolve user-user and user-provider conflicts of interest (Ijiri 1975) involving economic and social rights and consequences. It is thus not surprising that varied criticisms from diverse quarters abound (Bromwich 1981) and that calls for a conceptual framework for financial reporting are made. However, the very diversity of interests prevents general agreement on accounting theory (Watts and Zimmerman 1979) and, particularly in regulatory environments, each interested group employs convenient accounting theories or 'public interest' arguments to support and protect its position. The standard-setting arena just described thus allows managements to pursue their self-interests, which sometimes are congruent with owners', by lobbying, by being in positions of veto, by funding and exploiting theory development, and through the structural biases of standard-setting bodies.

Underlying many of these issues are questions of accountability. A stewardship view of accountability to investors was fostered by British nineteenth-century company legislation and subsequently by both Companies and Securities Acts in the UK and US. The FASB (1978) also identified present and future investors and creditors as the targets of financial statement, whilst the ASC (1981) has been less certain, stating that whatever the objectives might be, financial accounts should be useful to users. The Corporate Report, a discussion document, identified eight user groups, preferring to talk of those who had a reasonable right to accounting information (ASC 1975). EC Directives and recent UK government legislation are providing for piecemeal disclosure to employees, the state, and then, public, whilst pressure groups have sought to broaden accountability by producing alternative reports (Medawar 1976). Effectively then, financial accounting bodies officially have barely moved away from an investor model of accountability, wider interests having been represented by governments or non-accountants. The reality of corporate reporting, therefore, may well be one of power relationships where a financial nexus, the law, or concerted pressure creates accountability. Investors have sanctions, governments can act, but tend to give considerable discretion to corporations, whilst other stakeholders, because of their diffusion

(Tricker 1981), have limited impact. Managements thus can adopt a policy of reactive discretion.

Economic theory can contribute to this analysis. The theory of agency (Jensen and Meckling 1976) sees financial reporting, accounting performance-based compensation schemes, and auditing, as bonding and monitoring costs which the principals, or owners, and the agents, or managers, incur and accept in resolution of the asymmetry of information that arises from the separation of ownership and control (Berle and Means 1968, Galbraith 1967). This asymmetry provides management with opportunities and incentives to manipulate accounting reports (Williamson 1964, Watts and Zimmerman 1978, Dhaliwal et al. 1982). Thus accounting technologies, such as standards and audits, have to be cost-effectively designed to ensure truthful reporting, yet satisfy the utility-maximizing interests of the owners, managers, and public accountants concerned (Ng 1977 and 1978, Ng and Stoeckenhuis 1979, Benston 1980). Whether this is achieved is not proven.

Manipulation of accounting information, however, may not influence investors according to the 'efficient market' hypothesis (Fama 1970, Gonedes 1972, Downes and Dyckman 1973). Whilst there appears to be a general association between share prices and the announcement of accounting profits, the impact of particular accounting methods is rarely clear and the market seems not to be fooled by accounting treatments that do not represent significant economic differences. The foundations of this theory and its accounting implications can be overplayed (Lee 1979, Keane 1980, Benston and Krasney 1978), but it would seem to apply 'on average'. Nevertheless, firms do lobby for 'favourable' accounting standards, and managements do seek to smooth earnings figures by operational, financial, and accounting means (Gordon 1964, Beidleman 1973, Koch 1981), in part to influence capital markets. Indeed, according to my own enquiries (Earl 1983), managers and their accountants tend to *believe* that capital markets are inefficient and thus try to 'manage' external reporting and capital market relations where they can.

Not all corporate reporting, however, is aimed at capital markets; nor is it all supported or overseen by accounting's institutions. Many recent social reporting innovations have been driven by firms. Not surprisingly, managerialist motives can be observed. Value-added reporting (Morley 1978, Gray and Maunders 1980,

ASC 1975) and employee reporting (Maunders 1980) in practice tend to foreground the need for wealth creation, productivity, 'economic realities', and unitary team-work, and background the accounting enigmas involved and the possible alternative interpretations—all legitimated by neutral claims of simplifying and improving financial reporting. Social accounting (Estes 1976, Epstein *et al.* 1976) and human-resource accounting (Cherns 1978) can be seen as pre-emptive moves against internal or external criticism, as minimalist or opportunist responses to societal pressures and expectations, or as justifications of existing practice—as much as pro-active deeds of social responsibility. Often experimental, vague, varied, subjective, and ambiguous, these accountings afford management considerable flexibility and are unlikely to be institutionalized too soon by the profession.

Managerialist interests have also intruded on the technical arguments of the inflation accounting debate. Management preference for entity rather than equity concepts of capital maintenance, state industries' selection of methods which produce earnings figures in their best interest, pleas for special circumstances, concerns about subjective valuation, antithesis towards standard-setting, and concern for information production costs all suggest limited concern for accounts users. Perhaps a conversation on the inflation accounting question reported to me recently is indicative:

Chief accountant: Will we introduce current cost accounting?
Finance director: Does it improve profits?
Chief accountant: No.
Finance director: Does it improve cash flow then?
Chief accountant: No.
Finance director: Well will it reduce taxation?
Chief accountant: No.
Finance director: It isn't much good then is it?

But have we not overlooked the independence of accountants, a trait expected of any group that has cultivated its professional status for so long (Chambers 1966)? The reality is that industrial accountants work within management whilst public accountants have to work closely with managers in their accounting and auditing activities. Accounting firms have depended on, and exploited business for their growth in traditional accounting services and management consultancy. Business has been the profession's major client so that management's influence would seem to make the interests of owners secondary and of other stakeholders residual or insignificant. Although created to protect investor interests, public accountants joined an accountancy which for centuries had been the concern and tool of merchants and traders (Chambers 1966) and thus had its own momentum. Nearly a century later the Metcalfe Report went so far as to charge the large US accounting firms of being neither independent nor public but, through their own self-interest, of being tied to business. Others have reported on senior public accountants' close identification with the managements of their clients (Chatov 1975, Lafferty 1982). Even in auditing, where accountants have standards, laws, and sanctions to protect them, audit scandals persist and accounts users remain sceptical of audit efficacy and believe that audit competition, management consultancy services, and business associations impair auditor independence (Firth 1980, Shockley 1981). Despite all these traits, however, governments and capital market bodies continue to rely on accountants to solve disclosure problems and introduce reporting initiatives, and accountants succeed in fostering the notion that they are well equipped for these tasks (Tinker et al. 1982). Meanwhile, the corporate control of accounting that existed last century (Matheson 1893) and into this century (Paton 1922, Sweeney 1936) has continued to prevail (Johnson 1972).

Thus the function of financial accounting seems to be one of self-interest. It serves managers first, by furthering their interests directly or by protecting them from owners, and serves owners second, either where ownership's interests are congruent with management's, or where regulation has intervened. The financial accountant is therefore primarily a 'protector' of managers, and accounts *for* management. We can predict therefore that managers will use accounting in their external reporting activities where they can manage it, will calculate when they might benefit from its regulation, and will seek to manage any regulation process. Fortunately, accounts users may recognize the managerial nature of financial accounting and discount and adjust for it accordingly, so that it does in fact serve several purposes and users reasonably well (Macve 1981). Nevertheless we may prefer to curb corporate control by opening up accounting's institutions, by creating safeguards for other interests (Baxter 1953), by cultivating public accountants' independence and, despite the obvious risks (Benston 1980, Stamp 1969), by seeking greater government intervention. It also may be realistic to accept that accountancy, through its history, and our expectations of it, can only be concerned with a limited view of accountability and that wider concerns and interests can be better served by other means.

Accounting to Management

This and the next two 'accountings' describe the relationship between managers and management accounting. The thesis behind this second accounting is that many of an organization's financial planning and control systems are not designed for line and operating managers, but exist to serve top management. These systems and procedures thus are accounting *to* management in that their function is *'surveillance'* of the business and its operating managers. The role of the accountant, in this case of group controllers and the like, is accordingly one of *'prefect'* on behalf of top and corporate management. Etymologically, these two metaphors do seem to fit the relationship and situations to be described. From its historical use, 'prefect' suggests variously the role of officer, disciplinarian, overseer, and administrator all roles which both accountants and managers might recognize in typical group controllers. Equally, 'surveillance' suggests supervision, observation, intelligence, invigilation, and monitoring—all functions of many conventional financial control systems.

Indeed, much of management accounting has been seen as a technology reinforcing hierarchical control by specification and evaluation of business and management performance (Caplan 1971, Hopwood 1974). Simon *et al.* (1954) saw the function of score-card activities, and of much of attention-directing, as influencing managerial behaviour, persuading managers that corporate goals are worth pursuing, and that deviations from plan are worth correcting. The accountant is often portrayed as being primarily concerned with such corporate ends and means, conceiving and applying mechanistic models of control (Caplan 1971, Argyris 1952). Studies of particular techniques provide specific evidence of these claims.

Vancil and Buddrus (1978) suggest that two of the four functions of divisional performance measurement systems are concerned with central or corporate control rather than with devolution. First, such systems seek to co-ordinate and integrate decentralized units by planning and budgeting allocation of corporate resources and by providing a formal, aggregated, financial structure for the decentralized management process. Second, divisional performance measurement techniques and procedures seek to monitor each unit's organizational effectiveness, often by adopting 'management by exception' principles. Otley (1977) describes budget systems too as essentially integrative devices whose function is to enable senior management to regulate the activities of an organization so as to better achieve organizational objectives. To this end, Argyris (1952) saw many accountants imposing and using budgets as performance measures, deviations from the budget plan being reported directly up the hierarchy and interaction between the accountants and the line being limited, conflict-laden, and defensive.

Resource allocation techniques too, perhaps because of their corporate strategic implications, seem to take on similar emphases in use. DCF analysis of investment project nowadays is regarded with suspicion by large corporations, and divisional autonomy in capital-budgeting is frequently weak (Tomkins 1973, Coates *et al.* 1980, McCosh *et al.* 1981). Investment proposals typically are submitted by line and divisional managements for review by corporate officers or committees. Then, rather than focus on the future cash flow profitability of projects, corporate decision makers seem to be as much influenced, according to my own enquiries (Earl 1983), by the historical performance of the unit submitting the proposal. Thus group accountants and planners place emphasis on 'track record' and 'post-audits', both being products of surveillance exercises. Their use of DCF analysis and its sophisticated adjuncts then focuses on disproving project viability and highlighting the risks and uncertainties in the sure knowledge that the project's sponsors have massaged the data to good effect.

Studies of financial information flows paint a similar picture. Simon *et al.* (1954) observed that accountants generally analysed operations not to aid operating managers but to provide valid and objective data for higher levels of management. Much score-card and attention-directing information was used to judge subordinates, and was designed to provide an independent check on what was happening at operating level. It also was designed to keep operating managers alert and to convince them that top management knew what was going on. Argyris (1977) sees these traits as inherent in all systems of management control. The complexities and scale of the organizational control problem ensure that senior managers have to set rigid and simplified programmes for operating management, and have to monitor them through comprehensive but manageable information reports. Thus financial information flows are predominantly upward, and top management reports are necessarily abstract, quantitative, results-oriented, explicitly rational, generalizable, exception-based, and independently verifiable. Finally, Lorsch and Allen (1973) also discovered that financial information systems generally emphasized vertical and upwards communication in management.

Many of these surveillance systems are borne out of financial accounting (Simon *et al.* 1954). This is not surprising, since it is hard to ignore mandatory and mature accounting data which can be converted, at low cost, into a management tool (Vancil and Buddrus 1978). Indeed, since financial accounting data are in summary, results-oriented, and quantitative form they meet, if provided periodically, some of the essential criteria of top-management information. Of course, more external future-oriented, multidimensional, and disaggregated information might be recommended, but that can be provided by supplementary reports. Above all, it may be important to corporate management that its performance-tracking data can be easily related to both last year's published results and this year's likely, or forecast, accounts—and thus this financial accounting connection, although often critized, is understandable. Furthermore, the underlying cash basis of any financial information suits top management's surveillance needs. It provides a managerial discipline, a uniform business measure, and the ultimate mechanism for controlling resource allocation and consumption.

Recently, many of the surveillance and prefect characteristics of management accounting and accountants may well have been reinforced as businesses have sought to cope with inflationary, and now 'stagflationary', conditions. Under financial pressures, managements are likely to centralize control, as they conserve resources, monitor performance more closely, and limit divisional degrees of freedom. Emphasis on cash and liquidity management has prompted rapid reporting of gross numbers, disregard, in both planning and monitoring, of functional and divisional boundaries, and heavy usage of cash-flow modelling systems. Indeed, corporate modelling has not only become *de rigeur* but has emphasized short-term planning, examining the impact of external events on likely business results and aggregating, analysing, and extrapolating subsidiaries' financial reports. This type of 'planning', which is essentially a control technique, has impacted on, and involved, all management functions. However, it has been driven by group accountants and it is accountants who now do most corporate modelling (Grinyer and Wooller 1980). Top management has needed to probe variances, to anticipate events, to continually explore the impact of environmental uncertainties, and to revise budgets and expectations. As operating managers often have to supply the input data for these exercises and be confronted with the outputs and consequences (often via the accountants), they may well become irritated and defensive, and regard this extra invest-ment in information-processing as irrelevant and expensive. Fur-thermore, the traditional inter-dependence of planning and control becomes strained. Frequently, and perhaps simplistically, revised budgets cease to be good motivators for control, and short-term planning in the large seems to be unhelpful to those who have to plan in the small. Of course, these tensions have always existed in large organisations, but they may have been exacerbated by economic pressures so that operating mangers perceive surveillance and prefects more negatively than in the past.

For the accountants, however, such activities may have facilitated the cultivation and preservation of traditional values. Surveillance is essentially bookkeeping, even modelling exercises are based on conventional financial statements, so that the professional values of quantification, exactitude, rationality, and freedom from bias (Hastings and Hinings 1970) can be protected, and interaction with line management and wider aspects of business can be limited. Indeed, it is noticeable when interviewing management accoun-tants, whose task is to design, produce, and disseminate periodic accounting reports, how often they talk of 'reporting to manage-ment', 'information for management', 'if management is...', and 'when management says...'. These accountants not only see themselves as outside management, but often at arm's length from management. Perhaps this is necessary for their 'prefect' role; it may also explain some of the tensions between line managers and accountants.

Finally, besides being top management's technology of perfor-mance-tracking and diagnosis, surveillance systems and prefect roles are also the principal mechanisms through which they can select and emphasize certain measures, choices, and goals (Batstone 1978), reinforce asymmetrical patterns of influence and control (Birchell *et al.* 1980), and articulate what are their expectations, what is acceptable behaviour, and what are preferred decision criteria.

The traits attributed to this second relationship between accounting and managers, that is to accounting *to* management, might be seen to be particularly associated with functional and centralized organization structures (Perrow 1970). However, they can also be found in decentralized organizations, both in corporate controllers' departments and in subsidiary controllers with strong reporting ties to the centre (Sathe 1978). In short, all organizations probably have prefect accountants and surveillance accounting information systems in some form. They are the means of co-ordination and monitoring for corporate-wide regulation, and thus are oriented towards top management, financial performance, and the short run. It is inevitable that functional and line managers find these technologies of limited relevance and that they react negatively and defensively. It is even inevitable that these accounting systems have mechanistic tendencies in design and use. When managers say of accountants 'to them it is all figures' (Argyris 1952), they are describing prefects and surveillance, and perhaps are revealing that this is the accounting role that such accountants seek, top managers demand, and line managers would actually expect. The important design implication of the task of accounting *to* management, therefore, may be to recognize these realities whilst trying to limit any particular dysfunctional consequences.

Accounting in Management

This 'accounting' describes the relationship between lower and middle managers and management accounting. Labelled 'accounting *in* management', it describes the function of management accounting and the role of management accountants when they are located in line or functional departments, or in divisions and factories. Significant differences in this relationship are observed from that depicted by accounting *to* management. In accounting *in* management, accounting information systems are seen as 'support' systems, serving autonomy needs of divisional managements, meeting control needs of departmental managers, satisfying decision-making information requirements of line and operating managers, and supporting and complementing local information systems. These support functions are often associated with decentralized units (Dew and Gee 1973, Hofstede 1967, Simon *et al.* 1954), the local accountants being required to provide a 'service' to lower and middle management (Hopper 1980). However, the divisional or unit accountant often has a more complex, ambiguous, and conflicting role than the word 'service' implies. At many levels, it is a dual and conflicting role, for the accountant *in* management is not only serving middle managers, but is also representing senior management, and therefore retaining some surveillance and prefect responsibilities. Equally, he is representing finance and financial control, as well as serving operations and 'getting on with the job'. For these reasons, the accountant in management is here termed a 'pivot'. He has to face two ways with managers and keep a balance between accounting and management.

The pivotal nature of divisional accountants and the like is clear from studies of decentralized management systems. Inherent in decentralization is a fundamental contradiction (Sloan 1964), since on the one hand divisional autonomy has to be encouraged, and on the other hand central planning and control is essential. There is therefore a tension, or contradiction, between devolution, behavioural theories of the firm, and adaptability and effectiveness, as represented by the creation of divisions, and regulation, economic theories of the firm, and optimization and effieiciency, which are the concerns of the corporate centre. Decentralization thus produces contradictory and ambiguous roles for divisional managers by design (Vancil and Buddrus 1978); their responsibility exceeds their authority.

Divisional performance measurement systems, therefore, are required to support divisional managements by providing both operational guidance, through the specification of responsibilities, boundaries, costs and revenues, divisional relationships and performance measures, and motivation, through emphasizing autonomous financial responsbilities, involvement in goal-setting as well as goal achievement, and perhaps linking of rewards to performance. In addition, they must serve the two top-management functions described in the last section, namely co-ordination and monitoring (Vancil and Buddrus 1978). Thus divisional management's sense of autonomy is cultivated and local decision-making is encouraged by the accounting information system, but central controls and reporting also have to be designed to ensure corporate goal congruence and to minimize the sub-optimization.

Cordiner (1965) suggested that decentralization depended on teamwork, integration, balanced effort, and a shared philosophy between corporate and divisional management. The divisional accountant was seen by Simon *et al.* (1954) to be a key actor in this relationship. Direct communication between divisional accountants and divisional managements (and between functional accountants and functional managements) was essential to good controllership and effective and efficient divisional (or functional) performance. The divisional accountant was also the crucial link between corporate managers and unit mangers, in both management and accounting terms, in the pursuit of efficient and effective group performance. Accountants *in* management, therefore, had to give priority to these interactions, be located in the divisions, and possess the appropriate qualities and status to meet these demands. They are then likely to become influenced by, and share and accept, the values of the business and management needs of their unit (Rosenberg *et al.* 1982), but will also need to retain their prefect, or corporate, attitudes and responsibilities.

Under decentralization, therefore, the performance measurement system is very important. Its design has to support the degree of divisional autonomy being sought. In reality this is a constrained autonomy, but divisional managers need to perceive it to be relatively high, and apparently do so (Dittman and Ferris 1978, Vancil and Buddrus 1978). it is generally recognized, therefore, that the design of these systems is a considerable challenge (Solomons 1968, Dearden 1969). It is perhaps less widely recognized that, however cunning, subtle, or sophisticated is the divisional peformance measurement system, the role of the divisional accountant is crucial. The system depends on him and he has to serve two sets of management. His role is even more ambiguous than that of the divisional manager.

Similar issues have been raised in studies of budgetary control. Hofstede (1967) suggested that the co-ordination and control function of budgeting could easily destroy the motivation side. It was essential, he claimed, that budgetary control and reporting followed the responsbility structure, and that consequently the budget accountant, who was supplying a service to line managers without formal authority over them, had a very important and powerful, but sensitive, position. Furthermore, at most levels of line management, the accountant is required to provide budgeting assistance to managers who are both 'being controlled' by their superiors and are 'controlling over' their subordinates—another pivotal task. Simon *et al.* (1954) again emphasized the need for direct and active channels of communication between controller and operating staff. This was essential to create line-management confidence in both budget plans and budget reports. Management participation, with accountants' help, in making budgets was seen to be beneficial in ensuring relevant, controllable, reasonably attainable, and internalized targets. Assistance from accountants in managers' use of budgetary reports was seen to be beneficial in interpreting accounting language, correcting data errors, and helping to explain and probe variances. Hopwood (1973) agreed and suggested also that if budgetary control systems were to be useful to managers and were to meet their needs, managers should also participate in the system design process. However, such involvement with, or in, management is not the traditional role that the accountant has cultivated. Indeed the scorekeeping, evaluative, and arm's length tradition of many accountants has been blamed for budgeting failures, for example PPBS systems (Schick 1971). In many cases, accountants have been more concerned with meeting the budget than with maximizing economic performance (Drucker 1964, Hopwood 1973), with the method of measuring than with the context of what was measured (Hofstede 1967), and with performance evaluation than with the information needs of managers (Simon *et al.* 1954, Hopwood 1973).

Furthermore, accountants can easily overlook the fact that how information is used is as important as how to provide it. First, it is only of value if it is used. Thus if managers received educative and interpretative help from accountants, they might become 'users' rather than 'rejectors' or 'believers' of accounting information (Hopwood 1973). Second, the style of information use seems to influence both financial performance and managerial behaviour (Hopwood 1973, Otley 1978), the effects depending perhaps on the type of responsibility centre, management style, and the mix of other administrative, social, and self-controls in operation. Therefore, in designing and operating budget systems, the accountant needs to understand these relationships and this requires involvement in management at all levels.

Budgeting remains of course a management. rather than an accounting, tool and process, and for this reason Hofstede (1967) emphasized the 'hygiene' role of accountants. Their role, he suggested, was that of catalyst. If accountants and their systems were seen as judges, pressure devices, and controllers their impact would be negative. Instead, the accountant's task was to advise on the technical systems design and to facilitate system use through education and communication. He was expected to err on the side of self-restraint, rather than intervention, in order to gain managerial acceptance, and of divisional viewpoints, rather than corporate demands, in order to gain credibility. In short, a budgeting system is likely to be both used and useful if it is seen to help managers, if performance evaluation makes it important, and if the accountants give help (Simon et al. 1954).

According to conventional wisdom, accountants in management are also required to provide information for decision-making. However, it is frequently reported that emphasis on control-oriented accounting drives out this activity and that in turn managers do not seek accounting help in problem-solving, and textbook decision accounting techniques are not used in practice (Hofstede 1967, Simon et al. 1954, Hopwood 1973). Accountants, therefore, are exhorted to bring new data and skills into investment, product profitability, pricing, and similar decisions, instead of relying on elaboration of periodic accounting reports; at the minimum, for example, encouraging use of relevant costs rather than of absorption costs. Eclectic use of analytical techniques and user-based, problem-oriented, evolutionary methodologies are frequently recommended, much as has become the hallmark of developing decision support systems (Keen and Scott-Morton 1978). Such co-operation with operating managers on solving microeconomic problems plus the, probably, resultant collusion in the negotiation and bargaining that surrounds resource allocation decisions (Bower 1970, Pondy 1964, Lowe and Shaw 1968), may well be a departure from conventional accounting into 'entrepreneurial accounting' (Rosenberg et al. 1980), demanding a rather different combination of management, political, analytical, as well as accounting, skills.

Accountants in management may be able to meet some of their

service and support responsibilities better if they accept the limitations of their control accounting systems, present and future. Usually other local non-accounting information systems will exist and be at the core of operating managers' control technology. They will be in the local idiom, stress physical and concrete measurement, focus on efficiency and causality, and be unique, if not private (Simon *et al.* 1954, Argyris 1977), designed and operated to serve local needs only. Thus they are not generalizable or transferable, neither suitable for incorporation into accounting nor for standardization. Some of these systems will be informal and unofficial (Clancy and Collins 1979, Earl and Hopwood 1980), compensating for the inadequacies of the formal and official (often accounting) systems, sometimes experimental and temporary, and at other times defensive and maintained 'just in case'. The unit accountant is likely to be most effective if he accepts the advantages and legitimacy of these systems, and if he has the authority and propensity to provide other local information systems within the framework of company-wide accounting. He may need to accept that the principal purpose of most accounting information systems is to confirm and remind managers of what they know already, and to provide financial and corporate consciousness.

Thus the function of accounting information systems *in* management is to support not only the corporate management system, but also the local managers, their systems, and their decision-making. The accountant *in* management has therefore to maintain a balance in both the design and operation of these systems. The horizontal and vertical communication that this entails, the educational and supportive role implied, and the breadth of information-processing skills required—all can create job stresses for the accountant. Stress is also likely because his efforts do not show up directly in business results and thus are not easily reflected in either his extrinsic or intrinsic rewards. Indeed, this difficulty, together with the ambiguity over accounting's ends and means, may prevent his performance from being formally measured—much to the annoyance of line managers, but creating still more stress for the accountant (Gowler and Legge 1975). He may then fall back on procedural and professional success criteria which do not equate with a support role. He also runs the risk of being 'dogsbody' or 'scapegoat'; if his services are beneficial to management performance, management takes the credit, if his advice and assistance have no effect, he takes the blame (Gowler and Legge 1975). Furthermore, the more he is involved with management, the less he may be valued by his accounting superiors as an accountant, to the detriment of his career prospects (Rosenberg *et al.* 1982). These stresses, the periodic work-flow pressures of accounting, and the role ambiguity in general, then can impede the unit accountant's ability to meet his management's service expectations (Hopper 1980) and so he retreats into accounting's traditional role and values.

However, these role conflicts are not necessarily universal. With decentralized structures, with accountants who have service and support orientations, and where the job is appropriately designed and resourced, role conflicts can be low and service levels high (Hopper 1980). Nevertheless, it is likely that most accountants *in* management will need to accept and relish the pivotal nature of their job, with all its ambiguity. Both accountants and managers may have to work at creating conditions to reduce the conflicts of the role and to show concern about the accounting and management relationship. The accountant in management then becomes half specialist and half manager (Hofstede 1967), with loyalties half to the division and to service, and half to the centre and to surveillance (Simon *et al.* 1954), and with skills in both accounting and management, plus insights into the relationships between the two (Hopwood 1973).

Accounting as Management

This 'accounting' describes the relationship between management and management accounting at the organizational level. Here the function of accounting information systems is seen to be the provision and maintenance of *stability*—of ensuring both organization order and organizational continuity. It is suggested that accounting is a key element of the culture by which organizations (or societies) are held together and survive.

By observing the ways in which accounting information systems contribute to organizational decision-making, as described by behavioural rather than economic theories of the firm (Cyert and March 1963, Cohen *et al.* 1972), to organizational processes of legitimization and rationalization (Earl and Hopwood 1980, Feldman and March 1981), and to construction of managerial facades inside and outside the organization (Becker and Neuhauser 1975,

Meyer and Rowan 1977), it is suggested that accounting serves *as* management at the organizational level. Thus, whilst many accounting practices and procedures, as enacted in organizations, can seem 'irrational' to both participants and observers, from this more anthropological perspective they appear to fulfil quite 'rational' functions, helping organizations to cope with conditions of great complexity and uncertainty, conditions which often would seem inherently unmanageable. Once this functional interpretation of accounting *as* management is recognized and accepted, accounting technologies might then be managed accordingly, that is in the cause of stability. This view of accounting is based on studies of accounting in use, rather than of its espoused purposes and benefits. Essentially, it describes the symbolic role of accounting in organizations, namely its magical properties of myth, language, and ritual. By analogy, using a metaphor first popularized by Cleverley (1971), the role of the accountant, espcially at senior levels, becomes one of *priest,* as he designs and preserves the accounting language, acts the lead roles in accounting rituals, and publicly believes in accounting's efficacy.

In part, this view of accounting *as* management reflects recent behavioural theories of organizational decision-making. A normative view of management accounting might emphasize its role both as a decision calculus based on 'economic rationality', and as an organizational tool of planning and control based on Weberian 'formal rationality'. Indeed, such may be said of the 'surveillance' and 'support' functions of management accounting. In contrast, this more descriptive view of accounting *as* management, providing stability in large organizations, might reflect the *bounded rationality* model of organizational decision-making (Simon 1955, March and Simon 1958), where both the ability and the capacity of organizational information-processing are limited, and the decision environment is both inherently uncertain and complex. For example, many accounting activities have been described as standard operating procedures (Cyert and March 1963), or as rules, records, and plans, which provide organizational direction and stability, and which also tend to affect decision-making in general, by influencing goal formation, perceptions of the environment, generation and consideration of alternatives, and specification of decision criteria. Second, the 'bounded rationality' of ostensibly rational financial control systems has been highlighted in studies of budgeting and resource allocation procedures. Examples include biasing of estimates (Lowe and Shaw 1968, Berry and Otley 1975), incremental target-setting and budgeting (Wildavsky 1974, Danziger 1978, Davies *et al.* 1966), elaborate resolution of multiple objectives (Pondy 1964) and simplification of search procedures (Hopwood 1974).

Moreover, the function of accounting *as* management may also be explained within the *garbage-can* model of organizational decision-making (Cooper *et al.* 1981). This sees decisions being made by happenstance in an organizational arena of 'choices looking for problems, issues and feelings looking for decision situations . . . solutions looking for issues . . . and decision makers looking for work' (Cohen *et al.* 1972). In particular, there is strong evidence that management accounting systems, rather than embodying and facilitating the normative goal-setting, goal-directed, and goal-achievement management paradigm, frequently are used to make sense of past actions and decisions taken, thereby discovering rationales and goals retrospectively. Budgeting and resource allocation procedures frequently have been reported to serve as justification and rationalization devices, for example in capital-budgeting (Bower 1970), in PPBS and MBO systems (Dirsmith and Jablonsky 1979, Covaleski and Dirsmith 1980, Wildavsky 1976) and in cost benefit analysis and systems analysis exercises (Pringle 1978, Hoos 1969). This use of accounting procedures in a sense is retrospectively writing the organization's history and provides both an authoritative explanation of the past and a convenient guide for the future (Cooper *et al.* 1981), again, providing continuity and stability.

These studies also demonstrate the *mythical* qualities of accounting. Stability relies on making myths, since myths sustain and justify rights, institutions, and notions of what is legitimate and acceptable, secure commitment and obedience to leadership and hierarchy, and above all explain the world and its events. The accounting technologies described above can be, and are, used to provide a rational facade around organizational behaviour, a picture of respectability, competence, and control, legitimation of current managerial practice, explanations of irregular events, and confidence in future survival. Furthermore, accounting information systems, through the mystique and abstraction of their language, calculus and procedures, also provide the sacredness and mystery that myth requires in order to be able to cope with the complex, disastrous, and unforeseen, and yet not appear too nonsensical or irrelevant in more normal and routine situations. As Gambling (1977) puts it: 'What is sometimes sought from accounting is not so much absolute truth (if that can be found!) but something to which all parties can assent, albeit temporarily and with many interior reservations. As a result, they can keep moving—at least until next week.' This sacred aspect of myth also provides a charter for ritual (Malinowski 1922).

In primitive societies, magic *ritual* is employed in protection against uncertainty and in explanation of unfortunate events (Evans-Pritchard 1937). Given both the scant evidence that adoption of conventional accounting technologies actually brings financial success, and the substantial evidence of managers' subversion and manipulation of accounting systems, it has been suggested that many accounting practices are rituals that modern organizations devise in order to protect themselves from uncertainty (Cleverley 1971, Gambling 1977). The ever-increasing sophistication of capital investment appraisal is perhaps a rite employed to influence events in a favourable direction, for many accountants and planners recognize that DCF techniques and risk analysis cannot tackle the important uncertainties involved, whilst at the same time many managers seek from these exercises solutions and probabilities rather than learning and sensitivities. Equally, it is often very difficult to see a firm's budgeting system and long-range planning procedure being efficacious in delineating feasible business programmes, in forecasting future results, and in providing realistic and acceptable control targets. Especially in today's uncertain environments, the correspondence between the planned results and means of achieving them, and the actual out-turn and methods employed, is remote. Rather, the value of these accounting information systems may be their ritual quality. They provide confidence in future survival, suggest that the firm has the means to cope, and demonstrate that management knows what it is doing. At least doing something is better than doing nothing, and it is often claimed that the analytical processes involved in these exercises are perhaps where the benefits really lie. Furthermore, budgeting procedures and planning exercises, together with periodic reporting and management audits, have expressive, placatory, and ceremonial traits. Thus, as Cooper *et al.* (1981) suggest, these systems 'may be adopted ceremonially in order to convince the environment of the legitimacy and rationality of organizational activities. Organizations without formal accounting systems are vulnerable to claims that they are negligent, irrational, illegitimate and even unnecessary'. Thus, to the internal and external environments, these accounting systems are seen *as* management and without them both organizational members and external stakeholders would lose confidence and the total management system—indeed the business —would be unstable. Meyer and Rowan (1977) suggest that firms' use of professional economists has a similar legitimizing and stabilizing rationale, and Ackoff (1981) observes that many corporate planning procedures are not more than a 'ritual rain-dance'. Certainly, without ceremony, organizational life might be somewhat dull, and rituals do provide a sense of identity, belonging, and predictability, thereby reinforcing goals, values, and authority. Thus, we may need to evaluate the effectiveness of all these technologies as much by their ritual quality as by more tangible criteria.

An organization's culture is also created through the *language* of accounting, for its terminology of business and management fosters and reinforces shared meanings. Accounting terms and coding systems help fashion and sustain an organization's image (Daft and Wiginton 1979). A firm's financial controls, techniques, and information flows create a rhetoric for articulating its espoused objectives, its preferred means of management, and its organizational protocols (Pettigrew 1979). This accounting rhetoric, by its apparently clear, fundamental, and inarguable expression of organizational ends and means, is particularly suited for justification and legitimation of actual or potential power and exchange relationships, with their inherent contradictions that cannot be openly admitted or in many cases resolved, and for elimination of any challenges to them (Gowler and Legge 1981). Much of the potency of accounting rhetoric probably lies in its continuous influencing and delimiting of ends, means, values, problems, solutions, and patterns of authority, all of which can be covert, unobservable, or latent, much as suggested by Lukes' (1974) third dimension of power.

The language of accounting in day-to-day action also helps to foster economic consciousness, ensuring that costs, revenues, and profits pervade management discourse and decision-making. Even then, however, the apparent unambiguity of accounting terms provides just the flexibility of interpretation that organizational realities from time to time require. For example, 'profit' or 'profitability' has a definite, ultimate ring about it, even though accountants and others recognize that it is a construct and that there are many ways of defining it. Consequently, managements can use 'profit' in discourse to motivate, justify, and integrate, whilst individual managers can continue to satisfy their local goals and constraints behind its very imprecision. Today, an even more powerful term has entered management jargon. 'The bottom line' gives an impression both of the ultimate financial criterion and of the harshest, no-nonsense management watchword. Yet of course it is even more imprecise than 'profit'; it can mean anything and provides a perfect rhetoric for 'satisficing'.

Myth, ritual, and language, therefore, are all forms of symbolism which, with ideology and beliefs, make up a culture (Pettigrew 1979) by which organizations are held together and survive. There may be, however, a more obvious symbolic value of accounting as management. Record-keeping and reporting have an inherent control effect just because, as Cyert and March (1963) point out, records and reports are being kept and distributed and because managers imagine that they serve some purpose, or that a purpose will be found for them. Indeed, if such accounting exercises were discontinued, middle managers would probably sense a vacuum and lose confidence in their superiors and the organization. Likewise, if top management admitted that much of the financial control apparatus of organizations did not achieve its designed ends, or was disregarded and abused by middle managers, it would feel uncomfortable at best, and be concerned about apparent anarchy at worst. Thus, all managers may privately question the contribution of accounting but, like most doubters of religions, they prefer to remain agnostic. Indeed, the simile is appropriate, since formal actions which are symbolic are often associated with religion, and so anthropologists might see accounting as magic or religion.

Magic is the superstitious or religious method, as opposed to the scientific method, employed in controlling nature for a definite practical end, particularly to aid the functioning, binding, and survival of a society. It comprises beliefs that cannot be destroyed by presentation of contrary evidence, and practices whose continuance is independent of their efficacy (Cleverley 1971). It was argued earlier that accounting myths produce tolerable explanations of actions and events and provide necessary facades of legitimacy and control. In tandem, accounting rituals help to release our insecurity and to express our solidarity, but also seem important for their own sakes. Thus myth and ritual are very necessary but, because managements should be objective and rational, myths and ritual cannot be invented and discussed openly; they are taboo (Cleverley 1971). Fortunately, accounting as a language provides much of the ambiguity required to manage this conundrum. Accounting, therefore, not only serves *as* management in a symbolic sense, it can be managed accordingly. It is a magico-religious system, both instrumental and expressive, and accounting in design and operation perhaps should be judged and managed on both these dimensions.

If accounting at the organizational level is seen as a magico-religious system, the accountant by analogy becomes *priest*. Cleverley points out that accountants are usually hierarchical thinkers who develop and protect arcane knowledge and specialist, mystical skills, and who publicly emphasize and practice stewardship, discipline, and caution. Shareholders and auditors, he suggests, are the gods, and the accountant mediates between these divines and management (perhaps even 'protecting' managers, as argued earlier). Certainly, managers frequently accuse accountants of being priest-like in their roles of custodian and judge and in being above organizational evaluation and control. Indeed, managers may expect accountants to say 'no', to recommend caution, to represent financial probity, and to be evaluative. Certainly, the more management-oriented or entrepreneurial accountants often suggest that managers dislike them breaking out of this age-old role behaviour. Managers also do defer to accountants, are reluctant to develop accounting skills, and have firm views on when accountants should and should not be involved in decision-making. This tendency, together with the professionalization of accountancy, then allows the priests to presume to tell organizations and, directly and indirectly, society, what is good and right. They even presume to prophesy. Such prestige and status protects accountants from challenge and encourages and permits them to take over planning and control techniques that others have invented, often to the extent of giving them respectability. So, although others can perform some accounting tasks, for example systems analysts or corporate planners, in the end such usurpers need either to receive the accountants' blessing or be absorbed into the priesthood. The implication of this analysis of accounting information systems is clear. Their comparative advantage is their ability to provide organizational stability. Accounting takes on simplification, rationalization, and legitimation roles in organizational decision-making, providing order and continuity. Accounting also has symbolic value, as through myth, ritual, and language it provides legitimation, security, cohesion, and a facade of planning and control. In recent years, prescriptions have been offered for rendering management information systems more effective in helping organizations to survive and adapt in rapidly changing environments. These prescriptions, often based on claims that accounting systems beget rigidity (Cyert and March 1963, Hedberg *et al.* 1976) and alienation (Cherns 1978), include design of semi-confusing (Hedberg and Jonsson 1978), informal (Clancy and Collins 1979), dialectical (Churchman 1971), and decentralized (Zaltman *et al.* 1973) information systems. Certainly these characteristics may all be conducive to enquiry, experimentation, innovation, creativity, and intelligence, which in turn appear to be qualities necessary for organizational adaptation and growth in uncertain environments. However, they are neither the natural traits of accounting information systems, nor what managers expect of such systems. Consequently, we may do better to expect accounting systems only to provide stability in organizations and to set about designing and encouraging alternative, complementary, and non-accounting information systems to provide the major challenge and adaptation. Amey (1979), Hedberg *et al.* (1976), Buckley (1968), and others have argued for joint pursuit, in management information systems design, of stability and flexibility, but it may be that accounting's natural role is to provide only one side of this balance. Moreover, to reduce or remove the magical activities of accounting would seem likely to put the culture of organizations, and thus their stability, at risk.

Likewise, the implications for accountants are clear, particularly for those in senior positions. When they are accused of being conservative, traditional, ritualistic, above criticism, and interested only in financial numbers, they should not be overly concerned, for such accusations describe the role of priest which has evolved for them. Rather than cultivating qualities of entrepreneurship, dynamism, analysis, breadth of vision, and other seemingly desirable traits, they should remember their priestly role and not change their spots too readily—otherwise their management colleagues may be confused and insecure. Indeed, neither should managers demand radical changes in accountants or accounting at the organizational level. They should recognize, perhaps, that whilst they may never quite have the measure of accountants or their systems, accounting does serve as management in a rather subtle way. Accounting appears, and is espoused, to be rational and actively employed in management. It thus is able to provide a formal and official superstructure in which the bounded rationality, garbage can, and symbolic processes of management then can be enacted. These seemingly irrational management processes are quite rational once we recognize the complexity and uncertainty of organizations and organizational behaviour, but this cannot be publicly admitted. Accounting provides the facades necessary to maintain the rational fictions; in this sense it serves *as* management.

Conclusion

Accounting is a significant activity in the functioning of modern industrial societies, taking on a variety of roles, and having diverse consequences. To understand accounting in action, it would seem important, *inter alia,* to study the relationship between accounting and management, and it is hoped that this paper may be of value to accountants, managers, researchers, and policymakers as they seek to practice, work with, investigate, and improve accounting in organizations and society.

Four relationships between accounting and management have been identified, comprising four different functions of accounting information systems with four complementary roles of accountants. The assumption has been that these are universal, but some caveats may be necessary. These four accountings could differ in detail according to both societal and organizational context. For example, evidence cited is mainly drawn from large organizations, accounting institutions described are principally American or Britain, and management practices and styles assumed also may be culturally dependent.

Implications that flow from the analysis of each relationship have been discussed in the appropriate section, in particular emphasizing what are the distinctive characteristics, indicating what is required of accounting and accountants, and suggesting what can and cannot be expected of them both. In general, we might conclude from all four 'accountings' that accounting is both capitalist and managerialist, and that on balance, within and without organizations, it serves 'managerial capitalism'. This is only partly due to the inherent characteristics of accounting, being equally the result of the close juxtaposition of accountants and managers. In all four accountings, accounting information systems and accountants serve the interests of corporate and managerial control, and their comparative advantage over other information-processing is their appropriateness for, and heritage of, providing organizational security and stability. This is achieved in quite subtle, complex, and political ways. The principal implication of these generalizations is that accounting is not an appropriate mechanism through which to seek radical change in either organizations or society. If wider external accountability of organizations is sought, if alternative management structures or systems are required, if more devolved, eclectic information, analysis, and control are necessary, and if organizational flexibility and adaptation are essential, then the potential contribution of accounting is limited.

Nevertheless, accounting does seem to serve a variety of interests and purposes reasonably well. Indeed, analysis of these four accountings does suggest how accounting information systems and accountants should be 'managed' for effectiveness within their conventional roles. It is clear that the self-interest, surveillance, support, and stability functions of accounting information systems differ from each other. They require different emphases in design, different methods of use, and different criteria for evaluation. All four accountings, for different reasons, are necessary in organizations, but, especially in the case of the three internal accountings, they can overlap. Nevertheless, the differences often are sufficient to ensure that one particular function can only be achieved by one purpose-built accounting information system. Conversely, many financial planning and control systems are required simultaneously to relate to external reporting, provide overall surveillance, encourage local autonomy, and possess symbolic value. In this case, the lesson is to ensure a balance of all four functions in system design, use, and evaluation.

Similar implications follow for accountants in their roles of protector, prefect, pivot, and priest. Some accountants are required to fulfil only, or predominantly, one of these roles. Indeed, Simon *et al.* (1954) proposed organizational separation of the three roles they identified, in order to ensure each was properly fulfilled and to avoid role conflict and stress. Clearly, organizations do have financial accountants or protectors, group controllers or prefects, divisional accountants or pivots, and finance directors, chief accountants and the like, acting as priests. In reality, all these accountants do have to play all the roles some of the time—and in some organizations accountants are multi-purpose by design. Therefore it is important for them (and their management colleagues) either to decide which particular role they are most required to adopt, or to work out which situations require which role.

In general, from observing the conventional career progression of accountants, we can conclude that as accountants ascend the organizational hierarchy their role becomes more and more managerial. The four-accountings model, 'for', 'to', 'in', and 'as' management, also represents, in that sequence, more and more integration of accounting into management. Thus, except for those in positions of technical expertise and specialism, accountants can expect their role to change as they advance, and thus they will need new and different skills. Over time, they need broader and deeper understanding of management and business and will need to complement their traditional accounting skills with functional, communication, political, educational, analytical, and even dramatic skills and knowledge. Not only does this represent a conflict with many of the values and principles of 'the profession' (Hastings and Hinings 1970), but it scarcely corresponds with the professional training that accountants receive. At the same time, the stress and ambiguity of these roles increases as they represent greater integration with management. Thus certain personalities may not be suited to certain roles, and most accountants will need to learn to cope with these special forms of stress.

It would seem sensible for the accounting profession to consider the education and development implications of this analysis. It may be that it is actually in organizations that solutions can be found. Planned career development, involving both horizontal and vertical job rotation, management education, and fitting of personalities and experience to roles, would seem a promising prescription. At the same time, further research into the organization of accounting—in its broadest sense—might be worthwhile. If so, this paper perhaps has demonstrated that descriptive, sociological enquiry could be as relevant as normative, economic research. (There are also signposts to research which might be less interpretative and less functionalist in approach.) Finally, other taxonomies of accounting of course exist. This one is perhaps different in that it is based on a descriptive analysis of the relationships between accounting and management.

REFERENCES

Accounting Standards Steering Committee (1975), *The Corporate Report,* A.S.S.C.

Accounting Standards Committee (1981), *Setting Accounting Standards,* A.S.C.

Ackoff, R.L. (1981), 'On the Use of Models in Corporate Planning', *Strategic Management Journal,* 2/4.

Amey, L.R. (1979), 'Towards a New Perspective on Accounting Control', *Accounting, Organizations and Society,* 4/4.

Anthony, R.N. (1964), *Planning and Control Systems: A Framework for Analysis,* Harvard Business School, Division of Research.

Argyris, C. (1952), *The Impact of Budgets on People,* School of Business and Public Administration, Cornell University.

Argyris, C. (1977), 'Organizational Learning and Management Information Systems', *Accounting, Organizations and Society,* 2/2.

Banbury, J. and Nahapiet, J.E. (1979), 'Towards a Framework for the Study of the Antecedents and Consequences of Information Systems in Organizations', *Accounting, Organizations and Society,* 4/3.

Bariff, M.L. and Galbraith, J.R. (1978), 'Intra-Organizational Power Considerations for Designing Information Systems', *Accounting, Organizations and Society,* 3/1.

Batstone, E. (1978), 'Management and Industrial Democracy' in *Industrial Democracy: International Views,* Warwick University, Industrial Relations Research Unit.

Baxter, W.T. (1953), 'Recommendations 'On Accounting Theory', *The Accountant,* (October).

Becker, S. and Neuhauser, (1975), *The Efficient Organisation,* New York, North-Holland.

Beidleman, C.R. (1973), Income-Smoothing: The Role 'Of Management', *Accounting Review,* XLVIII (October).

Benston, G.J. (1980), 'The Establishment and Enforcement of Accounting

Standards: Methods, Benefits and Costs', *Accounting and Business Research*, 11/41 (Winter).

Benston, G.J. and Krasney, M.A. (1978), 'The Economic Consequences of Financial Accounting Statements' in *Ecoomic Consequences of Financial Accounting Standard* (research report), Financial Accounting Standards Board (July).

Berle, A.E. and Means, G.C. (1968), *The Modern Corporation and Private Property*, New York, Harcourt, Brace and World.

Berry, A.T. and Otley, D.T. (1975), 'The Aggregation of Estimates in Hierarchical Organisations', *Journal of Management Studies* (May).

Birchell, S., Clubb, C., Hopwood, A.G., Hughes, J., and Nahapiet, J. (1980), 'The Roles of Accounting in Organizations and Society', *Accounting, Organizations and Society*, 5/1.

Birnberg, J.G. (1980), 'The Role of Accounting In Financial Disclosure', *Accounting, Organizations and Society*, 5/1.

Bower, J.L. (1970), *Managing. The Resource Allocation Process: A Study of Corporate Planning and Investment*, Boston, Mass., Division of Research, Graduate School of Business Administration, Harvard University.

Bromwich, M. (1981), 'The Setting of Accounting Standards' in *Essays in British Accounting Research* (eds. M. Bromwich and A.G. Hopwood), Pitman.

Bruns, W.J. and Waterhouse, J.H. (1975), 'Budgetary Control and Organisation Structure', *Journal of Accounting Research* (Autumn).

Buckley, W. (1968), 'Society as a Complex Adaptive System', in *Modern Systems Research for the Behavioural Scientist* (ed. W. Buckley), Chicago, Aldine.

Caplan, E.H. (1971), *Management Accounting and Behavioural Science*, Reading, Mass., Addison Wesley.

Carsberg, D. (1977), 'Directions Into the Future: The Prospects for Research' in *Current Issues In Accounting* (eds. B. Carsberg and T. Hope), Deddington, Oxford, Philip Allan.

Chambers, R.J. (1966), *Accounting Evaluation and Economic Behaviour*, Englewood Cliffs N.J., Prentice-Hall.

Chandler, A. (1966), *Strategy and Structure*, New York, Anchor Books.

Chandler, A. and Daems, H. (1979), 'Administrative Co-odination, Allocation and Monitoring: A Comparative Analysis of the Emergence of Accounting in Organization in the USA and Europe', *Accounting, Organizations and Society*, 4/1/2.

Chatov, R. (1975), *Corporate Financial Reporting*, New York, Free Press.

Cherns, A.B. (1978), 'Alienation and Accountancy', *Accounting, Organizations and Society*, 3/2.

Choi, F.D.S., and Mueller, G.G. (1978), *An Introduction to Multinational Accounting*, Englewood Cliffs, N.J., Prentice-Hall.

Churchman, C.W. (1971), *The Design of Enquiring Systems*, New York, Basic Books Inc.

Clancy, D.K. and Collins, F. (1979), 'Informal Accounting Information Systems: Some Tentative Findings', *Accounting, Organizations and Society*, 4/1–2.

Cleverley, G. (1971), *Managers and Magic,* London, Longmans.

Coarse, R.H. (1968), 'The Nature of Costs' in *Studies in Cost Analysis* (ed. D. Solomons), Sweet and Maxwell.

Coates, J.B., Smith, J.E., and Stacey, R.J. (1980), 'Results of a Preliminary Survey into the Structure of Divisionalised Companies, Divisional Performance Appraisal, and the Associated Role of Management Accounting', (working paper), Aston University.

Coch, L. and French, J.R.P. (1948), 'Overcoming Resistance to Change', *Human Relations,* 1/4 (October).

Cohen, M.D., March, J.G., and Olsen, J.P. (1972), 'A Garbage-Can Model of Organizational Choice', *Administrative Science Quarterly* (March).

Cooper, D. (1981), 'A Social and Organisational View of Management Accounting', in *Essays in British Accounting Research* (eds. M. Bromwich and A.G. Hopwood), Pitman.

Cooper, D.J., Hayes, D., and Wolfe, F. (1981), 'Accounting in Organized Anarchies: Understanding and Designing Accounting Systems in Ambiguous Situations', *Accounting, Organizations and Society,* 6/3.

Cordiner, R.J. (1965), *New Frontiers for Professional Managers,* New York, McGraw-Hill.

Covaleski, N. and Dirsmith, M. (1980), *Budgeting as a Means for Control and Loose Coupling in Nursing Services,* Pennsylvania State University.

Cyert, R.M. and March, J.G. (1963), *A Behavioural Theory of the Firm,* Englewood Cliffs, N.J., Prentice-Hall.

Daft, R.L. and MacIntosh, N.B. (1978), 'A New Approach to Design and Use of Management Information', *California Management Review* (Fall).

Daft, R.L. and Wiginton, J.C. (1979),'Language and Organisation', *The Academy of Management Review* (April).

Danziger, J.N. (1978), *Making Budgets: Public Resource Allocation,* California, Sage Publications.

Davis, O.A., Dempster, M.A.H., and Wildavsky, A. (1966), 'On the Process of Budgeting: An Empirical Study of Congressional Appropriations', in *Papers on Non-Market Decision Making,* Vol. 1.

Dearden, J. (1969), 'The Case Against R.O.I. Control', *Harvard Business Review,* (May/June).

Dew, R.B. and Gee, K.P. (1973), *Management Control and Information,* London, Macmillan.

Dhaliwal, D.S., Solomon, G.L. and Smith, E.D. (1982), 'The Effect of Owner Versus Management Control on the Choice of Accounting Methods', *Journal of Accounting and Economics,* 4/1.

Dirsmith, M. and Jablonsky, S. (1979), 'M.B.O., Political Rationality and Information Inductance', *Accounting, Organizations and Society,* 4/1/2.

Dittman, D.A. and Ferris, K.R. (1978), 'Profit Centre: A Satisfaction Generating Concept', *Accounting and Business Research,* 8/32.

Downes, D. and Dyckman, T.R. (1973), 'Efficient Market Research and Accounting Information: A Critical Look', *Accounting Review* (April).

Drucker, P. (1964), 'Control, Controls and Management' in *Management Controls: New Directions in Basic Research* (ed. C.P. Bonini), New York, McGraw-Hill.

Dupoch, N. and Sunder, S. (1980), 'F.A.S.B.'s Statements on Objectives and Elements of Financial Accounting: A Review', *Accounting Review* (January).

Earl, M.J. (1978), 'Prototype Systems for Accounting, Information and Control', *Accounting, Organizations and Society*, 3/2.

Earl, M.J. (1983), 'Measurement and Management of Foreign Exchange Exposure in UK Multinationals' (a research report), Oxford Centre for Management Studies.

Earl, M.J. and Hopwood, A.G. (1980), 'From Management Information to Information Management' in *The Information Systems Environmental* (eds. H.C. Lucas (Jun.) *et al.*), Amsterdam, North-Holland.

Emerson, H. (1908–9), 'Efficiency as a Basis for Operation and Wages', *Engineering Magazine* (July/March).

Epstein, M., Flamholtz, E., and McDonough, J.J. (1976), 'Corporate Social Accounting in the USA: State of the Art and Future Prospects', *Accounting, Organizations and Society*, 1/1.

Estes, R.W. (1976), *Corporate Social Accounting*, New York, J. Wiley.

Evans-Pritchard, P.E. (1937), *Witchcraft, Oracles and Magic Among The Azande*, Oxford University Press.

Fama, E.F. (1970), 'Efficient Capital Markets: A Review of Theory and Empirical Work', *Journal of Finance* (May).

Feldman, M.S. and March, J.G. (1981), 'Information in Organisations as Signal and Symbol', *Administrative Science Quarterly*, 26/2.

Financial Accounting Standards Board (1978), *Statement Number One: Objectives of Financial Reporting by Business Enterprises* (November).

Firth, M. (1980), 'Perceptions of Auditor Independence and Official Ethical Guidelines', *Accounting Review*, LV/3 (July).

Flint, J. (1977), 'Historical Background to Accounting' in *Current Issues in Accounting* (eds. B. Carsberg and T. Hope), Deddington, Oxford, Philip Allan.

Galbraith, J.K. (1967), *The New Industrial State*, London, Hamish Hamilton.

Gambling, T. (1977), 'Magic, Accounting and Morale', *Accounting, Organizations and Society*, 2/2.

Gonedes, N.J. (1972), 'Efficient Capital Markets and External Accounting', *Accounting Review* (January).

Gordon, L.A. and Miller, D. (1976), 'A Contingency Framework with a Design of Accounting Information Systems', *Accounting, Organizations and Society*, 1/1.

Gordon, M.J. (1964), 'Postulates, Principles and Research in Accounting', *The Accounting Review* (April).

Gowler, D. and Legge, K. (1975), 'Stress, success and Legitimacy' in *Managerial Stress* (eds. D. Gowler and K. Legge), Aldershot, Hants. Gower.

Gowler, D. and Legge K. (1981), 'Negation, Synthesis and Abomination in Rhetoric' (Management Research Paper 1), Oxford Centre for Management Studies.

Gray, S.J. and Maunders, K.T. (1980), *Value-Added Reporting: Uses and Measurement,* Association of Certified Accountants.

Grinyer, P.H. and Wooller, J. (1980), 'An Overview of a Decade of Corporate Modelling in the UK', *Accounting and Business Research,* 11/41 (Winter).

Hastings, A. and Hinings, C.R. (1970), 'Role Relations and Value Adaptation: A Study of the Professional Accountant in Industry', *Sociology,* 4/3 (September).

Hayes, D.C. (1977), 'The Contingency Theory of Managerial Accounting', *Accounting Review,* LII/1 (January).

Hedberg, B. and Jonsson, S. (1978), 'Designing Semiconfusing Information Systems for Organizations in Changing Environment', *Accounting, Organizations and Society,* 3/1.

Hedberg, B.L.T., Nystrom, P.C., and Starbuck, W.H. (1976), Camping on Seesaws: Prescriptions for a Self-designing Organization, *Administrative Science Quarterly* (March).

Hertz, D.B. (1964), 'Risk Analysis in Capital Investment', *Harvard Business Review* (January/February).

Hoepfner, F.G. (1973), 'What Behavioural Science Implies for Cost Accounting', *Management International Review,* pp. 51–63.

Hofstede, G.H. (1967), *The Game of Budget Control,* van Gorcum.

Hostede, G.H. (1978), 'The Poverty of Management Control Philosophy', *Academy of Management Review,* 3/3.

Hoos, I.R. (1969), *Systems Analysis in Social Policy: A Critical Review,* London, I.E.A.

Hopper, T.M. (1980), 'Role Conflicts of Management Accountants and Their Position within Organizational Structures', *Accounting, Organizations and Society,* 5/4.

Hopwood, A.G. (1973), *An Accounting System and Managerial Behaviour,* Farnborough, Hants., Saxon House.

Hopwood, A.G. (1974), *Accounting and Human Behaviour,* Teddington, Middx., Haymarket Publishing.

Hopwood, A.G. (1978), 'Towards an Organizational Perspective with a Study of Accounting and Information Systems', *Accounting, Organizations and Society,* 3/1.

Hopwood, A.G., Birchell, S., and Clubb, C. (1979), 'A Development of Accounting in its International Context: Past Concerns and Emerging Issues', (paper presented in April at The Third Charles Waldo Haskins Seminar On Accounting History, Atlanta).

Horngren, C.T. (1973), 'The Marketing of Accounting Standards', *Journal of Accountancy* (October).

Ijiri, Y. (1975), *A Theory of Accounting Measurement,* Sarasota Fla., American Accounting Association.

Jensen, M.C. and Meckling, W.H. (1976), 'Theory of the Firm, Managerial Costs and Ownership Structure', *Journal of Financial Economics* (October).

Johnson, H.T. (1978), 'Managerial Accounting in an Early Multinational

Organisation: General Motors in the 1920s', *Business History Review*, pp. 490–517.

Johnson, T. (1972), *Professions and Power*, London, Macmillan.

Keane, S.M. (1980), *Efficient Market, Hypothesis and the Implications for Financial Reporting*, Scotland, Institute of Chartered Accountants.

Keen, P.G.W. and Scott-Morton, M.S. (1978), *Decision Support Systems: An Organisational Perspective*, Reading, Mass., Addison-Wesley.

Khandwalla, P.N. (1972), 'The Effect of Different Types of Competition on the Use of Management Controls', *Journal of Accounting Research* (Autumn).

Knight, K. (1977), *Matrix Management*, Farnborough, Hants., Gower Press.

Koch, B.S. (1981), 'Income-Smoothing: An Experiment', *Accounting Review*, LVI/3 (July).

Lafferty, M. (1982), in 'Survey of Accountancy', *Financial Times* (17 June).

Lee, T.A. (1979), 'The Role of Accounting and Evidence of Efficient Markets', *The Accountant's Magazine*, LXXXIII (June).

Lee, T.A. (1981), 'Development in Company Financial Reporting: A History and an Introduction' in *Developments in Financial* (ed. T.A. Lee), Deddington, Oxford, Philip Allan.

Litterer, J.A. (1961), 'Systematic Management: The Search for Order and Integration', *Business History Review*, pp. 369–91.

Lorsch, J. and Allen, S. (The 3rd) (1973), *Managing Diversity and Independence*, Boston, Mass., Harvard University, Division of Research, Graduate School of Business.

Lowe, E.A. and Shaw, R.W. (1968), 'An Analysis of Managerial Biasing: Evidence from a Company's Budgeting Process', *Journal of Management Studies* 5/3.

Lukes, S. (1974), *Power—A Radical View*, London, Macmillan.

Macve, R. (1981), *A Conceptual Framework for Financial Accounting and Reporting: The Possibilities for an Agreed Structure*, Institute of Chartered Accountants of England and Wales.

Malinowski, B. (1922), *Argonauts of the Western Pacific*, London, (Reprinted Dutton, 1961.)

March, J.G. and Olsen, J.P. (1976), *Ambiguity and Choice in Organisations*, Bergen, Norway, Universitets Forlaget.

March, J.G. and Simon, H.A. (1958), *Organizations*, New York, Wiley.

Matheson, E. (1893), *The Depreciation of Factories, Mines and Industrial Undertakings and Their Evaluation*. (Reprinted Arnot Press 1976).

Maunders, K.T. (1981), 'Disclosure of Company Financial Information to Employees and Unions: The State of the Art', *A.U.T.A. Review*, 13/2 (Autumn).

McCosh, A.M., Whiting, E., and Howell, S. (1981), 'Planning and Control Systems and Their Evolution during Inflation' (working paper 71), Manchester Business School and Centre for Business Research.

McKenna, E.F. (1978), *The Management Style of the Chief Accountant: A Situational Perspective*, Farnborough, Hants., Saxon House.

Medawar, C. (1976), 'The Social Audit: A Political View', *Accounting, Organizations and Society,* 1/4.

Metcalfe, L. (1976), *The Accounting Establishment,* US Senate Committee on Government Operations.

Meyer, J.W. and Rowan, B. (1977), 'Institutionalized Organization: Formal Structure as Myth and Ceremony', *American Journal of Sociology,* pp. 340–63.

Moonitz, M. (1974), *Obtaining Agreement On Standards In The Accounting Profession,* Sarasota, Fla. American Accounting Association.

Morley, M.F. (1978), *The Value-Added Statement: A Review of its Use in Corporate Reports,* Scotland, Institute of Chartered Accountants.

Ng, D. (1977), 'Financial Reporting. External Auditing and Managerial Decisions' (working paper), Stanford University.

Ng, D.S. (1978), 'An Information Economics Analysis of Financial Reporting and External Auditing', *The Accounting Review,* LIII/4.

Ng, D.S. and Stoeckenhuis, J. (1979), 'Auditing: Incentives and Truthful Reporting', *Journal of Accounting Research,* 17 (Supplement).

Otley, D.T. (1977), 'Behavioural Aspects of Budgeting', *The Accountant's Digest,* 49.

Otley, D.T. (1978), 'Budget Use and Managerial Performance', *Journal of Accounting Research* (Spring).

Otley, D.T. (1980), 'The Contingency Theory of Management Accounting: Achievement and Prognosis, *Accounting, Organizations and Society,* 5/4.

Parker, R.H. (1981), 'The Study of Accounting History' in *Essays in British Accounting Research* (eds. M. Bromwich and A.G. Hopwood), Pitman.

Paton, W.A. (1922), *Accounting Theory.* (Reprinted Chicago, Accounting Studies Press 1962.)

Perrow, C. (1970), 'Departmental Power and Perspective in Industrial Firms' in *Power in Organisations* (ed. M.N. Zald), Vanderbilt University Press.

Pettigrew, A.M. (1973), *The Politics of Organisational Decision-Making,* London, Tavistock.

Pettigrew, A.M. (1979), 'On Studying Organisational Culture', *Administrative Science Quarterly,* 24/4 (December).

Piper, J.A. (1980), 'Determinants of Financial Control Systems for multiple Retailers—Case Study Evidence', *Managerial Finance,* 6/1.

Pondy, L.R. (1964), 'Budgeting an Inter-Group Conflict in Organizations', *Pittsburgh Business Review,* 34/3 (April).

Pope, P.F. and Peel, D.A. (1981), 'Information Disclosure to Employees and Rational Expectations', *Journal of Business Finance and Accounting,* 8/1 (Spring).

Pringle, C. (1978), 'The Early Development of Cost Benefit Analysis', *Journal of Agricultural Economics* (January).

Rosenberg, D., Tomkins, C., and Day, P. (1982), 'A Work Role Perspective of Accountants in Local Government Service Departments', *Accounting, Organizations and Society,* 7/2.

Samuels, J.M. (1965), 'Opportunity Costing: An Application of Mathematical Programming', *Journal of Accounting Research,* 3/2.

Sathe, V. (1978), 'Who Should Control Divisional Controllers?', *Harvard Business Review* (September/October).

Sayles, L.R. and Chandler, M.K. (1971), *Managing Large Systems: Organizations For The Future,* New York, Harper and Row.

Scapens, R. (1980), 'An Overview of Current Trends and Directions for the Future' in *Topics in Management Accounting* (J. Arnold, B. Carsberg, and R. Scapens), Deddington, Oxford, Philip Allan.

Schick, A. (1971), *Budget Innovation in the States,* Washington, The Brookings Institution.

Shockley, R.A. (1981), 'Perceptions of Auditors' Independence: An Empirical Analysis', *Accounting Review,* LVI/4 (October).

Selto, F.H. and Neumann, B.R. (1981), 'A Further Guide to Research on the Economic Consequences of Accounting Information', *Accounting and Business Research,* 11/44 (Autumn).

Simon, H.A. (1955), 'The Behavioural Model of Rational Choice', *Quarterly Journal of Economics* (February).

Simon, H.A., Kozmetsky, G., Guetskow, H., and Tyndall, T. (1954), *Centralisation Versus Decentralisation in Organising the Controller's Department,* New York, The Controllership Foundation.

Sloan, A.P. (Jun.) (1964), *My Years With General Motors,* New York, Doubleday.

Smith, E.A. (1982), 'Corporate Secrecy: Management Misinformation or Misinformation Management?' (Unpublished M.Litt. Thesis), Oxford University.

Solomons, D. (1968), 'Historical Development of Costing' in *Studies In Cost Analysis* (D. Solomons), Sweet and Maxwell.

Solomons, D. (1978), 'The Politicisation of Accounting', *Journal of Accountancy* (November).

Solomons, D. (1965), *Divisional Performance: Measurement and Control,* New York, Financial Executives Research Foundation.

Stamp, E. (1969), 'The Public Accountant and the Public Interest', *Journal of Business Finance,* 1.

Stedry, A.C. (1962), 'Aspiration Levels, Attitudes and Performance in a Goal-Oriented Situation', *Industrial Management Review,* 3/2.

Sweeney, H.W. (1936), *Stabilised Accounting,* New York, Harper and Bros.

Tinker, A.M., Merino, B.D., and Neimark, M.D. (1982), 'The Normative Origins of Positive Theories: Ideology and Accounting Thought', *Accounting, Organizations and Society,* 7/2.

Tomkins, C. (1973), *Financial Planning in Divisionalised Companies, Teddington, Middx., Haymarket Publishing.*

Tricker, R.I. (1967), *The Accountant in Management,* London, Batsford.

Tricker, R.I. (1981), 'Corporate Accountability and the Role of the Audit Function' (discussion paper pp. 5), Oxford, Corporate Policy Group.

Vancil, R.F. and Buddrus, L.E. (1978), *Decentralisation: Managerial Ambiguity by Design,* Illinois, Dow-Jones-Irwin.

Waterhouse, J.H. and Tiessen, P. (1978), 'A Contingency Framework for Management Accounting Systems Research', *Accounting, Organizations and Society,* 3/1.

Watts, R.L. and Zimmerman, J.L. 'Towards a Positive Theory of the Determination of Accounting Standards', *The Accounting Review*, LIII/1 (January).

Watts, R.L. and Zimmerman, J.L. (1979), 'The Demand for and Supply of Accounting Theories: The Market for Excuses', *The Accounting Review*, LIV/2 (April).

Watts, T. (1981), *'The Watts Report'—Setting Accounting Standards*, London, Accounting Standards Committee.

Wildavsky, A. (1964), *The Politics of the Budgetary Process*, Boston, Little Brown.

Wildavsky, A. (1976), 'Economy and Environment/Rationality and Ritual: A Review Essay', *Accounting, Organizations and Society* 1/1.

Williamson, O.E. (1964), *The Economics of Discretionary Behaviour: Managerial Objectives in a Theory of a Firm*, Englewood Cliffs, N.J., Prentice-Hall.

Zaltman, G., Duncan, R., and Holbeck, J. (1978), *Innovations And Organisations*, New York, Wiley.

Zeff, S.A. (1974), 'The Impact of Inflation on Accounting: A Review of the Response of the Accounting Profession in Ten Countries', *Management Decision*, 14/3.

Zeff, S.A. (1972), *Forging Accounting Principles in Five Countries*, Champaign, Ill., Stipes Publishing Company.

Zeff, S.A. (ed.) (1976), *Asset Appreciation, Business Income and Price Level 'Accounting: 1918-1935*, Arnot Press.

Zeff, S.A. (1978), 'The Rise of Economic Consequences', *Journal of Accountancy* (December).

6

Perspectives on Corporate Governance: intellectual influences in the exercise of corporate governance

R. I. TRICKER

John Maynard Keynes was convinced that it was ideas that ultimately determined the affairs of men: by contrast, John Stuart Mill argued for 'conspiring circumstance', and Karl Marx believed it was vested interests. But what if crucial ideas no longer lead events, but trail behind them? The theme of this essay, which endeavours to give some perspectives on top management, is that the reality of business today is ahead of contemporary concepts of the corporation. Consequently, fundamental issues in the direction of companies, in the regulation of companies, and in determining the legitimacy of their behaviour in modern society, are misconceived and can be badly handled.

It is argued that corporate governance, the processes by which companies are run, is in need of a fundamental rethink, and should not be confused with the management of the various businesses involved. The evolution of ideas about companies is shown to be rooted in out-of-date ideologies which emphasize structure. The alternative framework proposed focuses on process and power. Ideas, not organizations, change events.

This essay therefore seeks to discuss established and emerging concepts of corporate governance, examining their intellectual heritage, and proposes an alternative framework based on ideas of process and power. It provides an opportunity to explore various ideas about boards of directors. The different perspectives, from

This paper is based on studies of The Corporate Policy Group, Oxford, which is devoted to the study of corporate direction, control, and governance. It is intended as a contribution to discussion. It does not necessarily represent the views of the trustees or the corporate sponsors of the group.

which the work of directors can be viewed, are recognized; as is the need for a conceptual framework that adequately relates to the practices of corporate direction, control, and accountability in the context of the diversity and complexity of modern corporations.

On Corporate Governance

THE NOTION OF CORPORATE GOVERNANCE

Corporate governance is concerned with the processes by which corporate entities are governed. Who is responsible, to whom, for what, in the direction of the enterprise, the supervision and control of executive actions, the acceptance of accountability, and the recognition of regulation? By what mechanisms are such responsibilities pursued? By what authority and power are such duties exercised or rights demanded?

Obviously, corporate governance has to be set within the company law and regulatory systems of the states in which the corporate entity operates. But corporate governance is far wider than legal, regulatory processes: it addresses the entirety of a company's impact on the society in which it exists. It legitimizes the power of a company to affect the lives and the interests of others. It refers to the linkages between the company and other parts of a society that are affected by it, whether they be providers of capital or credit, labour or other services, whether their interests are as consumers of the company's products or users of its services, whether they are affected in any other way.

From case evidence, it is apparent that, in Britain at least, there is some difficulty with the word 'governance', as applied to companies. Some executives fear an attack on their perceived right and duty to manage the enterprise, an erosion of the managerial prerogative by even recognising the concept. Others, executives and civil servants alike, would prefer to identify governance solely with the government of the state (Wilson 1977).

However, the word 'governance' has a totally valid Anglo-Saxon, indeed Chaucerian, ancestry. More to the point, it pertinently and appropriately covers processes which every corporate entity has to undertake and which need to be distinguished from managing and management.

DISTINGUISHING GOVERNANCE FROM MANAGING

The classical management literature has not differentiated managing from governance. None of the three main streams of management thinking—the traditional, functional focus on the activities of managers such as planning, controlling, organizing, leading, and co-ordinating; the human behavioural and organizational theoretical approaches; and the systematic, information-oriented focus on decision-making—recognize a separate area of interest in matters of governance. Issues that might arise are considered properly the field of corporate jurisprudence or bureaucratic, regulatory mechanisms. Consequently, any action that is necessary is a technical task for the company secretary, the auditors, or the lawyers.

Obviously if a company is run and dominated by a single, entrepreneurial figure, or the board of directors is composed entirely of company executives, the focus will be on managing the business and there is unlikely to be any differentiation between managing and governance. The thesis of this paper is that the demands on the modern, complex corporation necessitate a differentiation of the roles.

> The chairman of a public company, quoted on the London Stock Exchange, writes formally to any executive who is appointed to the board, outlining his expectations on the role to be adopted by directors. 'It is necessary for an executive director to "wear two hats"—the one as an executive responsible for specific duties within the business, the other as a director responsible with the rest of the board members for directing the company.' 'In the board room you should not be wearing your executive hat,' he comments.

Again, management control in the classical literature is identified as a management task (Anthony 1965), through which ongoing, operational business activities are kept in line with management's longer-term strategic plans. The emphasis is on performance measures and managerial control.

In the context of corporate governance, control has a wider scope. It concerns the exercise of supervision, monitoring, and control of the corporate executives, by whom, and by what means. It raises questions about the separation of function between execution and supervision, which we shall see shortly are fundamental to ideas about two-tier boards, non-executive directors, audit committees, and the like.

> A company chairman put the matter succinctly: 'On an executive board they are marking their own examination papers.'

> Or as Juvenal explained the problem much earlier: 'Quis custodes ipsos custodiat'; although he was worrying about who should guard his wife's guard when he went to the wars.

Thus, whilst management is concerned with running the business efficiently and effectively, corporate governance is concerned with the company's overall direction, the oversight and control of executive actions, and the satisfaction of legitimate expectations of accountability and regulation.

It is apparent, from the management literature, that the management role is perceived as managing the business operations within the boundaries of the company under which it trades, referring to activities that are internal or external to the company. By contrast, corporate governance is less involved with the operations of the enterprise itself, more with the interactions across the boundary, between the company and those who affect it and are affected by it. Consequently, an important aspect of corporate governance is the exercise of authority and the wielding of power. Yet organizational power is a topic conspicuous by its absence in the relevant management literature. (Pfeffer 1981, Allen *et al.* 1979.) Why should this be? Because the matter has been relatively unimportant? When there is no challenge to the exercise of managerial prerogative, no questioning of corporate power, no demand for accountability, participation, or disclosure—then one would expect scant attention to be paid to governance issues.

THE IMPORTANCE OF CORPORATE GOVERNANCE

In recent years, however, there have been developments which point to the significance of corporate governance. Consider the following examples, which are in no way exhaustive, but do illustrate the issues that are challenging company directors and corporate regulators.

1. *The structure and role of boards*

The original draft Fifth Directive of the European Community (October 1972) called for companies over a certain size to create two-tier boards, the upper or supervisory board to be comprised equally of representatives of employees and shareholders, the lower or executive board to be responsible for running the business. The primary duty of the supervisory board would be the monitoring and supervision of executive action, its prime sanction being the hiring and, if necessary, firing of the executives.

The British government formed a committee, under the chairmanship of Lord Bullock (1977), to report on industrial democracy. Its report Cmnd. 6707, advocated the unitary board, but with equal representation of shareholders and employees (appointed through trade union mechanisms) and a third, balancing element, of independent members. [The '$2x+y$' formula.]

Both the original draft Fifth Directive and the Bullock Report were strongly attacked by British management. Indeed, the industrial members of the Bullock Committee produced a minority report, which advocated a separation of function between executive and independent supervision. But the debate focused more specifically on ideas for worker involvement at board level, than on the restructuring of boards.

The subsequent revised draft Fifth Directive (1978) widens the scope for alternative board structures, permitting the original two-tier board (the 'German' model), or an alternative two-tier board (the 'Dutch' model, with a tripartite grouping of interests sympathetic to labour, capital, and the general good). The draft directive also permits the unitary board with a mandatory works council system or with independent, non executive membership.

Considerable interest has been shown in the use of non-executive directors in Britain (*The Conduct of Company Directors,* 1977; Tricker 1978). Institutional support has been given to the encouragement of adding non-executives to boards (PRO NED 1982), although the conventional view is that such non-executive membership should form a minority on the board. However, an essential element has not been widely explored—that is whether non-executives should be genuinely independent.

By contrast, the boards of public companies in the US tend to have a majority of outside directors. Moreover, for a listing on the

New York Stock Exchange, an audit committee, comprised of independent, outside directors is required; and independence is carefully defined (New York Stock Exchange 1976a and 1976b). Typical problems of US boards have been suggested by Andrews (1979):

—the chairman's defensiveness against challenge or question;
—the reluctance of outside directors, especially when new, to do the challenging that is needed if they are to meet their legal liability and make substantive contributions;
—the continuing need to define the boundary between the roles of the board and the management;
—the latent hostility that is inherent between a competent management and an independent board, even when both sides have the friendliest intentions.

With predominantly executive boards, as in Britain, other problems can arise; such as distinguishing the roles of chairman and chief executive (Tricker 1981).

2. *Structure and relationships in complex groups*

A modern, international group of companies may include within the corporate galaxy:

—wholly owned subsidiaries, registered under different jurisdictions;
—partly owned subsidiaries, with minority shareholders;
—associated companies, with less than a formal, ownership control but over which executive authority and control is exercised;
—joint ventures with other groups of companies or governments;
—network consortiums or federations with other companies, involving the holding of shares in each other.

Under such circumstances who is responsible for direction and where is strategy formulated? What is the responsibility of directors in each of the various companies, to whom are they accountable?

In practical terms, large corporate groups, operating multi-plant, multi-product, and international activities, have also to consider whether to organize through subsidiary companies, divisions, or strategic business units.

Our case notes show a number of groups in which the business organization structure no longer equates with the corporate structure. Subsidiary companies are retained for legal protection, reporting, and taxation purposes, but the management processes are organized on divisional or product group lines.

The draft Ninth Directive of the European Community (1981 'Wurdinger Report') would require the dominant company in a complex group to assume responsibility for the actions of subordinate companies which affect creditors, employees, and others. Such an approach, though probably reflecting the reality of corporate power, is contrary to the position in British company law, which treats each corporate entity, as autonomous. Creditors of a UK subsidiary company have no right of access to funds of the holding company or other companies in the group. Under the Ninth Directive they *would* have, unless the dominant company had clearly denied responsibility at the time of contracting.

3. *Participation and involvement of employees*

An important element of the draft Fifth Directive, and of the Bullock Report (1977), was to facilitate wider involvement and participation of company employees in the affairs of the company.

The last twenty years have seen the growth of the giant industrial enterprise, and the concentration of economic power in the hands of fewer and fewer such companies. For example, in 1953 the 100 largest manufacturing enterprises in the UK accounted for 25 per cent of the total net output; in 1971 the corresponding figure was 40 per cent.

There has been a growing recognition of the influence of such companies on many aspects of people's lives at home as well as at work. As companies have grown in size and complexity, they have also tended to become remote from the communities in which they operate and from the people whom they employ. Major decisions about the nature of a company's or plant's organisation, affecting closely the future of the local community or the jobs of the employees, may often be taken far away from the site by the directors of a parent or holding company, sometimes by the management of a parent company overseas.

The power and complexity of the industrial enterprise and the remoteness of decision-making have led to demands for large companies to be more responsive to the needs of society in general and of their employees in particular.

New concepts of the role of employees in decision-making at company level are not just reactions to economic trends. They also derive from social changes which have taken place since the war, especially rising standards of education and higher standards of living. The significance of the educational developments is not just that more people have received a basic education; it is the nature of that education which has changed. There is now less concentration on formal authoritarian teaching methods and more encouragement to children to adopt independent and questioning approaches in order to develop individual initiative and ability. It is only since World War II that we have seen the end of the deferential society, in which working people rarely aspired to positions of power or authority in local or national life. The coming of age of democracy in our society is a process that inevitably affects the whole of people's lives; it cannot be excluded from the workplace. The parallel increase in standards of living has also been important. Most people now live in more comfortable homes and have more money and leisure to enjoy them. They have come to expect a higher and rising standard of material comfort and are therefore naturally less tolerant of low standards, discomfort, boredom and lack of proper provisions for safety and health in their working environment as well as less prepared to accept the prospect of redundancy and unemployment (Bullock 1977).

Another draft directive of the European Community is associated with the former Commissioner, Mr Vredeling, and concerns procedures for informing and consulting the employees in undertakings with a complex structure, in particular trans-national firms. Management, in such groups, would be obliged to provide information at least every six months to employees' representatives about the activities of the concern as a whole. Prior consultation would also be required 'with a view to reaching agreement' about major decisions liable to affect employee interests directly, such as plant closures, major organizational changes, or long-term strategic changes. Where local managements fail to fulfil such obligations, employee representatives would have the right to apply directly to the 'dominant' undertaking.

4. Supervision and accountability

In 1975 the Accounting Standards (Steering) Committee produced *The Corporate Report,* a research study which advocated widespread disclosure of information by all economic entities to interest groups affected by the activities of the entity. Such an orientation suggested responsibilities far wider than the present practice, in

MGT FOSTER : KNOWLEDGE / CAPABILITY / RECOGNITION
IN EXCHANGE FOR
INFORMED / COMPETENT / MOTIVATED EMPLOYEES
TO DELIVER LONG TERM ORG SUCCESS

which corporate disclosure is required under various Companies Acts (1948 and 1981 particularly) and, for listed companies, under the Stock Exchange rules.

In the US, audit committees have been widely used as vehicles for ensuring supervision and accountability at board level (Mautz and Neumann 1977). An audit committee is a main board committee, wholly or mainly composed of independent, outside directors, with the main responsibility to:
—discuss with independent auditors any problems and experience in completing the audit;
—discuss scope and timing of independent audit work;
—discuss effectiveness of internal controls;
—discuss meaning and significance of audited figures and notes therefore;
—approve or nominate independent auditors;
—discuss adequacy of staffing for internal audit;
—discuss findings and recommendations of internal audit;
—discuss adequacy of staffing for accounting and financial responsibilities;
—discuss organization and independence of internal auditors;
—discuss plans of internal audit function;
—review accounting principles and practices followed by the company;
—discuss effectiveness of procedures to prevent conflicts of interest, political contributions, bribes or other improper payments;
—discuss effectiveness of use and control of data-processing.
There have been endeavours to introduce non-executive directors and audit committees into British companies. However, the practice, though increasing, is not widespread (Tricker 1978; Bank of England 1979).

In terms of financial accountability, the establishment of accounting standards is felt to be necessary for comparable reporting (*Accounting Standards Committee* 1981). But establishing standards, obtaining acceptance by accountants, and requiring conformance by companies has raised political problems in the accountancy profession that were previously unimaginable.

For example in Britain, SSAP16, the standard requiring large companies to publish current cost accounting reports, was introduced for an initial, exploratory three-year period. Yet even during that period, members of the Institute of Chartered Accountants in England and Wales called for a special meeting to debate the matter, and very nearly carried the vote on a motion 'deploring' the standard and calling for its immediate withdrawal.

The Accounting Standards Committee, which is a committee of the Consultative Committee of Accountancy Bodies representing the six senior UK accounting bodies, appointed lay (non-accountant) members for the first time in 1982.

5. *Corporate regulation*

In countries which base company law on common law the tendency is to emphasize self-regulation by companies and institutions and the tradition of a minimum of legislative control. In the US, with companies incorporated under the jurisdiction of specific states, there has been a call for 'federal chartering'. The Securities and Exchange Commission also exercises a significant authority in regulating public companies (Williams 1981).

In Britain, the systems of corporate self-regulation have been put under pressure by various corporate collapses and undesirable activities (Clarke 1981). As a result, the Council for the Securities Industry was created to:

—maintain the highest ethical standards in the conduct of business within the securities industry;
—keep under constant review the evolution of the securities industry, market practice and related codes of conduct, and to scrutinize the effectiveness of existing forms of regulation and the machinery for their administration;
—maintain arrangements for the investigation of cases of alleged misconduct within the securities industry and breaches of codes of conduct or best practice, and to keep these arrangements under review;
—to initiate new policies and codes as necessary concerning activities in the securities industry, other than those properly within the domestic province of each individual constituent member;
—resolve differences on matters of principle between constituent parts of the securities industry;
—consider the need for changes in legislation affecting the activities

of the securities industry and to examine any proposals for such legislation;

—ensure liaison with the European Commission on securities industry matters and the implementation of the EEC Capital Markets Code of Conduct.

By contrast, the basis of Continental European company law is predominantly Roman; consequently the emphasis is on prescription for behaviour, rather than self-regulation. The effect of such thinking can be seen affecting the UK in the 1981 Companies Act, which lays down a detailed prescription for company reporting, in response to the Fourth Directive of the European Community. The law, not the institutions, lays down the rules.

Self-regulation versus state regulation seems likely to remain an important topic in matters of corporate governance. The challenge is to demonstrate legitimacy in a pluralistic world.

6. *Corporate social responsibility*

The aspect of corporate governance that has received the greatest prominence, particularly in the American literature, is the concept of corporate social responsibility. (For a survey, see Child 1969.)

Much has been written on the idea of stakeholders. Essentially, stakeholder theory perceives the modern (particularly the large and public) company being surrounded by a circle of interest groups which have a legitimate interest in the activities of the company because, by its actions, the company can affect their interests. Although authorities do not agree precisely on the composition of such interest groups they typically embrace some or all of the shareholders, employees, managers, customers and end consumers, suppliers, communities—at the local, state, and federal levels—and the public generally. From such a perception the stakeholder theorists argue for an acceptance of responsibility, whether based on legal, ethical, or moral grounds, for the activities of the company to recognize responsibilities to their stakeholders.

However, there are serious limitations in the stakeholder model. First, the view of a company surrounded by a set of discrete interest groups is naïve. In practice these interest groups themselves may interact: some will be found to have members in common. The network of interacting interests can be highly dynamic; the sets are constantly being redefined. Moreover, the active membership of any group is likely to be but a small part of that entire class, and the interests of the vocal minority may not be representative of the interests of the class as a whole. Second, groups are not homogeneous. In some cases, suppliers for example, there are precise and legally pursuable contracts between the company and the stakeholder. In other cases, the general public for example, only the most peripheral and general case may be advanced. In other circumstances, for example with employees, whilst the legal case for accountability by the company may be limited there is a considerable compatibility of interest between the company and its employees which can be seen—not least because many of them are committing their working life to the enterprise. Some authorities argue that thereby they acquire a property which should become a basis for *de jure* power.

The modern enterprise, in reality, is itself loosely bounded and involves complex and interacting networks of relationships. It is better perceived as a set of dynamic open systems—coalitions of interests between various parties. Indeed, a modern public company, operating internationally, may well involve groups of wholly and partially owned subsidiaries and be, itself, enmeshed in joint ventures with other public companies and governments. In these circumstances the concept of 'the company' surrounded by a precisely bounded set of stakeholders is an abstraction at a very high level, and probably unhelpful in practice in thinking through corporate responsibilities.

These current examples indicate the significance of corporate governance today. Before exploring possible approaches, it will be interesting to remind ourselves of the underpinning ideas in corporate governance.

On the Intellectual Heritage of Corporate Governance

THE HISTORICAL ROOTS

A company is a legal entity, a 'fictitious legal persona', created under the company law of a specific state or country. It is able to contract, to own property, to sue and be sued in its own right. It has an existence outside that of its founders and current members. It may enjoy perpetuity. Property represented in it may be transferred by the sale of shares. In most cases the liability of the subscribing members of a company for corporate debts is limited to the amount of the capital subscribed. The creation of the concept of the company, and the provision of limited liability, were among the great, imaginative developments of the mid-nineteenth-century. Business growth was encouraged, capital formation facilitated, and wealth and employment created.

The concept was derived from nineteenth-century culture and ideology. The rights of property were significant and ownership formed the basis of power in a company. Even today the underpinning, *de jure* view of the company is of the members nominating and electing the directors, who are held accountable for performance, and report on their stewardship, through the accounts, audited by independent auditors, at the annual members' meeting. In contrast, the *de facto* model of governance in the modern company (except the proprietorial company in which owners and executives are synonymous) bears little relation to the *de jure* ideal.

The evolution of these ideas is informative, as can be seen in the following sections.

THE ORIGINS OF CORPORATE ENTERPRISE (1850–1900) IN BRITAIN

Before the mid-nineteenth-century, the dominant forms of business organization were the sole trader, the partnership, and the unincorporated company. Only the Crown or an act of Parliament could create a separate legal entity, with limited liability, such as those bastions of monopoly power, the East India Company or the Hudson Bay Company. At the beginning of the nineteenth-century to limit the liability of owners for business debts they incurred seemed immoral; to separate ownership from management control, madness. By the end of that century both were totally accepted. The 1855 and 1856 Companies Acts were surprisingly liberal—allowing the formation of companies with limited liability, completely separating the owners from the company and enabling the legal entity thus created to sue and be sued in its own right, as though it were an artificial person. Insurance companies, gas and water companies, markets, banks, and many other undertakings were incorporated in increasing numbers from the mid-nineteenth-century.

In 1852 there was a Companies Consolidating Act and in 1870 the Joint Stock Company Arrangements Act, which laid down disclosure requirements before seeking new members. In 1888 the Liquidation Act enforced further controls and in 1900, following the Davey Committee, came another Companies Act which required registration of mortgages. In the later years of the nineteenth-century, cotton-spinning companies, coal mines, cycle manufacturers, breweries, and iron steel works were all trading as joint-stock companies with limited liability. This period also saw the first voluntary corporate mergers: the Salt Union was created to avoid cut-throat competition, and the alkali manufacturers merged nearly fifty separate companies into one industrial combine.

SCALE, COMPLEXITY AND CONCENTRATION

In the 1907 Companies Act, private and public companies were distinguished for the first time—a feature to be reappraised seventy years later in the 1980 Companies Act. The first half of the twentieth-century saw corporate growth, concentration, and in-creasing complexity. Companies grew larger by internally gener-ated growth, new issues of capital, and by merger. Initially, such mergers hoped to achieve scale economies and reduce competition within an industry, but subsequently they aimed to reduce the dependence on a single market or industry, and companies became multi-product, multi-plant and, more recently, multinational.

Berle and Means (1932 (revised edn. 1967)), in their definitive 1932 study, showed the separation that had arisen between members of public companies and their management. The power of the shareholders, acting by majority in company meetings, to elect the board and demand stewardship of their resources became eroded as the shareholder base became large and diffuse whilst management became dominant. Nominations to fill directorships and to appoint the auditors now came from the management with routine ratification by the members.

There was another Companies Act in 1929 and the major Reforming and Consolidating Act in 1948. Amongst this latter's many provisions was the requirement for the first time for consolidated accounts for groups of companies, thus recognizing the increasing significance of large corporate groupings. It is a requirement that some member countries in the European Commu-nity have yet to recognize.

Hayek, in an interesting paper written in 1960 about corporate power, raised an important point about companies owning and controlling other companies:

I must admit that I have never quite understood the rationale or justification of allowing corporations to have voting rights in other corporations of which they own shares. So far as I can discover, this was never deliberately decided upon in full awareness of all its implications, but came about simply as a result of the conception that if legal personality was conferred upon the corporation, it was natural to confer upon it all powers which natural persons possessed. But this seems to me by no means a natural or obvious consequence. On the contrary, it turns the institution of property into something quite different from what it is normally supposed to be. The corporation thereby becomes, instead of an association of partners with a common interest, an association of groups whose interests may be in strong conflict; and the possibility appears of a group who directly own assets amounting only to a small fraction of those of the corporation, through a pyramiding of holdings, acquiring control of assets amounting to a multiple of what they own themselves (Hayek 1960).

INFLUENCES IN THE LITERATURE

The two principal threads of study in corporate governance might be classified as legal and normative.

The legal, constitutional literature is based on jurisprudence and is directly concerned with the company law and its impact on the company and its directors. Inevitably, in such a large field of law, the literature is voluminous. But its primary orientation is explanatory. There is little which addresses the underlying assumptions, or which questions the philosophical underpinnings of company law. There is a sub-set of the legal literature which is concerned with socio-political issues, particularly the reform of company law. Such contributions recognize that the political, social, and economic foundations of company law are based on philosophies which are seldom made explicit and which tend to owe more to nineteenth-century ideas of capitalism and the exercise of power based on property, rather than the contemporary commercial reality of the modern group of companies (see Hadden 1977).

The normative literature is, typically, concerned with descriptions of recommended good practice, case histories of corporate direction, and exhortation and discussions of how directors and boards should behave. (For examples see Sloan 1963, Drucker 1946 and (revised edn. 1964), and Wright and De Lorean 1979.) A more scholarly study of the work of boards, and one of the few pieces of research, is Mace (1971), in which he attacks the mythology of boards as policy-formulating mechanisms. His sample was of US public companies.

Mace found that most boards do provide a source of advice and counsel to the president. The role of outside directors was perceived as largely advisory and not decision-making. The inputs of such outside directors were valued by top management, who generally regarded them as 'additional windows to the outside world'. Outside directors, who were members of a peer group with the president, were typically accustomed to dealing with business problems of considerable magnitude, and thus able to bring a worthwhile point of view to such issues in board discussions. Mace also found that in most companies the boards of directors provided a discipline for the management. The need to appear periodically before a board of professional peers did cause executives to review their operating results, identify problems and give explanations. The feeling of accountability to a legally constituted body such as the board resulted in a closer examination and analysis of results.

It was also found that most boards of directors exercise a decision-making power only in the event of a crisis, such as the sudden death of the president or the recognition by the board that the management performance has become so unsatisfactory that a change must be made in the presidency. However, Mace also found that the boards of most companies do not do an effective job in evaluating, appraising, and measuring the company president until the financial and other results are so dismal that some remedial action is forced upon the board. The president's instinct is to attribute poor results to factors over which he has no control. The inclination of friendly directors is to go along with these apparently plausible explanations. Only when the company's results deteriorate to a fatal point does the board step in and face the unpleasant task of asking the president to resign.

A third strand of literature, however, does address matters of direct interest in corporate governance. This strand might be classified as the socio-political literature.

In their pioneering book, Berle and Means (1932) argued that as companies grew and increased their share capital, and as national prosperity increased and more people invested in shares, so the proportion of voting stock held by the largest shareholders decreased. Consequently, the power of the shareholders to control large corporations had diminished. Directors, who were originally the agents for the owners, would develop policies of their own and assume a self-perpetuating power. Berle further believed that, freed from shareholder control, managers would act with social responsibility for a range of interests.

Burnham (1941) took the same theme but went much further and suggested a society dominated by management. He was more concerned than Berle with state enterprise and the rise of a new ruling class, a managerial meritocracy. The concepts of managerial power and the separation of ownership from control developed by Berle and Burnham have been influential in forming managerial opinion; Burnham's views were also influential in the Labour Party in the late 1950s and 60s.

There is an alternative view, however, well expressed by Crosland (1962), arguing that ownership has, in fact, not become dissipated but is increasingly concentrated in institutional owners and that this concentration ensures control. Moreover, owner control can be reinforced through interlocking directorships and, even where control does rest in the management, it is exercised in the interests of the owning class. In other words, he argues that there has not been a real divorce of ownership and control so much as a 'managerial reorganization of the propertied classes'.

Dahrendorf (1959), having pin-pointed the distinction between the two schools of thought described above, takes a different line. He agrees that ownership has been superseded by management as the spread of shareholdings has reduced the power of property. Like Berle, he believes that the joint-stock company has broken with earlier capitalist traditions: 'separating ownership and control... gives rise to a new group of managers who are utterly different from their predecessors'. However, he also believes that the absence of owner-managers in industry is virtually irrelevant. Authority, he argues, determines class and class conflict. Property ownership is not a prerequisite for class membership, rather it is the ability to exercise authority. Consequently he advances the view that modern advanced industrial nations are 'pluralist societies with power being exercised between a plurality of the ruling class (those with authority)'.

As Nichols (1969) comments:

Dahrendorf... entertains the possibility that conflict may develop both within the industrial enterprise and also between the ruling classes of business and the other ruling classes. Other writers, however, whilst they are eager to assert that businessmen may have their power delimited by other groups outside the enterprise are equally keen to imply that there is no conflict of interests within the enterprise itself. Such theories ... have a high degree of ideological potential. Large-corporation directors often assert that their interests are identical with those of their employees which means that 'we must do away with this idea that there are two sides of industry'.

It is apparent, therefore, that alternative views can be held about the nature of managerial prerogative and power in a modern society. However, the socio-political literature tends to address managerial power and fails to distinguish the basis of corporate governance for management prerogative.

CULTURAL ASSUMPTIONS IN CORPORATE GOVERNANCE

The practice of corporate governance is set within the cultural norms, the expectations of behaviour, of society. What people believe influences how they think and, thus, behave in all matters—including the governance of companies. There are historical and cultural determinants in developing such frameworks. As Hofstede (1978) puts it: 'Culture is the collective programming of the human mind, obtained in the course of life, which is common to the members of one group as opposed to another.' However, in matters of corporate governance, we find a mismatch between the underlying assumptions of British company law as it now exists and the cultural, ideological expectations of that society about business. The underpinning of company law has not kept pace with cultural changes. Nor does it adequately reflect the socio-economic reality of the modern corporation.

Moreover, we conclude that ideological assumptions about corporate affairs can differ significantly between cultures. Weiner (1981) shows an English frame of mind conditioned by an aristocratic and rural idyll, anti-industrial prejudice in education and amongst intellectuals, a way of life in which even the successful businessman becomes 'gentrified'. He contrasts such attitudes with pro-business ideologies in Germany and the US. Consequently, attempts to harmonize company law, or to develop common international standards, are destined to create adversarial circumstances, unless an attempt is made to understand and then to harmonize the underlying ideological assumptions about desired and acceptable company behaviour.

The essential arguments of this essay can now be simply stated:
—that the exercise of corporate governance depends on the availability of necessary power;
—that such power may be based on authority legitimized by law, or power derived from culturally accepted behaviour or available sanctions;
—that the availability of such power depends on the underlying assumptions about acceptable behaviour, that is on the ideological, cultural underpinnings;
—that significant differences are apparent between the ideologies evidenced in different legal systems, and between company law and expected company behaviour. Thus harmonization of law is likely to be fraught with difficulties unless the underlying ideas are recognized, rethought, and harmonized first;
—that there is a need for a coherent, conceptual framework to understand corporate governance, to improve efficiency and effectiveness in exercising corporate governance, and to regulate and legislate for corporate behaviour.

To put the theme in the vernacular, 'unless we all know and agree on what we want companies to do, we had better not try to legislate on their behaviour'.

An Alternative Conceptual Framework for Corporate Governance

The existing conceptual frameworks for corporate governance are structurally oriented; that is, they focus on the roles and responsibilities of specific offices and entities. (For example, with the structure of boards, audit committees, non-executive directors, auditors, dominant and subsidiary companies, responses to employees, stakeholders, institutions, and regulatory bodies.) An alternative approach would be to focus on the activities and underlying ideas involved in corporate governance; that is an orientation on process, not structure.

The work of Mace (1971) emphasizes that boards do not devote their major efforts to the tasks advocated in the normative literature. This has been supported by the studies of The Corporate Policy Group. In interview and group discussion, directors were invited to indicate what they believed would be the appropriate emphases of board attention shown in Figure 6.1.

External matters
(outward-looking   A | D
orientation)

Internal matters
(internal-looking   B | C
orientation)

Concern for the   Concern for the
business   shareholders and
                         external parties

FIG 6.1

Intuitively the respondents tended to emphasize the importance of the external orientation for the business (quadrant A). This is a strategic view—the business in its external environment. However, asked to give an estimate of actual board emphasis, they recognized that a lot of time was devoted to internal business matters (quadrant B).

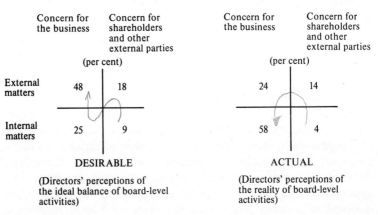

Concern for   Concern for   Concern for   Concern for
the business   shareholders   the business   shareholders
                 and other   and other
                 external parties   external parties
      (per cent)   (per cent)

External   48   18   24   14
matters

Internal   25   9   58   4
matters

        DESIRABLE   ACTUAL

(Directors' perceptions of   (Directors' perceptions of
the ideal balance of board-level   the reality of board-level
activities)   activities)

FIG. 6.2

The actual data have to be treated cautiously, as there was significant variability as the sample included directors from different types of company—public, wholly and partly owned subsidiaries, and private, proprietorial companies, because one would expect significant differences. Notwithstanding, the responses were as shown in Figure 6.2.

Within the limits of the data, they do show a significant difference between the belief that directors have of desirable activities, and actual activities. Also they emphasize the greater focus on business matters rather than a concern for matters affecting shareholders or other external parties.

The quadrant can also be used to provide us with the basis for an alternative conceptual framework for corporate governance, as shown in Figure 6.3.

	Concern for the business	Concern for shareholders and other external parties
External matters	DIRECTION	ACCOUNTABILITY
Internal matters	EXECUTIVE ACTION	SUPERVISION

Fig. 6.3

AN ALTERNATIVE CONCEPTUAL FRAMEWORK

This framework focuses on processes in governance, rather than on the structures through which it is carried out. By determining the activities first, alternative means of fulfilling them can be evaluated.

The *direction* of a company involves the formulation of strategy and allocation of overall resources, setting policies which guide and constrain management action and, broadly, establishing the direction the company is to take. It emphasizes the mission of the business—the shared vision of possible futures and desirable directions for the enterprise. It is concerned with instigating changes in the direction of the enterprise and the setting of overall corporate direction and policy. Direction will inevitably be longer term and oriented towards the commercial, economic, social, technological, and political environments in which the business exists. Strategy formulation involves the assessment of the threats and opportunities external to the business and the understanding of the strengths and weaknesses of internal resources. It includes the setting of corporate objectives and the identification, evaluation, and choice of strategies to be pursued.

Executive action involves the running of the business—day-to-day operational matters of financial, production, and market management, keeping an eye on performance throughout the enterprise and taking decisions consistent with the strategies. It includes planning the ongoing operations, and organizing, co-ordinating, motivating, and leading. Industrial relations, procurement, production, marketing, accounting, and the control of operations, are all part of the executive-management task. The orientation will tend to be shorter term.

Supervision, on the other hand, implies a monitoring of executive action, with a view to ensuring it is appropriate to the interests of the shareholders and other groups with legitimate interests in the company. Supervision is an activity carried out to control executive action.

Accountability is the response of the company to be held accountable to the legitimate expectations of interest groups external to the company.

APPLYING THE ALTERNATIVE CONCEPTUAL FRAMEWORK

Before applying the conceptual framework to the various alternative structures now under discussion, it is important to differentiate between types of enterprise. Unless companies are distinguished, discussion of corporate governance can become over-generalized. Governance processes will differ in emphasis for the public quoted company with a widespread dispersion of shareholding, the public company with a significant proportion of shares in a few hands, a subsidiary company (whether wholly owned or with minority holdings), the associated company, and a private, proprietorial company with little separation of ownership from management. Further consideration is also necessary in the case of joint ventures between companies and federations of companies linked with cross-shareholdings.

Let us now apply the four-part framework to some of the corporate structures under discussion. First, with the *two-tier board,* the direction and management both fall to the executive management team, whilst governance and control are the responsibility of the supervisory board. In the German approach, which formed the basis for the original EEC draft Fifth Directive, both strategy formulation and operational management are the responsibility of the management board. The supervisory board has no executive power for strategy or operations. Its power lies in the right to appoint, approve, or remove the management board. The supervisory board also combines responsibility for monitoring and supervision with the responsibility for governance. This is largely achieved by representative membership of the supervisory board elected from shareholders, employees and management.

With *the dominated unitary board,* typical of most companies in Britain, there is a majority of executive directors on the main board. Governance is exercised by the annual general meeting of members, whilst the predominantly executive board is concerned with direction, management, and control.

Recognizing the apparent weaknesses of dominated boards, various ideas have been advanced to introduce separation and independence into the top processes of companies. The most favoured model retains governance by members in the annual general meeting, but emphasizes the separate functions of executive management and board-level responsibilities for both strategic direction and control. Where a director holds an executive managerial post and a directorship he is, in effect, expected to wear two hats. The board is not there to run the business: it is there to see that the business is being well run. This is the concept behind the *unitary board,* and a number of recent proposals for greater independence at board level can be better understood from the four-part analysis of the top-management processes in a company. For example, the audit committee of non-executive directors, the idea of a non-executive report to the members, proposals for wider use of non-executives, questioning the degree of independence of non-executives, and the proposal that non-executives form a majority on the board, can all be seen to be attempts to strengthen the separation of direction, control, and executive management, and to emphasize independence.

The dilemma of board-level activity in *subsidiary companies* is clearly seen when the four-part model is applied to their direction, management, control, and accountability, that is to their governance. In the UK, the subsidiary-company board is likely to be executive—responsible for executive management—but the direction, control, and governance is often undertaken or dominated by its holding company. This is not in accord with the *de jure* responsibilities of the directors which, since the subsidiary company is an autonomous entity, have the full duties of a board. The law, at the moment in Britain, maintains the 'corporate veil' around each separate company.

We would argue for a complete reformulation of the concept of a subsidiary company which would recognize the naïvity of the *de jure* position in the subsidiary and emphasize the subordination of subsidiaries to the holding company. Where it is shown that a subsidiary does have sufficient autonomy to undertake direction and perhaps control, in addition to management, then we would look for greater visibility and accountability.

The ultimate differentiation would obviously be one in which each of the four functions were identified and allocated to different sets of people, even though they met together as a unitary board. This might be termed the *independent board.*

Conclusions

Corporate governance was defined as the processes by which a company was governed and made responsive to legitimate interests in it. Governance was distinguished from management. Governance is about running the company: management is about running the businesses within the company. We have seen that there is no generally accepted conceptual framework for understanding the governance of companies. In Britain, the basis of company law is founded on nineteenth-century culture, whereas present attitudes towards companies are rooted in a changed ideology. The development of company law and the agreement on accounting standards require an alternative conceptual framework for governance. Moreover, cultural and ideological differences between countries create difficulties in the harmonization of company law and the establishment of international accounting standards.

An alternative framework of corporate governance is needed to improve the direction and top management of business, to influence the development of company law and corporate regulation, and to understand the reality of the processes by which companies are governed, rather than the structures through which governance is exercised. The alternative framework proposed is based on four key activities of corporate governance; namely 'direction', 'executive action', 'supervision' and 'accountability'.

The thorough exploration of these activities, in the context of a specific type of company, would enable the various alternative structural approaches to governance to be appraised, and relevant concepts of independence and objectivity, participation and involvement, information and disclosure, and corporate regulation, to be determined. If such a conceptual framework was applied to ideas in governance, it might be possible to return to the earlier, golden days of the corporate concept, when it was significant in encouraging the formation of capital, facilitating business growth, and generating wealth in the widest way for society. Ideas might again be the prime mover in corporate affairs. The alternative is governance based at best on an expensive bureaucracy of regulation or, at worst, the adversarial emphasis of vested interests.

REFERENCES

Accounting Standards Committee (1981), *Setting Accounting Standards,* London, Institute of Chartered Accountants.

Allen, R.W., Madison, D.L., Porter, L.W., Renwick, P.A. and Mayes, B.T. (1979), 'Organizational Politics—Tactics and Characteristics of Its Actors', *California Management Review,* Vol. 22 No. 1 pp. 77–83.

Andrews, K. (1979), 'Born-Again Boards of Directors', *Harvard Business School Bulletin* (March/April).

Anthony, R.N. (1965), *Planning and Control Systems: A Framework for Analysis,* Boston, Harvard University.

Bank of England (1979), *Quarterly Review* (December).

Berle, A.A. and Means, G.C. (1932), (revised 1967), *The Modern Corporation and Private Property,* New York, Harcourt, Brace World.

Brown, C. (1976), *Putting the Corporate Board to Work,* New York, Macmillan.

Brown, S.R. and Grogan, P.R. (1951), *Company Directors—in Australia* (3rd edn. 1974), Sydney, The Law Book Company.

Bullock, Lord A. (1977), *Report of the Committee of Enquiry on Industrial Democracy,* Cmnd. 6707, London, HMSO.

Burnham, J. (1941), *The Managerial Revolution* (revised 1962), New York, Day & Co.

Child, J. (1969), *The Business Enterprise in Modern Industrial Society,* London, Collier-Macmillan.

Clarke, M. (1981), *Fallen Idols,* London, Junction.

Copeman, G. (1978), *The Managing Director,* Newton Abbot, David & Charles.

The Council for the Securities Industry (1979), *Report on the Year to 31 March 1979,* London, Council for the Securities Industry.

Crosland, C.A.R. (1962), *The Conservative Enemy,* London, Jonathan Cape.

Dahrendorf, R. (1959), *Class and Class Conflict in Industrial Society,* London, Routledge & Kegan Paul.

Drucker, P.F. (1946), *Concept of the Corporation* (revised 1964 and 1972), New York, John Day and Mentor.

Franks, J.A. (1973), *The Company Director and the Law* (3rd edn. 1981), London, Oyez Publishing.

Hadden, T. (1977), *Company Law and Capitalism* (2nd edn. 1977), London, Weidenfeld & Nicolson.

Hayek, F.A. (1960), 'The Corporation in a Democratic Society' in *Management and the Corporation 1985* (eds. M. Aushen and G.L. Bach), New York, McGraw-Hill.

Hofstede, G. (1978), 'Culture and Organisation—A Literature Review Study', *Journal of Enterprise Management,* 1 pp. 127–35.

Juran, J.M. and Louden, J.K. (1966), *The Corporate Director,* New York, The American Management Association.

Mace, L. (1971), *Directors: Myth and Reality,* Boston, Harvard University Press.

Mautz, R.K. and Neumann, F.L. (1977), *Corporate Audit Committees: Policies and Practices,* Cleveland, Ernst & Ernst.

Nichols, T. (1969), *Ownership, Control and Ideology,* London, George Allen & Unwin.

New York Stock Exchange (1976a), *Proposals for Audit Committees* (3 September).

New York Stock Exchange (1976b), *Requirement for Listing* (9 December).

Pfeffer, J. (1981), *Power in Organisations,* Massachusetts, Pitman.

PRO NED, (1982), *Role of the Non-Executive Director,* London, Promotion of Non-Executive Directors.

Sloan, A.P. (Jun.) (1963), *My Years with General Motors,* New York, Macfadden-Bartell.

The Conduct of Company Directors (1977) (White Paper), Cmnd. 7037, London, HMSO.

Tricker, R.I. (1978), *The Independent Director,* London, Tolley.

Tricker, R.I. (1981), 'Chairman of the Board' (discussion paper PP6), Oxford, The Corporate Policy Group.

Tricker, R.I. (1982), 'Corporate Accountability: The Context and the Concept' (discussion paper PP7), Oxford, The Corporate Policy Group.

Weiner, M.J. (1981), *English Culture in the Decline of the Industrial Spirit, 1850-1980,* New York, Cambridge University Press.

Williams, H.M. (1981), 'Corporate Regulation—The Role of the SEC in
    Overseeing the Accounting Profession' (discussion paper PP4), Oxford,
    The Corporate Policy Group.
Wilson, H. (1977), *The Governance of Britain,* London, Sphere.
Wright, J.P. and De Lorean J.Z. (1979), *On a Clear Day You Can See
    General Motors,* New York, Avon Books Hearst Corporation.

7

Management in Government

NEVIL JOHNSON

From Administration to the Management Idiom

During the past twenty years or so there has occurred a major change in the vocabulary of British public administration. This is the replacement of 'administration' as a key concept by 'management'. Naturally, it is possible to find references to the problems of management in the public services in the literature on administration of the year preceding the Second World War, whilst we also encounter plenty of concern with administration and with administrative methods and structures in contemporary writing about government and the role of the public services. Nevertheless, there can be little doubt that administration, which used to be the crucial term characterizing both structures and activities in the public sector, has for some time now been in retreat before the notion of management. Already in 1961, the Plowden Report[1] gave an impetus to a much keener preoccupation with how resources are used and the methods by which public-spending programmes are planned. In 1965 the report of the Estimates Committee of the House of Commons on Recruitment to the Civil Service[2] marked another step in the questioning of traditional administrative assumptions, pointing in its turn to the more comprehensive investigation of the Civil Service by the Fulton Committee which was launched in 1966. By the end of the 1960s the language of management was 'in', and that of administration, if not quite 'out', was looking distinctly old-fashioned.

The basic issue with which I am concerned here is how far and with what kind of qualifications the management concept can be applied in the sphere of government. In dealing with these issues within the limits of a short essay my aim is first to comment on how the idea of management in public administration has been formulated and, in particular, the manner in which there has been in recent years in Britain a shift of perspective which tends to disguise important continuities in the 'principles of management' tradition. This leads me then to consider some of the reasons why, in public administration, the appropriateness of the management concept in its modern dress may have to be qualified in various ways which are grounded in the purpose and conditions of government viewed as a set of political functions.

It is not intended to consider these questions on the basis of a rigorous definition of management, and certainly not one which takes account of the many technical elements in the management function and in the skills related to its performance. Management will simply be taken in its broad sense as the activity of organizing the use of human abilities and material resources for the efficient and effective performance of predetermined tasks. It will be noticed immediately that one feature distinguishing management in this broad sense from administration is the emphasis placed on using people—the personnel function, to use more formal language—and on efficiency in the transformation of material resources, whatever they may be, into output or results. Another feature is the stress on defining and, where possible, quantifying the tasks or objectives themselves. In contrast, administration suggests looking after certain requirements and the effective performance of tasks according to whatever may be the operating conditions prescribed. There is less overt stress on the personnel factor and the explicit definition of objectives, as well as less emphasis on the efficient transformation of resources into outputs.[3] Indeed, it is doubtful whether administration as traditionally conceived had much use for the notion of outputs at all, though it plainly embodied the achievement of effects and results.

The contrast just drawn between management and administration is, of course, too sharp. Indeed, it is of some interest to note that in the early writing on management both in Europe and in the US it was administration rather than management that was assumed to be the object of theoretical analysis. Henri Fayol illustrates this very clearly in the title of his seminal essay, *Administration Industrielle et Générale* (1916), translated first as *Industrial and General Administration* and later in a 1949 edition as *General and Industrial Management*. In the work of L.F. Urwick and L. Gulick we also find that management is very often discussed under the heading of administration, and even Chester Barnard's major work, *The*

Functions of the Executive (1938), is written to some extent in the language of government rather than in that of private business management.[4]

No doubt these pioneers of administrative theory were influenced by the fact that governmental institutions were then regarded as outstanding and even unique examples of complex hierarchically organized institutions, and to some extent they argued that from this area of experience it was possible to deduce principles of organization applicable to a very wide range of activities and organizational forms present throughout society. Thus for them 'management' was to a considerable extent synonymous with 'the principles of organization or administration'. In recent years not much attention has been paid in Britain to the close links which originally existed between administration and management, no doubt in part because the public and private sectors have for some time been seen in dichotomous terms. Whether the revival of a concern for management in public administration will bridge the gap still remains to be seen. What is striking is that during the past two decades management and administration were pushed apart, with the former seen increasingly as an operational remedy for the defects of the latter. Management is held to have dynamic overtones and to put the emphasis on the effective use of resources of all kinds—materials, finance, and personnel. In addition, it has ideological overtones derived from its application to commercial operations in the private sector, and perhaps from the fact that so much writing on management theory and techniques has drawn on the experience and needs of business organizations. Thus management, at any rate in Britain, is now often associated with private enterprise and the constraints of the market. In contrast, administration is commonly identified with rule-bound organizations and bureaucratic behaviour, conditions naively believed to be chiefly characteristic of the sphere of government or of what is generally referred to as the public sector. Not surprisingly, as administration has acquired this negative flavour, so is has become part of the conventional criticism to argue that the way to administrative reform and improvement in the public sector is by the introduction of management concepts and practices: management has been widely seen as the key to a more dynamic and efficient public service. Thus, the idea of management in government is intertwined in recent years with the evolution of the reform movement in public administration, particularly in the Civil Service and in local government.

The concern with management in the services of government has many roots. At a general level it is possible to identify at least three principle influences. First, there is in Britain the traditionally critical attitude towards bureaucracy which has probably been reinforced during recent decades by the extension of public regulation, the decline in respect for authority, and the growing gulf between elected politicians and the various groups of officials who serve them. If a scapegoat is wanted to bear the responsibility for shortcomings in the provision of public services and for mistaken decisions in government, the bureaucracy remains a popular candidate. It follows that there is always plenty of support for the idea that with the right therapy the bureaucracy could be cured of its weaknesses: less bureaucracy and more efficient management by the bureaucrats that remain, has become a popular slogan. Second, there has been the steadily growing impact of changes in the scale and character of government functions. In essence, it is the transition from a primarily regulatory state to one seen predominantly in terms of service provision. The concept of administration acquired most of its definition at a time when much of the work of government was more obviously regulatory. In this context, administration came to be seen more or less in Weberian terms as the activitiy of implementing a system of rules, what Webor himself conceptualized as a rational legal order possessing authority in virtue of its rule-based quality. The extension of welfare services provided for the citizen, and of activities directly concerned with producing goods or services, has persuaded many people to put a question mark over the appropriateness of traditional administrative methods, structures, and styles to the performance of the tasks of the modern welfare state.[5] Third, there has been a growing demand for greater efficiency in administration. No doubt the intense preoccupation in recent years with this problem reflects in some degree Britain's relative economic decline: a country with shrinking resources and a high demand for public goods becomes more sensitive to the costs of government than those which have found it easier to finance expanding services out of increasing tax revenues. It is the call for greater efficiency in government that represents the principal practical conclusion drawn from the other two factors at work: bureaucracy might be made at least tolerable if

rendered more efficient, whilst to achieve more efficient performance it becomes necessary to recognize the changed character of
many contemporary public services and the need to apply
maximizing criteria to them.

Aspects of the Management Movement in Government

The diffusion of these influences can be charted by reference to
many stages in the review and change of British administrative
practices and structures during the past twenty years. Running
through so many of the reports produced, decisions made, and
reorganizations undertaken, there is the management theme. Even
before the Fulton Committee on the Civil Service reported in 1968,
there was an investigation of management in local government,[6] the
findings of which undoubtedly had some effect in modifying
perceptions of how local authority administration should be
conducted. Gradually the emphasis moved towards a perception of
the local authority as a corporate entity engaged in producing
service outputs and requiring for that purpose new styles of
management and organization, corporate planning and corporate
management methods. Within the local government sector this
tendency was reinforced by the 1969 Royal Commission *Report on
Local Government in England* with its preoccupation with efficiency
in local government[7], the structural reorganization of local government between 1972 and 1974 throughout the country, and the 1972
Bains Report, *The New Authorities: Management and Structure*.
This is not the place to attempt any evaluation of how far the
management concept has indeed completely changed local authority administrative behaviour:[8] it is sufficient to note that in this part
of the public sector the terms in which the work and organization of
local authorities are considered have changed substantially.

More dramatic in some ways was the reception of the management idea in the Civil Service, no doubt in part because the idea of a
specific administrative function was more deeply embedded in that
branch of public service. The Fulton Report gave a decisive impetus
to this change, partly through its sharp criticism of the traditional
administrative ethos in central government and of the class of
officials regarded as its bearers, partly through the attention it
devoted to the identification of tasks and job analysis. Indeed, one
of the appendices to the report was the 'Report of a Management

Consultancy Group', prepared by a team of management consultants working with a member of the committee and a Treasury official. One of the immediate effects of acceptance of the Fulton Report was the creation in late 1968 of the Civil Service Department (CSD) to which the management of the civil service responsibilities of the Treasury were transferred. But it was more than a matter of transfer of functions: the CSD was intended positively to develop the management services available to central government, to give the lead in implementing the Fulton proposals, and to advise the departments in the improvement of their management methods. Shortly after the Fulton Report appeared, the management movement received a further stimulus from the arrival of a Conservative Government (1970) which was ostensibly committed both to a reduction in government activity and to a programme of rationalization and greater efficiency in the public sector. The White Paper on the reorganization of central government (1970),[9] the establishment of a central policy review staff, the initiation in 1971 of exercises in programme analysis review, and the introduction of a small number of advisers from private business into Whitehall, all bore witness to a commitment to improve the efficiency of public administration and to a belief in improved management as a cardinal requirement of such a development. Nor was the Heath Government's endorsement of this managerial approach limited to its own sphere of central administration. As already mentioned, encouragement was given to a management orientation in local authorities, whilst in other parts of the public sector a variety of schemes of administrative reorganization were carried out, in some cases after seeking guidance from private management consultants. The restructuring of the National Health Service and the creation of regional water authorities can serve as examples.

Notwithstanding the great effort invested in administrative reorgnization, roughly in the period 1965 to 1975, the results have in terms of enhanced efficiency· been widely regarded as disappointing. The costs of the public sector continued to rise, at any rate until about 1978, a trend which admittedly owed more to the willingness of governments to allow expenditure to increase than to any demonstrable decline in the efficiency of the public sector (leaving out of account some of the nationalized industries, where different conditions have applied). Manpower totals in the public sector went on rising, as did pay levels in the wake of high levels of inflation. All this could hardly fail to suggest to the public that the principal beneficiaries of rising public expenditure were public employees themselves, rather than the community for which services were being provided. The general economic performance of the country during the 1970s was marked by yet more serious difficulties and weaknesses, a fact which was grist to the mill of those who argued that the public sector was both inefficient and too large. The implementation of the Fulton reforms in the Civil Service lost momentum by about 1975, and it was hard to assert with confidence that what had been done really had produced a major qualitative change in the performance of the Civil Service, or even established the foundation for such changes in the future.[10]

Yet these rather ambiguous developments tended to reinforce the call for more efficient and effective management in the public services. And it is a cause that has received support from widely separated points in the party-political spectrum. When the General Subcommittee of the House of Commons Expenditure Committee reported on the Civil Service in 1977 it renewed its call for more attention to be given to management methods and to the possibility of diffusing managerial responsibilities in the civil service more widely. This received support from both Conservative critics of growing public expenditure and Labour Party supporters of more extensive public planning and higher welfare spending. More vividly still, the approach adopted since 1979 by Mrs Thatcher's Government involved a vigorous reaffirmation of the importance of more efficient management in government. Much of the effort invested in the pursuit of this aim has been in individual departments and agencies, though the central role of the CSD and its relations with the Treasury also came under scrutiny, leading finally at the end of 1981 to the return to the Treasury of responsibility for staff costs, and the transformation of the CSD into something more like a purely personnel management unit in the Cabinet Office.[11] But there were in addition specific policy commitments which altered significantly the context in which the goal of improved management had to be pursued. Far more decisively than any government of recent years, that elected in 1979 was determined to reduce the level of public expenditure overall and to diminish the relative share of the public sector in the use of national resources. Despite the difficulties affecting realization of this aim—stemming most notably from the rise in transfer payments attendant on a rapidly growing level of unemployment—there can be no doubt that constraints on the resources available (coupled in many fields with cash limits) began to establish a more stringent framework within which to tackle the problems of management. In addition, a commitment to removing activities from the public to the private sector introduced a new challenge to well-established assumptions about the proper sphere of government. This bias in favour of private provision where practicable, and of market constraints, stimulated renewed efforts to investigate more actively within the public sector itself what scope might exist for providing services on a more efficient and cost-effective basis. To put the matter crudely, the government was seen by many as being involved extensively in a business operation, and for that reason it was concluded that its affairs should be administered in accordance with those managerial principles held to be conducive to efficiency in private business.

Symptomatic of the climate of opinion that sees improved management in government working hand in hand with firm ceilings on public expenditure to secure greater efficiency and enhanced effectiveness was the scrutiny programme initiated in 1979 by Sir Derek Rayner, appointed as adviser to the Prime Minister 'on ways to improve efficiency and eliminate waste in 'government'.[12] It should be noted that this is by no means the first time that an effort has been made to scrutinize programmes in the hope of reducing costs and raising efficiency: the initiation of programme analysis review in 1971 pointed in the same direction, as indeed have several exercises carried out in the 1970s both by the Civil Service Department and other departments. Experience has shown, however, that it is very difficult to maintain the momentum of such efforts, and that their effects constantly run the risk of being dissipated by new commitments or the reassertion of old ones. On this occasion the pressure for improved management was reinforced by a much keener emphasis on a critical approach to the question of whether the tasks under scrutiny really had to be carried out by government. Within the context of the present discussion it is not, however, the latter aspect of the Rayner scrutiny programme which will be pursued. My concern is rather to underline the importance attached to the achievement of better management as the key to 'promoting the quality of the service provided by government and the efficiency of the task undertaken by government'.[13] Amongst the phrases used by Sir Derek Rayner were 'a robust and tauter system of management', 'the emphasis I place on management information for ministers', 'accountability for the management of resources', 'to ensure good stewardship in each department under its managers', 'whether some ... rules are contrary to good management practices', and 'to assure departmental ministers and ministers collectively that the management systems do exist and do work'.[14] Here we have a vivid example of the language of the management enthusiast (and in this case of a successful business manager, let it be said) applied directly to the administration of public services. What are we to make of it? What exactly is being called for? How far, in fact, can management thinking, derived chiefly from the sphere of industry and commerce, apply to government?

Management and Administration: New wine in old bottles?

We need to begin unravelling these questions by recalling the obvious fact that government is involved in a multifarious range of activities, all of which result in the delivery of services of some kind to somebody, and all of which make demands on material resources and personnel. Of course, the services provided are infinitely various, many of them being internal to the organization of government itself (e.g. briefing a minister, running a registry, providing memoranda for Parliamentary committees), and many of them being directed to clients in the community or simply to the community at large (e.g. paying out unemployment benefit, administering planning regulations or exercising traffic control). Some functions are discharged by prohibitions and thus entail enforcement; some impose requirements with which citizens must comply before receiving certain benefits or becoming entitled to act in various ways; many entail the provision of services which clients can use (or are even required to use, such as schools for those between the ages of five and sixteen) and thus call for the deployment of substantial material resources and personnel; some functions consist chiefly in the paying out of cash benefits such as pensions; others involve governmental or public agencies in the production of goods and services which may be sold commercially or made generally available in different ways (as is, to some extent, the case with the work of research establishments); yet others produce pure public goods such as defence and policing.

What is quite clear from this list of examples is that in some important respects the organization of government does resemble other pieces of social organization: from one point of view it can be regarded as processing resources in order to produce outputs that people can use. From this perspective it follows that a rational method of organization and operation in government will seek to maximize outputs in relation to the resources used. Since government is financed out of taxes (which the citizen is obliged to pay) it is apparent that to operate on any other principle entails claiming more resources from citizens than would otherwise be necessary and thus is reducing the scope for the satisfaction of individual preferences in the society. On this argument, inefficient government might be characterized as a respectable form of organized robbery.

If we focus attention on only certain aspects of the similarity between what is done by and on behalf of government and what is done by other non-governmental organizations we are, therefore, pushed towards the conclusion that the *modus operandi* in government should resemble that held to be rational and efficient elsewhere, notably in the sphere of the production of goods and services for sale to consumers. This conclusion is supported by the changes that have taken placed in the role of government and what it is committed to undertake. It has become hard not to see many of the activities of government as in some sense analogous to those of a productive enterprise, rather than as being directed to the maintenance of a relatively simple regulatory framework for private action. As a result, it appears almost self-evident that the principles of management appropriate to a productive enterprise delivering goods to a market ought to be applied in the sphere of government too. If this is not done, so it has often been argued, there can be no hope of securing efficiency and little chance of stemming the tendency inherent in large and complex organizations, which are themselves largely able to determine the volume of resources they claim, to grow ever more demanding and ever more removed from the discipline of economy in the use of resources and of the need regularly to review the purposes being pursued.

Accepting this account of the problem (and without at this stage contemplating any of the qualifications which have to be made to it) we must next consider in rather more detail what view of management might be entailed by it in the sphere of government. It seems to me that something like the following operational requirements need to be met. First, it is necessary to know what the tasks being performed are and to specify them in some detail. Second, it is necessary to have some view of the purposes or objectives served by the tasks undertaken, in other words to define objectives. Third, it is essential to have as full information as possible about the resource inputs and their costs. Fourth, it is necessary to make judgments about the level of effort in task performance that it is reasonable to demand of personnel. Fifth, it is necessary to be able to foresee at least some of the ways in which the environment itself is likely to affect the performance of tasks. And sixth, there must be ways of determining, and as far as possible measuring, effectiveness in performance.

Given such requirements, effective management means taking appropriate action to fulfil them. It is a method of proceeding so that for a given demand on resources the most effective results are efficiently achieved in the performance of the tasks set. This implies, of course, that attention has to be paid to the processes or steps by which tasks are carried out, and such an analysis is likely to include reference to planning, organization, deployment of personnel, direction and co-ordination, financial control, and the provision of information for monitoring purposes. All this is very close to Gulick's famous PODSCORB formulation,[15] itself derived largely from Fayol. But lest this sounds hopelessly old-fashioned, its modernity can be demonstrated by turning to Sir Derek Rayner's recommendations for the structure of reports called for by the scrutiny programme referred to above. Here we find very familiar headings—the nature and purpose of activities and functions, the costs involved in task performance and their breakdown, aspects of organization, methods of operation, and arrangements for the appraisal of effectiveness and efficiency in performance.[16]

It might well now be asked whether management in government in this sense adds up to anything substantially different from what were recognized a long time ago as the principles of effective and cost-conscious administration. Are we not concerned largely with a change in vocabulary rather than with anything fundamentally new in the diagnosis of what is required for the efficient discharge of public business? For the most part, the answer must be that the changes now advocated do represent a rediscovery of earlier

wisdom rather than the formulation of new principles for the
performance of administrative tasks. At the same time, however,
they express important changes of attitude and approach inside
public administration, and in particular a curious reversal of
perspective as compared with that adopted in earlier organizational
theory. The pioneers of such theory were aiming at the formulation
of operating principles of general application and did not differentiate sharply between public and private organizations, assuming that
certain conditions were common to the rational design of organizations, regardless of important differences in external constraints and
operating conditions. In other words, they did not assume that the
absence or attenuation of market constraints was a crucial factor
differentiating public from private organizations in respect of the
requirements to be met in applying rational principles to the design
of organization. In contemporary Britain the perspective seems to
have changed to the extent that it is widely believed that only the
private, profit-making body provides a model of the conditions
which need, in various ways, to be simulated as far as is possible in
the public sector if efficiency in operations is to be attained. Thus
the management theory often recommended for application in
government is to some extent more narrowly based and more
particularist than was much of the earlier classical organization
theory, though much of its practical content can easily be shown to
be little different from the conclusions suggested by those who took
complex organizations in general as their field of inquiry rather
than the special case of the commercial enterprise.

There are, however, more straightforward reasons too for
doubting whether the management movement in modern British
administration is quite as original in its recommendations as the
language of its advocates sometimes appears to suggest.

There is first the tendency to underestimate the continuity which
has certainly existed in this country since the early 1920s in our
preoccupation with organization and methods in the public service,
and particularly at the level of the central government. It is true that
there has never emerged a science of organization and methods,
capable of providing general principles applicable across the whole
range of public administration.[17] But what did develop (and
especially during and after the Second World War), was a
substantial fund of received wisdom and practices bearing on the
possibilities of adapting organizations to tasks and of maintaining

efficient staffing levels (which generally meant low staffing levels). Closely related to O. & M. work in the traditional sense was the complementing and staff inspection function which was well developed in British central administration and became an important factor working in favour of economy in the use of staff. Much of what currently goes on as programme analysis or scrutiny is in fact a further development and intensification of an earlier habit of systematically reviewing organization and staffing levels.

A second point is that underpinning much of the contemporary preoccupation with improved management is a shift back to the enforcement of fixed expenditure limits. In the preceding outline of the basic operational requirements for efficient performance in government this condition was not underlined. This was deliberate, since the concern at that stage was to specify in general terms the basic operational requirements of efficient management viewed as an ongoing activity. In principle, the quantity of resources made available can be clearly distinguished as an issue for decision from the methods or procedures necessary to secure efficiency in their use. Indeed the allocation of resources can in some conditions be regarded as dependent on performance: how much finance an activity receives is an outcome of how efficiently it is carried out. Yet in the case of government and much of the public sector, we know from experience that if relatively firm financial limits are removed, we then lose the one over-arching constraint which, in relation to public services for which no direct payment is made, is the only constraint analogous in its effects to the private business's need to balance its books and secure a return on capital.

It is not without interest (and a touch of irony) that the early theorizing about efficiency in administration, to which reference has been made, occurred when balanced budgets were still the rule rather than the exception. Scientific principles of administration seemed to make sense within such a context: perhaps indeed it was unconsciously assumed that in government balanced budgets were the functional equivalent of market constraints elsewhere. Subsequently, much of the Western world lived through a long period in which rising prosperity and faith in demand management by government made balanced budgets sound like a quaint echo from the past. Yet even in such conditions the growing scale of public expenditure has eventually made it necessary to give renewed attention to the problem of how best to improve the operations of government and to increase the efficiency with which resources are managed. But so long as expenditure could rise (regardless of the reasons for this), the call for better management tended to amount to little more than moral exhortation, as indeed the experience of British public administration over the past fifteen years or so has often suggested. Now the wheel has turned full circle, or nearly so. Even if there can be no return to an epoch of balanced budgets, there is now in Britain and elsewhere a far keener realization than has existed for at least a generation that real limits need to be set to public budgets, not least as one of the conditions necessary for the control of inflation. It is precisely in this context, marked by a partial return to financial disciplines, that application of 'the principles of management' becomes a realistic undertaking. But if called such, they resemble fairly closely what, under comparable limits at an earlier time, would have been called the principles of efficient administration.

So far I have attempted to show that much that is presented as management in government in fact on closer inspection shows many similarities with what earlier was described in the language of administration. Certainly, some of the more perceptive writers on management in government appear to recognize this, even though they express themselves in the management idion which has become fashionable.[18] Their intention is not to treat government as if it were some gigantic business enterprise, but rather by analysis of processes in the public sector to show how administration can become more self-critical abouts its methods and objectives, and more cost-conscious. In some degree it is classical theory which has been revised, even though expressed in different terms, and then linked with a new awareness of the importance of financial limits. Equally, modern work on management practices has laid great emphasis on the personnel function, on the need to motivate staff, to use them effectively, and to maintain programmes for career development. On the whole British public administration has not been slow to adapt its methods of personnel management in ways which have resulted in a more deliberate effort to make better use of personnel. There has been growing recognition of the importance of personnel management in the repertoire of skills needed by the administrator. Insofar as the management idiom has helped to encourage progress in these directions and rendered public officials more sensitive to the need to seek the best results for the lower costs, its acceptance and diffusion have served a valuable purpose.

The Limits of Management in Government

The burden of the argument so far is that there are undoubtedly good reasons for attempting to improve management methods in government, but that the actual content of what are often recommended as sound management principles is somewhat less original than is sometimes assumed. However, the propagation of management in government as a concept and set of techniques also conceals certain dangers associated with over-simplification of the problems facing public organizations and underestimation of some of the very important ways in which a large part of public administration differs substantially from the private sector. These differences relate far less to what is being done than to the conditions under which tasks must be performed. The rest of this discussion will be chiefly concerned with some of the constraints affecting government, the special needs to which they give rise, and the extent to which they entail qualifications of the contemporary managerial message.

It is worth beginning with the obvious point that government at all levels serves politically sanctioned ends. In the conditions of political democracy this means that the effectiveness of public administration depends significantly on the continuing consent of the governed and on its capacity to respond to the environment of dispute and critical argument likely to exist in relation both to ends and means. It is also a fact of great significance that the top management in government consists principally of politicians who have been elected in competition with each other, and whose tenure is sometimes uncertain and usually short. The politician so appointed finds himself in an ambiguous position. On the one hand he (or she) is normally interested in securing results, both in order to fulfil promises made and to improve the prospects of re-election. But at the same time he must respect the interests present in the society and well-established expectations about the manner in which government will go about its business. These factors in turn impose very serious constraints on the capacity actually to achieve results. This indeed is often what is meant when we talk about the difficulty of finding administratively viable ways of pursuing particular policy objectives.

It is conditions of this kind that generally make it impossible for management in government to assume those dynamic characteristics which, at any rate in a vulgarized view of the matter, are often attributed to the management function in the business enterprise. Management in government means the achievement of efficient and effective performance under conditions which, to a substantial degree, express procedural values accepted both for their own sake and for the protection of the interests of the governed. These values are for the most part unrelated to the value of efficiency itself, and indeed may run counter to it. Management in government cannot, therefore, be a maximizing activity to the same extent that it is in principle in an enterprise organization of a commercial kind. It can be directed to maximization only in the narrower sense of seeking to promote the most effective results by the rational use of resources, but all the while remaining subject to the very varied conditions defining the kind of behaviour that the public expects of those in the service of its governmental institutions.

There are other blind spots, too, in the current preoccupation with management in government. One is the temptation to exaggerate the extent to which the activities carried on by government have, in fact, ceased to be regulatory, persuasive, and reactive: in other words, governments are still engaged in governing, and that is something different from the supply of goods. Another is the tendency to arouse or maintain ill-founded or naïvely optimistic expectations of the gains to be derived from good management in respect of levels of efficiency. Then there are the risks, inherent in any approach that tends to deny or minimize the multi-valued purposes served by government, of obscuring the political foundations of government and all that that may mean for the maintenance of values in society. And finally, there are considerations relating to professional ethics which, in the public service, remain of major importance and are likely to qualify the management approach in various ways. It is with some discussion of these matters that I will conclude.

It has become commonplace to assert that the functions of government have radically changed in character and purpose, and to some extent this is obviously true. Within the public sector broadly defined there are now many activities which consist essentially in the production of goods and services. These are produced and offered for sale, or in the case of many services (e.g. medical care or refuse collection) provided free to the client and paid for out of taxation. Education has become another of the great service-providing activities in which numerous semi-autonomous agencies are engaged. Most of these services are dependant financially on the decisions of the central government and are provided within statutory frameworks approved by Parliament. But the responsibility for providing them rests exclusively with non-central bodies such as local authorities, administrative boards and agencies of different kinds, and curiously 'private' bodies like universities. In the wake of these changes in the type of services provided it is not surprising that the conclusion is often drawn that in the sphere of government the predominant preoccupation must be with the management of resources, human and material, in such a way as will guarantee the most effective delivery of particular benefits. The whole process tends to be seen as active and creative, directed to the provision of an immensely varied range of outputs.

Yet, this is only one side of the coin, even if it is the side which is most visible to the individual who receives benefits, and perhaps employment too, from the public sector. When we turn our attention to the directing levels of the governmental system it is clear that the government and its immediate administrative agents are, in Britain, not often concerned directly with the provision of services, nor even with close control of the executive agencies. Ministers may claim credit for all kinds of concrete achievements, but in fact neither they nor their civil servants generally have an active role in such matters at all. Instead what they do is still extensively to maintain the framework within which others must operate. This involves the allocation of finance, the provision and amendment of legal powers, negotiation and consultation with many of those within and outside the public sector who are expected to provide the goods or services, and a continuing effort to maintain public support for whatever policies the government is pursuing. If we look closely at the kind of activity engaged in by most government departments, we find that a large part of it is still regulatory in a broad sense of that term: it does not consist in producing some service, but in facilitating the production of such services (or goods) by others. This is done by maintaining a complex framework for action which in turn has to be justified politically.

Moreover, many activities which result in the provision of welfare services (e.g. social security payments or unemployment benefit) do in fact contain a substantial regulatory element: much of the work of the administrative agencies concerned is directed to checking that the relevant legal conditions have been met by the claimants.

Thus we still have to take account of the fact that in many parts of the governmental system, and especially at the centre where many policy decisions are made, the functions to be performed are still extensively directive, regulatory, and persuasive. They appertain to the task of governing and differ in decisive qualitative respects from what is involved in, for example, the running of Marks & Spencer. Moreover, the government in a democratic society has to react to changing circumstances and opinion in a way not expected of private commercial organizations. Its actions are subject to continuing argument and criticism, and it is expected to react to an unpredictable range of problems and difficulties in society. (Political signals are different from market signals.) Government finds itself in the position of a fire brigade: it is constantly on call and is expected to be able to extinguish the fires which regularly occur. Yet the analogy is also inadequate, for there is little dispute about what a fire brigade should do. In contrast, how a government deals with the fires to which it is called is itself a mater for argument and debate.

The conclusion to be drawn from these remarks is that in government it is the regulation of a pattern of relationships, internal and external, that is just as essential as the ultimate provision of benefits and services.[19] This may indeed be true, in some degree, of any organization in society, but undoubtedly this fact constitutes a more decisive constraint in government than in many other spheres of social life. A danger implicit in applying the concept of management to government is that attention may then be focused too insistently on end results, whilst many of the conditions to which the achievement of results has to be subordinated may be neglected. Moreover, these conditions are for the most part complex and subtle, and to understand and express them calls for talents and abilities which may not be typically those of the manager of resources and the provider of goods and services. The capable politician and senior administrator need a capacity for abstract and generalized analysis and the effective use of written and spoken language, which may be of advantage in business management but hardly appears to be an essential condition of successful operation.[20] It should not be forgotten that ultimately the politician in a democracy depends on his ability to persuade, and that his first need is to maintain the fabric of institutions which enable him to do this. It follows that many of the official advisers of ministers and of local council leaders must share this preoccupation: they are administrators who minister to the needs of those they serve. It is important that preoccupation with management in government should not obscure these necessities.

The danger of exaggerated expectations of improved management in government can be illustrated in many ways. Such expectations arise chiefly because too little attention is paid to the limits affecting the ability of government both to change what it is doing and the terms on which it operates. The limits imposed on change stem both from the resistance of society to change and from the fact that the governmental system has at its different levels relatively little direct control over many of those, even within the public sector, who are responsible for the actual administration of regulations or the provision of goods and services. Thus within the structure of government there is enormous scope for seepage,[21] for the progressive attenuation of whatever managerial disciplines may be established at key points. Naturally this situation does not justify passivity in relation to the need to develop and maintain effective management systems. But it does remind us that the tasks of government are always tied back to a political function and require for their performance a system of organization of very great complexity. Thus there can be no royal highway to success and efficiency: getting things done remains a wearisome and frustrating business.

Moreover, the conditions of operation in the public sphere exclude the application of some of the controlling and disciplining mechanisms available elsewhere. A simple example is the elusiveness of the notion of accountable management which became so popular in the post-Fulton era. If accountable management means that an official (a 'manager') has to work within defined financial limits and to explain ('to account for') any infringement of these within his sector of responsibility, then no doubt the concept is a useful reassertion of the desirability of cost-conscious administration. In some activities it may even be practicable to operate trading funds (for example, in parts of the Property Services Agency of the

Department of the Environment) and then to require the managers to work within the constraints of such a fund, balancing their costs against their revenue earnings. All this makes sense. But what is much more questionable is the idea lying behind the call for accountable management units, that in some way the manager in public service can be made subject to exactly the same discipline as the business manager who is required, for the survival of his enterprise, to secure an adequate rate of profit. This hardly seems to be attainable in government where the threat of bankruptcy is absent. The nearest approach to such a situation is to be found in publicly owned industry, provided there are firm financial limits set and maintained by the government. Yet even here it is well known that the managers have only in the most attenuated way been held 'accountable' for the losses which most public enterprises have at different times incurred. Financial discipline is without doubt essential to effective management and the attainment of acceptable standards of efficiency in public service. But it is a mistake to believe that as a rule the public manager can, in virtue of being called an accountable manager, be exposed to the same kind of corrective discipline as the manager acting under market constraints and the pressures of a profit and loss account.[22]

Reference has already been made to the multi-valued character of so much of the activity of the government, and to the fact that it is often impossible to separate procedural values from the value attaching to particular objectives. Additionally, objectives are typically hard to define and appreciation of them will vary according to the standpoint of the person reacting to them. It is in this connection that the comparison with the world of private business may be particularly misleading. In private productive activity the objectives pursued tend to be relatively well-defined. This is at any rate true of many of the final products, even if the complexity of the incidental social purposes served by a privately owned business enterprise is a more debatable matter. A shoe factory is engaged in the production of shoes. Whilst there may be room for a lot of argument about what style and type of shoes to produce, for what markets and in what quantities, there can be little doubt that the factory is in the business of shoe production—at any rate so long as it remains a shoe factory. Even such an institution as a university, customarily thought to be concerned with more exalted activities than shoe production, nevertheless maintains at a certain level of discourse a reasonably clear understanding of what its members are there to do: they teach in particular subjects, offer courses, prepare students for examination, conduct research, and so on. It is relatively easy, in fact, to discern whether a university is generally pursuing its conventionally understood objectives or not.

In contrast, in many sphere of government it is far harder to pin down the objectives served by the numerous activities undertaken. Sometimes they will be elusive and obscure, especially when expressed at a high level of generality (e.g. in the case of the education or health services); sometimes they will be hotly contested and exposed to competing interpretations; and nearly always they will be multi-valued objectives, not always wholly compatible with each other and requiring to be kept in some kind of equilibrium one with another. Often, too, the objectives will be political in a purely tactical sense: to quieten criticism, to survive an awkward dispute, to convey the mere impression of concern or activity when those involved know that what they want to do is precisely nothing.

Conditions of this kind simply reflect the fact that government is more than 'a contrivance of human wisdom to provide for human wants', to quote Burke in one of his more utilitarian moods. It is just as much a contrivance to assist society in going about its business, and such business is infinitely various and subject to many different evaluations according to the position and interests of those in society. It follows that at any rate within a civilized and liberal system of government very many decisions, both of policy and implementation, are never cut and dried. A large degree of evaluative appreciation comes into them, there is much room for argument about what it is expedient and prudent to do, and there may well be many normative considerations expressed in law to be taken into account. The emphasis on management tends often to veil and underestimate the impact of the multi-valued choice situation in government. It encourages a search for simplification in the identification of tasks which may be wholly beneficial if and when the task to be performed can be clearly specified and its objectives are widely accepted. Classic examples would be provided by military operations in time of war. But far more typical is a condition of ambiguity and uncertainty in which it is a question of deciding what, on a balancing of advantage and disadvantage, it is practicable to do. In such circumstances it is not surprising that the cautious administrator may sometimes achieve more than the thrusting manager.

Here we can make the transition to the question of professional ethics in the service of government. In Britain, as in many other countries, the modern public service has developed as a profession, committed by its codes of behaviour to serve the political authority, to work in the interests of the public, and to act with due respect for the legal framework set for its activities. The professional standards which have been built up under such conditions inevitably subordinate the individual official to the requirements of his profession: generally he does not act as an individual, but as the representative of a public authority.

It is noticeable that many of those who advocate a managerial approach to the activities of government recommend a more independent, even aggressive, style of management, but ask few questions about the degree of autonomy which the manager in public service enjoys and can legitimately claim. Equally they tend to discount the significance of the various obligations which the public official—regarded often as the servant of the state—is expected to acknowledge. Yet in reality the autonomy of the public official in Britain is remarkably limited. For better or worse, the political traditions of the country have denied to him any significant share in political authority. He is appointed to perform a wide range of functions under the law and is usually subject to the control of ministers or elected councillors, although it must be noted that nowadays the relationship of many administrative agents with a politically accountable authority is very indirect. The strength of the idea that the proper status of officials is one of subordination is underlined by the persistent difficulty experienced in accommodating nationalized industry to the British governmental system. In principle, nationalized industry is exempt from day-to-day ministerial control over what has been called 'day-to-day management'. Yet it has been hard to allow to nationalized enterprises the degree of autonomy that may be required for efficient commercial operation, in part because there has been reluctance to accept that those who manage these enterprises should have such discretion in making policy decisions as appeared appropriate only to politically accountable persons, i.e. ministers.[23]

The relatively restricted scope for independent action and initiative enjoyed by the official is determined in the first place by his subordination to politically responsible authorities. But it is often reinforced by the legal limitations under which he operates as well as by the organizational characteristics of the public service. The legal dimension in government serves to circumscribe the conditions under which both officials and politicians must act, and in addition it generally makes explicit the exclusion of most officials from any personal share in the authority conferred by law. Instead, it is normal for powers to be vested in ministers, local councils, and a wide range of corporate bodies, with the consequence that responsibility is rarely in a legal sense seen to rest with the individual official who acts. Within the public service it suffices to refer to the formalization of conditions of service in a manner which excludes virtually all independent action by the personnel manager (or indeed by any other kind of manager). Consequently, in relation to the handling of personnel, the more senior official lacks even in principle many of the means of influencing behaviour and performance available to the manager in private businesses, though it is worth remembering that the influence of trade unions and staff associations now qualifies substantially in every sphere of employ-ment the discretion in the treatment of staff previously enjoyed.

The official works, therefore, within a structure of constraints which heavily qualify the discretion necessary for the application of purely results-oriented methods of management. It is in this context that the ethic of public service, embodying commitment to the public and its politically responsible representatives, has been important. On the one hand it has expressed many of the constraints under which the official works. Yet on the other it has served as a practical motivating force contributing to the energy and dedication applied to the performance of tasks. Professional standards in the public service have to some extent been a necessary substitute for different motivating conditions and operational constraints which in other spheres of social organization have been conducive to effective performance.

It must, however, be acknowledged that in the pursuit of ways of achieving operational effectiveness it may have become more difficult to appeal to the standards of professional ethics formerly regarded as so important in the public services. There is some evidence to suggest that in recent years the traditional professional ethos characteristic of many branches of public service has been in decline. There are many reasons for this, most of them connected with patterns of social and political change. The expansion and diversification of the public services have played a part in weakening commitment to professional standards as has the rapid growth of unionization amongst public employees at a time when high levels of inflation have encouraged more aggressiveness in pressing claims to higher pay. More generally, the public services cannot escape the impact of a widespread questioning of authority relationships in the society, nor the existing mood of criticism towards officials themselves. Finally, it is probable that the emphasis on a managerial approach also contributes to growing uncertainty within the public service about the role it is expected to perform.

Reflection on the political functions of government suggests that if acceptable standards of conduct and adequate levels of performance are to be maintained, then it is still necessary to be able to appeal to a set of professional commitments expressing an ethic of public service. In an important sense this has to be the cement which holds together the edifice of government. This means that effective and efficient management has to be developed and applied within a wider understanding of the purposes served by government and of the standards of behaviour which the administrative system ought to sustain.

What is called for here is a difficult and sensitive balancing of requirements. Undoubtedly, the official in public service is now engaged extensively in the use and deployment of resources taken away from the people he serves and returned to them as benefits and entitlements legitimated by the system of government. It is clear that in these circumstances he or she bears a responsibility for the efficient use of resources and to this end must be ready and able to use such methods of management as will offer the best prospect of optimal performance. But the function of officials cannot be exhaustively defined in terms of achieving results efficiently. There is also a duty to observe the varied limits imposed on action by public bodies and to satisfy the political imperatives of public service—loyalty to those who are politically responsible, responsiveness to parliamentary and public opinion, sensitivity to the complexity of the public interest, honesty in the formulation of advice, and so on. It is out of these commitments that a professional ethic was fashioned in the public services. Even if this has weakened in recent years we cannot afford to dispense with it. This is because a system of representative government does require officials to act as the custodians of the procedural values it embodies. The contemporary concern with efficient management, with performance, and with securing results, should not be allowed to obscure this fact. The pursuit of better management in government, important though it is, has to recognize the political limits to which it is subject. Otherwise the administrators and managers, along with the politicians they serve, may be bound for shipwreck.

NOTES

1 *Control of Public Expenditure,* Cmnd. 1432, London, HMSO (1961).

2 *Recruitment to the Civil Service* (6th Report from the Estimates Committee), HC 308 (1964–5).

3 'Efficient' in this context refers to an optimal ratio of resource inputs to outputs or results achieved, i.e. maximum results for minimum inputs. For further comments on efficiency and effectiveness, see the author's memorandum 'Efficiency and Effectiveness in the Civil Service' in *The Civil Service* (11th Report of the General sub-committee of the House of Commons Expenditure Committee), Vol. III, Appendix 26, HC 535 (1977), pp. 960–7.

4 It is also expressive of an older tradition that degrees in business administration are still awarded and that much of 'administrative science', especially as reflected in the *Administrative Science Quarterly* (an American journal of long standing) refers to problems encountered just as much in the business environment as in government.

5 The reception of the Weberian theory of bureaucracy was, of course, always highly qualified in Britain, chiefly because Britain lacked the systematic structure of public law which formed the basis for Weber's analysis. Thus administration has never been regarded as equivalent first and foremost to the application of legally binding codes and rules, but has always had strong overtones of the discretionary use of powers in the activity of ministering to needs.

6 *Report of the Committee on the Management of Local Government* (5 vols.), London, HMSO (1967).

7 *Report of the Royal Commission on Local Government in England,* Cmnd. 4040, London, HMSO (1969).

8 New management methods in local government are examined in: T. Eddison, *Local Government: management and corporate planning,* Aylesbury, Leonard Hill Books (1973); J.D. Stewart, *Management in Local Government: a viewpoint,* London, Charles Knight (1971); R. Greenwood, K. Walsh, C.R. Hinings and S. Ranson, *Patterns of Management in Local Government,* Oxford, Martin Robertson (1980).

9 *The Reorganisation of Central Government* (White Paper), Cmnd. 4506, London, HMSO (1970).

10 Many of the prevailing doubts about the effectiveness of the post-Fulton changes in the Civil Service were expressed, albeit in somewhat jejeune terms, in *The Civil Service* (11th Report of the General sub-committee of the House of Commons Expenditure Committee), HC 535 (1977). In particular this report noted the relatively weak position of the Civil Service Department *vis-à-vis* other Departments in respect of management and organization questions, the limited progress made towards the introduction of accountable management units, and the refusal to take specialization seriously, whether in career planning or in training arrangements. The Committee did not, however, consider that such evidence called for a serious reappraisal of what might be called the Fulton approach.

11 The Civil Service Department was wound up in 1981 in its 1968 form, and re-established as the Office of Personnel and Management attached to the Cabinet Office. Simultaneously the control of pay and levels of staffing went back to the Treasury.

12 Note by Sir Derek Rayner, submitted to the Treasury and Civil Service Committee of the House of Commons (Minutes of Evidence), HC 333-iv, February (1980).

13 Ibid., Q. 275, opening statement by Sir Derek Rayner.

14 Ibid., Q. 275.

15 L. Gulick, 'Notes on the Theory of Organization with special reference to Government in the United States', *Papers on the Science of Public Administration* (eds. L. Gulick and L.F. Urwick), New York, Institute of Public Administration (1937)

16 Op.cit. in note 12, p. 56.

17 R. Thomas, *The British Philosophy of Administration,* London & New York, Longman (1978), surveys British theorizing about the principles of administration in the years between the two world wars.

18 For a perceptive treatment of management in the public sector see C.D.E. Keeling, *Management in Government,* London, George Allen & Unwin (1972); also P.J.O. Self, *Administrative Theories and Politics,* London, George Allen & Unwin (1972).

19 For a penetrating analysis of administration as an activity concerned with the adjustment of relationship and the balancing of values see Sir G. Vickers, *The Art of Judgement,* London, Chapman & Hall (1965). See also Vickers, *Towards a Sociology of Management,* London, Chapman & Hall (1967), especially Ch. 5.

20 Evidence of the relatively limited use of the written word in private business management is provided by H. Mintzberg, *The Nature of Managerial Work,* New York & London, Harper & Row (1973). In contrast great reliance is placed on the spoken word.

21 For an impressive analysis of the obstacles in the way of achieving intended administrative effects, see C. Hood, *The Limits of Administration,* London & New York, Wiley (1976).

22 It should be noted that in addition the accountability of the manager in government is subject to constitutional qualifications: politically and legally it is, in general, elected persons (ministers or local councillors) who are ultimately accountable in the sense of being exposed to a vote of censure or rejection by the electorate.

23 During the later 1970s there is little doubt that the central government has made a substantial effort to withdraw from involvement in settling policy questions within the sphere of nationalized industries, though it cannot escape a measure of responsibility as a result of its obligation to fix borrowing levels and approve investment programmes. For comments on the difficulties of defining government responsibilities in the nationalized sector see N. Johnson, 'The Public Corporation: An Ambiguous Species' in *Policy and Politics* (essays in honour of Norman Chester, edited by David Butler and A.H. Halsey, London and Basingstoke, Macmillan (1978).

8

The Meaning of Management and the Management of Meaning: a view from social anthropology

DAN GOWLER AND KAREN LEGGE

... I quite fail to understand why it is a necessary imperative for any and every body of knowledge to disguise itself as a 'science', no matter what the cost or what damage is done to the vital spirit of that body of knowledge in itself (Ross 1982, p. 19).

The point is that rhetoric, like ritual, may be more than a symbolic reaffirmation of social relations. Through rhetoric people have licence, so to speak, to explain and evaluate the causes and consequences of social relations, sometimes to the point of distortion. Rhetoric is thereby dynamically involved in their organisation and perpetuation (Parkin 1975, p. 119).

Introduction

For the purposes of this chapter, 'management' is treated as that segment of the semantic order (subculture) of contemporary English-speaking societies which is characterized by the language of efficiency and control. In the following discussion, this relatively broad perspective is more narrowly focused on a proposition, derived from social anthropology, that *management may be viewed essentially as an oral tradition.* As illustrated in Figure 8.1, the significance of this perspective is that it highlights how this oral tradition simultaneously accomplishes the meaning of management and the management of meaning by use of plain speaking and rhetoric.

One justification for taking this position is that recent empirical research on managerial roles and work (Mintzberg 1973, Stewart 1976, Davis and Luthans 1980) has repeatedly shown that managerial activity has a high oral communication content. For example, Stewart (1976, p. 92) reports that 'management is a verbal world where people are usually instructed, assisted, and persuaded by personal contact rather than on paper'.

Similarly, Davis and Luthans (1980, p. 65) comment that:

Observational studies by researchers indicate that most managers operate at a very high activity level and spend most of their time in oral communication. These studies found that managers spend between two-thirds and three-fourths of their time communicating with others. Therefore, *it is clear that the modern manager's world is a verbal—specifically, oral—one.* Much time is spent in persuading, justifying, and legitimizing past, present, and future courses of action [emphasis added].

In this chapter, we go beyond this relatively uncontroversial assertion to contend that such verbal activity frequently involves the use of rhetoric, that is, *the use of a 'form of word-delivery'* (Parkin 1975, p. 114) *which is lavish in symbolism and, as such, involves several layers or textures of meaning* (Gowler and Legge 1981).

This view of management is explored in four sections, each of which deals with a theme in *the rhetoric of bureaucratic control,* i.e. highly expressive language that constructs and legitimizes managerial prerogatives in terms of a rational, goal-directed image of organizational effectiveness. The first section describes our general model, with particular reference to the distinction between plain speaking and rhetoric. The second, third, and fourth sections discuss the interrelated themes of hierarchy, accountability, and achievement respectively. Each of these themes has been selected to illustrate how *the rhetoric of bureaucratic control conflates management as a moral order with management as a technical-scientific order, whilst submerging the former.* They also demonstrate how, *through the management of meaning, the rhetoric of bureaucratic control contributes to management as a political activity* concerned with the creation, maintenance, and manipulation of power and exchange relations in formal work organizations. As Cohen and Comaroff (1976, p. 102) comment:

... a crucial variable in the construction of reality lies in the *management* of meaning: actors compete to contrive and propagate interpretations of social behavior and relationships ... The management of meaning is an expression of power, and the meanings so managed a crucial aspect of political relations.

Similarly, Golding (1980a, p. 43) reports that the management of meaning, with explicit and implicit appeals to 'the right to manage', becomes particularly evident in situations where those concerned perceive their managerial authority to be continually eroded and undermined. In exploring these themes, we are presenting a view which constructs management as a subculture, i.e. a social collectivity whose members share a set of implicit and explicit meanings acquired through innumerable communicative exchanges. Furthermore, the possession of these shared meanings

. . . can only be demonstrated or utilised in communication, or in acts related to communication. Further, it is only by usage that the set of meanings, and the system of symbols to which they are attached within the subculture, can change, develop and extend (Turner 1981, p. 61)

Thus, we present 'management' not only as an oral tradition in its literal sense, i.e. managers spend most of their time talking, but also in its anthropological sense, i.e. as a means by which culture is generated, maintained, and transmitted from one generation to another. This emphasis on language also stems from a commitment to the idea that '. . . semantic powers make human beings members of a self-defining species' (Crick 1976, p. 3). In other words, human beings are fundamentally creatures who use language to make and communicate meanings and who, as such, are *rhetoricians*, 'partly creations of their own talk and other social practices' (Harré 1980, p. 205).

We develop this 'semantic' approach to illustrate how, in the managerial subculture, meaning may be created through rituals, myths, magic, totemism, and taboo. Social anthropologists use these concepts to make sense of a wide range of cultural phenomena but, as yet, they are relatively little used in the serious description and interpretation of managerial constructions of reality. For it appears that, even when such ideas are put to 'serious' use, they often have negative connotations. Douglas (1970, pp. 1, 2), for example, points out that ritual has become 'a bad word signifying empty conformity' and a 'despised form of communication'. Similarly, Pym (1975a, p. 677) complains that 'industrial man gives precious little credibility to ritual. For him it belongs to Church, Army, and the Sepik River tribes, lesser societies than his own'—no doubt an observation which would also apply to contemporary lay views about myth, magic, totemism, taboo, and so on.

We turn now to a discussion of our general model.

1. PLAIN SPEAKING AND RHETORIC

Insofar as managers express views about their speech acts, they tend to emphasize the unambiguous articulation of aims, means, outcomes, and achievements. Indeed, that such plain speaking is necessary for the clear communication of managerial purposes is often asserted in the correspondence columns of professional and trade journals. For example:

For heaven's sake let us all stop trying to impress by using long words and jargon and start speaking and writing in plain English. Only then shall we really start to communicate with each other (Grant 1981, p. 52).

This letter is interesting not only because of its unequivocal call for clarity, but also because it makes a passing reference to literacy, i.e. 'speaking *and* writing'. It is this distinction that a social anthropologist, Leach (1964b), uses in making a comparison between the construction of meaning in different societies. He observes:

Because we are literate, we tend to credit words with exact meanings—dictionary meanings. Our whole education is designed to make language a precise scientific instrument. *The ordinary speech of an educated man is expected to conform to the canons of prose rather than of poetry; ambiguity of statement is deplored.* But in a primitive society the reverse may be the case; a faculty for making and understanding ambiguous statements may even be cultivated (Leach 1964b, p. 346, emphasis added).

We would argue, however, that whilst managers often *espouse* the virtues of, and a commitment to, plain speaking, they frequently *adopt* a type of speech that is highly ambiguous, i.e. rhetoric. Furthermore, they employ a form of rhetoric that associates two distinct orders of meaning in such a way as to preserve the *appearance* of plain speaking.

To convey this point, and following Parkin (1975), we represent plain speaking and rhetoric as two ends of a continuum (see Figure 8.1). Thus, with an increase in the symbolic content of a verbal or written statement one moves from plain speaking to rhetoric. Discussing this issue, Parkin states that rhetoric is:

. . . a type of ritual: it says *something about the speaker, the spoken-to, and the situation, which goes beyond what is contained in the surface message.* At the other end of the continuum we have plain speaking. Moving constantly around the half-way mark between these poles of flowery speech and stark statement we have the styles of delivery used by most of us, but with sometimes significant cultural, as well as situational differences as to the precise position on the continuum (Parkin 1975, p. 114, emphasis added).

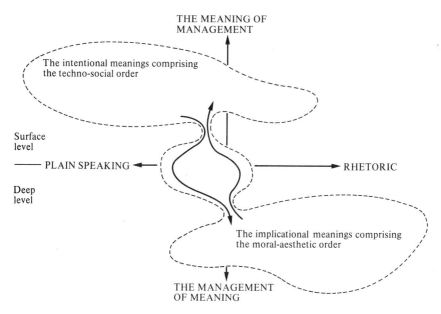

FIG. 9.1 The Rhetoric of Bureaucratic Control

Parkin (1975, p. 116) goes on to emphasize the point that, since rhetoric is lavish in symbolism it has the power to engage attention and arouse emotion. Furthermore, as symbols both reveal and conceal, they increase the degree and variety of ambiguity in any act of communication (Lewis 1977). Because, like the rest of us, managers constantly move 'around the half-way mark between these poles of flowery speech and stark statement', they are able, within the same statement, to use the ambiguity of rhetoric to arouse emotion and the clarity of plain speaking to direct behaviour. In other words, rapid shifts between plain speaking and rhetoric permit managers, *ceteris paribus,* to generate motivation, i.e. the arousal and direction of behaviour.

This essentially 'flip-flop' model of shifts between plain speaking and rhetoric, by varying the degree and variety of symbols and meanings, however, is too simple a view of the complexities of communication. This is because it emphasizes the *content* (degree and variety of symbols and meanings used) at the expense of the *structure* of statements (the relations between the symbols and meanings used). When the structure of a statement is examined, paradoxically, what might appear on the surface as plain speaking emerges from this deeper level of analysis as rhetoric (see Figure 8.2, Section 3).

The following example may help to illustrate this. During an animated discussion about the turnover of stock in the retail trade, one of the authors recorded the following comment made by a senior store manager: 'At Christmas, when the customer is not the consumer, you can shift a lot of stuff then.' Now at the surface level of meaning, this statement makes the relatively clear and incontrovertible assertion that, at a certain time of the year, it is easier to sell more goods and services. But, when analysing this statement at a deeper level of meaning, other more complex and controversial issues appear.

First, these comments are more than a simple piece of plain speaking; they comprise an attribution of cause and effect in the world of retail trading. Furthermore, this attribution is achieved by the use of a distinction drawn between 'customers' and 'consumers', which implies a theory of behaviour. In other words, when the customer is also the consumer, he or she will behave differently, possibly by being a more cautious shopper. Second, given this interpretation, the statement also functions as a covert *justification* for not being able to 'shift a lot of stuff' during those periods when the customer unfortunately insists on becoming the consumer. Third, the reference to 'Christmas' not only indicates a time of year, but evokes significant experiences and sentiments. Furthermore, the *evocative power* of the term Christmas is juxtaposed and then transformed by the 'rational', economistic distinction between customers and consumers.

Looked at this way, this apparently simple fragment of plain speaking has multiple functions and layers of meaning. In addition to providing an attribution, a theory of behaviour, and a justification, it relates the economic order to the moral order, by linking exchange relationships (buying and selling) to social obligations (the giving and receiving of gifts at Christmas) (Belk 1979). Finally, the structure and content of the statement combine the evocative power of a complex and ambiguous symbol with a rational means/ends explanation of events in the world of pragmatic affairs. This example is also instructive because it illustrates how *intentional meanings*, for example, the reasons given for variations in the turnover of stock, are enriched and embellished by *implicational meanings*, for example, the traditions and values of Christmas. Hanson (1975), from whom we have borrowed this distinction, comments:

> Human phenomena are intrinsically meaningful, and they are best understood and explained by making their meaning intelligible. However, one can ask different kinds of questions about human phenomena, and the answers involve different kinds of meanings. Individual questions are about the needs, motives, desires, aims, purposes of people; their answers are in terms of intentional meaning. Institutional questions are not about people at all. They inquire into ideas, beliefs, customs, forms of social organization as such, and their answers demonstrate implicational meaning (Hanson 1975, p. 10).

For Hanson, implicational meanings raise socio-cultural issues, since they involve a whole network of values, beliefs, norms, and so on. Thus, when our example is analysed in these terms, perhaps it is not surprising to find that this senior store manager's rhetoric surfaces intentional meanings, whilst submerging implicational meanings.

This example may now be used to explicate the model represented by Figure 8.1, where we identify meanings as comprising either the *techno-social* or *moral-aesthetic* order. The techno-social order is defined by Peacock (1975, p. 5) as those meanings which '...connect events, roles, groups, tools, and resources in *causal-functional relationships*' (emphasis added). Briefly, the meanings comprising this order invoke ideas about achievement and agency, for example 'getting things done' by 'rational decision-making' and 'effective managerial controls'. Indeed, the plain speaking of managers and management theorists is replete with references to, and admonitions about, goals, objectives, intentions, plans, outcomes, and effectiveness. What is more, many definitions of 'management' and 'managers' make direct use of these techno-social meanings. For instance, when discussing the work of a manager, Drucker (1974, p. 400) claims that:

A manager, in the first place, sets objectives. He determines what the objectives should be. He determines what the goals in each area of objectives should be. He decides what has to be done to reach these objectives. He makes the objectives effective by communicating them to the people whose performance is needed to attain them.

By contrast, the moral-aesthetic order is comprised of the implicational meanings referred to by Hanson (1975, p. 10). As Douglas (1973, p. 15) comments:

... the moral order and the knowledge which sustains it are created by social conventions. If their man-made origins were not hidden, they would be stripped of some of their authority. Therefore the conventions are not merely tacit, but extremely inaccessible to investigation.

As many social scientists argue, however, the tacit, ambiguous meanings comprising the moral-aesthetic order are emergent and constructed through social interaction, especially through such forms of talk as gossip and humour.

We contend that managers consistently invoke moral-aesthetic meanings, particularly in those situations where questions of control arise. For example, they surface when the issue of 'responsibility' emerges. While the meanings of this rather slippery term vary in the context concerned, for many managers it refers to a hierarchically organized set of priorities. And, when asked about *their jobs,* managers will often draw attention to their *responsibility for* profits, productivity, people, quality, service, and so on. But, when questioned about *their organizations,* they frequently refer to the roles and personalities of those *to whom* they claim to be *responsible.* In both instances, though, there emerges a hierarchy of duties, which also operates as a set of moral-aesthetic imperatives. In other words, the rhetoric of bureaucratic control relates the 'positive' field of rational purpose, i.e. the techno-social order, to the 'normative' field of ethical justification, i.e. the moral-aesthetic order.

While we elaborate upon the nature of this complex relationship in the following sections, at this point it is necessary to comment further upon the concept of an 'order of meaning' (see Figure 8.1). First, the abstract character of this concept is suggested by an indeterminable, amoeba-like shape. The dotted line defining this form represents the idea that orders of meaning do not have the concrete boundaries usually accredited to objects in the physical world. Second, the dotted line is also intended to make the point that these orders or provinces of meaning have been arbitrarily chosen from amongst the many others with which they are interwoven. As evidence of this point, the reverse arrows located in the 'waist' of the figure, represent the idea that orders of meaning may exercise an influence upon one another. As Douglas (1973, p. 13) puts it, 'There is a tendency for meaning to overflow and for distinct provinces to interpenetrate.' It is this fluidity of meaning that is central to the perspective being developed here. *In other words, it is from this ability to stimulate flows of meaning from one order to another that rhetoric derives its evocative and directive powers.* But it should be noted that the exercise of these powers requires that the rhetorician and his audience be 'on the same wavelength'. Consequently, like gossip, rhetoric is a parochial business by which, through language and social interaction, those involved participate in the creation and maintenance of shared meanings.

To recapitulate, then, the solid lines in Figure 8.1 represent an attempt to frame the indistinct and 'messy' processes described above in terms of a formal analysis. Thus, the solid horizontal line indicates how a move from plain-speaking to rhetoric increases the level of symbolic complexity. Furthermore, the solid reverse arrows in the waist of Figure 8.1 suggest that, with an increase in symbolic complexity, there is an increase in the flows of meaning from one order of meaning to another. Finally, the solid vertical line illustrates the idea that, *in the special case of the rhetoric of bureaucratic control,* the flows of meaning associate the surface intentional and the deep implicational meanings of management. It also is intended to suggest that these associations, conflations, and interpenetrations of meaning not only accomplish our everyday, taken-for-granted understanding of management, but simultaneously achieve the covert manipulation of these understandings in the flux of complex social interactions and contexts.

As with any formal analysis, generalizations tend to be too sharply drawn, and therefore any responsible commentary has to highlight where awkward exceptions undermine the certitude and elegance of formal models. In the following sections examples of the rhetoric of bureaucratic control clearly expose the gap between the ambiguity of everyday conversation and the relative clarity of formal analysis. And the extent to which we close this gap provides an indicator of the success of our own rhetoric.

The following sections discuss examples of these processes and consider three distinct though interrelated themes in the rhetoric of bureaucratic control, i.e. *management-as-hierarchy, management-as-accountability, and management-as-achievement.* But, before we embark upon this, it is necessary to introduce a methodological note. Briefly, we have taken our empirical data mainly from the conversation and correspondence of practising managers. As far as conversation is concerned, we have found that spontaneous discourse passes too quickly to be captured in full, simultaneous transcription. Consequently, the conversations reported here are comprised mainly of fragments just one or two sentences long. Nevertheless, they have all been collected by the authors, mainly on management courses, where those concerned had been labelled or had labelled themselves as 'managers', and were commenting, *inter alia,* on the many meanings of this role. Importantly, these comments were not collected for the purposes of research and publication, they were recorded because they seemed significant at the time.

The second source of data, i.e. letters to management, trade, and professional journals, has been selected because we believe this correspondence to be the *sine qua non* of written rhetoric. This is because these letters:

(a) tend to pose and then answer their own questions;
(b) are frequently couched in 'high-flown language';
(c) are directed at a given audience or community, with
(d) the express intention of influencing thoughts, feelings, and actions.

Furthermore, we believe these highly expressive letters come closer to oral communication than do more formal literary pieces, for example articles in learned journals, textbooks, and government reports. But it should be noted that, unlike the verbal comments we have casually collected over many years, the letters have been more recently sought out and selected for the purposes of this chapter, i.e. as examples of themes in the rhetoric of bureaucratic control.

2. THE MANAGEMENT-AS-HIERARCHY THEME

At the outset, it is useful to consider some recent comments made by academic observers of managerial and organizational life on the prevalence of hierarchy in organizational settings. For instance, when outlining their comparative approach to organizational control, Tannenbaum and Cooke (1979, p. 183) write:

Classical theories of organization are clear in asserting the importance of hierarchy for organizations. Even human relations theories that advocate 'participation' and that allude to 'power equalization' do not seriously challenge the essentially hierarchical character of control in organizations. ... *hierarchical control in one form or another is a universal feature of organization and it therefore provides the basis for comparative research* [emphasis added].

This echoes Chandler's (1977, p. 7) claim that '. . . the existence of a managerial hierarchy is a defining characteristic of the modern business enterprise'. Hunt (1981), however, goes beyond these empirical observations and, in fine rhetorical style, comments that:

The persistence of centralised hierarchies leads one to the question (of the) [*sic*] plausibility of designing participative or flatter structures. Are there, within organisations, the reinforcements of the centralisation of power that critics hope to change? Conversely, is hierarchy our 'natural' state and attempts to flatten it misguided? After all, this amazingly robust structural form has persisted for centuries. Would flatter structures be beneficial? Could we achieve them even if we wanted? (Hunt 1981, p. 21).

He goes on to answer some of these questions and states that:

, , , it is fashionable to argue that managers hog power to the detriment of the rest. I will argue that it is a two-way process: managers centralise power with the blatant connivance of their subordinates (ibid., p. 23).

In quite different vein, Golding (1979) raises issues of more direct relevance to the social anthropological perspective being developed here. For example, he writes:

The 'sovereignty of management' is generally regarded as in some way given (deriving inexorably from the 'essence' of hierarchy), and the fatalistic acceptance of this by 'actors', has led to the idea that the 'sovereignty of management' in an industrial hierarchical organisation is some kind of truism. The truism perspective is a teleological confusion originating from the failure to consider the elements of 'sovereignty' and 'hierarchy' which derive from the structuring of the actors' social worlds (Golding 1979, p. 169).

Finally, to give a word to the managers themselves, the following comment was rather sharply made when, during a management seminar, one of the authors raised the issue of what Herbst (1976) has termed 'alternatives to hierarchies': 'But management is hierarchy!' With this went quite warm support for the contention that any challenge to the idea of hierarchy is also a challenge to the 'sacred' right to manage commented upon above.

We consider, overall, that 'academic' commentators tend to treat hierarchy in a more explicit manner than managers. For example, until very recently, academic commentators have been inclined to highlight the origins, functions, and malleability of social and organizational hierarchies. On the other hand, like other laymen, managers tend to allude to hierarchy in a more oblique and implicit fashion, for example when referring to such issues as delegation, participation, leadership, motivation, responsibility, and performance. For instance, the following quotations have been taken from two letters appearing in the same correspondence column of a monthly, professional journal:

A The art of delegation as I see it is to know the strengths and weaknesses of subordinates and to delegate those jobs which the subordinates can perform. Not because they do them better but for the reason that, because you can complete the task anyway there is no need for you to do it. By thoroughly understanding all aspects of his department's work in this way, the manager should be free for more important tasks which his subordinates cannot yet do.
Under this system, continual delegation of work should allow the department to grow and expand its capabilities. Delegation can only come from the top and must be completely controlled from the top (Clark 1979, p. 51).

B It is nonsense to suggest that officials delegate to their staff because they feel the latter can do a better job or because they wish to get rid of unwanted tasks. Officials delegate certain tasks because in their opinion such tasks are better suited to a subordinate because such work does not require the higher ability and experience of themselves. To undertake such work themselves would be wasting their own time, the company's money and reducing their own efficiency. An experienced departmental head needs no authority to delegate; it is a matter of personnel [sic] judgement.
Departmental heads in general are fully aware of the ability of their subordinates and selection for delegation of work is an easy task. They normally treat their staff as human beings and at times praise their efforts, but under no circumstances do they treat them as equals in the running of a department (Fleet 1979, p. 51).

At first glance, these letters might appear to be pieces of plain speaking about the efficient allocation of work in formal organizations. However, when viewed in terms of the perspective being developed here it is possible to offer alternative interpretations.

First, as suggested above, comments about 'subordinates', 'heads of departments', 'officials', and so on imply the existence of a hierarchy of roles and controls. Second, in both letters it is explicitly stated that such structures are or should be hierarchies of abilities and expertise. Indeed, in letter A the correspondent concludes that, if this is not the case '. . . it is a sad reflection of [sic] business organisations'. Third, these letters explicitly refer to the delegation of tasks as opposed, for example, to the delegation of powers and responsibilities. Finally, they clearly attribute departmental and organizational efficiency to these bureaucratic arrangements.

When analysed in this way, the rhetoric of bureaucratic control becomes more apparent. For example, these letters fail to draw the distinction between what might be termed the normative and positive approaches to delegation. In other words, one is not sure whether delegation *does, or should* take the form these correspondents describe. In the light of this, we suggest that the generation of such ambiguity is a major characteristic of rhetoric, where the rhetorician conflates the intentional meanings associated with *actual* causes and effects in the world with the implicational meanings associated with *proper* causes and effects in the world. Thus, like ritual, rhetoric expresses what is as what should be.

This becomes more significant when one examines the empirical evidence on managerial behaviour. For, despite the claims and strictures of the correspondents quoted above, observations of managerial activities reveal a somewhat 'informal' state of affairs. When discussing questions about managerial authority, Pym (1975b, pp. 140–1) comments:

My own researches over the past decade among the executives of large concerns show the great majority of critical events, as privately reported by managers, are most significantly influenced by information *incidental* and *peripheral* to those more 'legitimate' sources like professional reports, computer print-outs, company and government records, balance sheets and the like. Furthermore, as other researchers have shown, the patterns of communication between people engaged on and around these events are *informal* and *lateral* in direction. They are seldom dealt with in formal situations through the hierarchy.

Consequently, it seems reasonable to suggest that the blurring of 'real' and 'preferred' states of affairs is partially accomplished by backgrounding informal and lateral interaction, whilst foregrounding formal and vertical interaction.

To summarize this section, some 'everyday' views on the forms and functions of delegation have been used to illustrate how an implied hierarchy of roles positively relates control to efficiency. Moreover, by conflating a hierarchy of power relationships with a hierarchy of expertise, this link between control and efficiency reinforces 'the right to manage', i.e. helps to legitimate managerial prerogatives. Finally, the hierarchy theme in the rhetoric of bureaucratic control is interwoven with those of accountability and achievement, and, as such, contributes to the creation and maintenance of the meaning of management in a highly uncertain world.

3. THE MANAGEMENT-AS-ACCOUNTABILITY THEME

In her review and interpretation of Evans-Pritchard's influential corpus of work, Douglas (1980, p. 71) observes that:

The foundation of meaning, according to my reconstruction upon his work, is *the system of accountability.* As people decide to hold others accountable and as they allow the same principles to extend universally, even to apply to themselves, they set up a particular kind of moral environment for each other [emphasis added].

In this section, we examine this 'foundation of meaning' and discuss how the rhetoric of bureaucratic control uses 'accountability' to present a rational, goal-oriented image of managerial action as 'a particular kind of moral environment'. Furthermore, we define 'accountability' as a form of moral and technical reckoning, where the careful husbandry of scarce resources is not only treated as a sign of managerial competence but also of moral superiority.

This approach to the management-as-accountability theme is influenced too by the observation that the rhetoric of bureaucratic control is permeated by the logic and language of accounting. This reflects the increasing significance that accountants and accounting practices have in contemporary market-oriented societies. For example, Burchell *et al.* (1980, p. 5) claim that:

Accounting has come to occupy an ever more significant position in the functioning of modern industrial societies. Emerging from the management practices of the estate, the trader and the embryonic corporation . . . it has developed into an influential component of modern organizational and social management . . . What is accounted for can shape organizational participants' view of what is important, with the categories of dominant economic discourse and organizational functioning that are implicit within the accounting framework *helping to create a particular conception of organizational reality* [emphasis added].

When looked at in terms of the model developed in Figure 8.1, two issues come into high relief. First, the computational practices that comprise accounting rest upon a system of symbolic classification, i.e. number of plausible binary distinctions, for example debits and credits, expenditure and revenue, profits and losses, assets and liabilities, which go beyond a mere description of objective conditions in the world. This is because when such terms are used in everyday conversation, apart from their doubtful specificity, they involve moral-aesthetic judgements about the proper order of things. Indeed, Colville (1981) goes so far as to suggest that this issue should provide a focus for research on 'behavioural accounting':

> . . . talking and acting is the very stuff of organizations and it is my contention that we would know more about the behavioural implications of accounting in organizations if research were directed to listening to such talk and observing such acting. In this way, *it may be possible to discern the organizational scripts which facilitate the talking and acting and to see the role accounting plays in such a process: whether or not accounting terminology has entered into and become part of the organizational language* . . . (Colville 1981, p. 131, emphasis added).

Second, it is central to our argument that not only has accounting terminology become part of organizational language, for example people are said to be 'written off' or labelled 'a liability', but when incorporated in the rhetoric of bureaucratic control it also appears to clarify results and resolve problems by reducing individuals, things, acts, and events to a common denominator, i.e. money. Then, by the use of a variety of polarities, for example costs and benefits (Chambers, 1980), it interprets the past, forecasts trends, determines ends, means, and the relationships between them. As suggested above, such modes of transformation, i.e. turning the intangible into the tangible and the normative into the positive, help managers to evoke a sense of 'blissful clarity' in their world (Barthes

1972, p. 143). Through such reification, simplification, abstraction, and rhetorical manipulation, managers (like the rest of us) construct a relatively concrete world. However, it has been argued that such achievements are not without their dangers. For example, Golding (1980b), following Barthes, asserts:

The process of abstraction and simplification enables 'a world' to be constructed and given meaning, but in a way which tends to result in a viewing of the construction as the only possible world. The whole transaction has a tendency to become self-fulfilling. The 'views of the world' produced by the abstraction and simplification process in fact achieve the continuing confirmation required to perpetuate their existence, by the transformation of 'the possible' into the 'absolute'. This 'defining as absolute' thereby works to prevent (although never *totally* achieves) access to alternative possible views. The particular is made general and becomes accepted to the extent that the access to the totality of the larger world, in the shape of possible alternative views, is blocked. Perspectives tend to become ossified (Golding 1980b, p. 763).

This discussion of the construction of a simplifying 'absolute' view of the world may be illuminated by considering rhetoric-as-myth as well as as-ritual (see Figure 8.2).

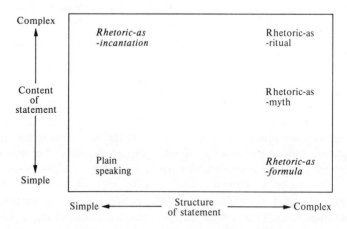

FIG. 8.2 Rhetoric-as-Ritual and Rhetoric-as-Myth

Myth and ritual are closely associated in laymen's eyes and, indeed, Leach (1964a, p. 13) has argued that essentially ritual is the

THE MEANING OF MANAGEMENT   213

action counterpart of the stories embodied in myth. But when both are seen as communicative and hence potentially rhetorical statements (Tambiah 1979), an interesting functional distinction emerges, which may be clarified by analysing the following example in terms of the model outlined in Figure 8.1.

During a discussion about creativity, a member of a senior management course firmly told one of the authors that: 'There are no good ideas until there's cash in the till.' Now, when analysed in terms of Figure 8.1, this statement is clearly an example of the rhetoric of bureaucratic control, since it (a) juxtaposes and associates moral-aesthetic meanings ('good ideas') with socio-technical meanings ('cash in the till'), and (b) by implying that the status of knowledge is solely determined by its use in the world, it foregrounds socio-economical interpretations whilst backgrounding moral-aesthetic ones. But this statement may also be treated as a myth because, following Golding, it defines the many forms and possibilities of 'good ideas' in terms of the one absolute explanatory criterion, i.e. 'cash in the till'. Additionally, this statement has other mythic properties because it also backgrounds potential dangers, impurities, and abominations (Gowler and Legge 1981), for example the possibility that there are no good ideas until money is *taken* from the till.

In order to accomplish these mythic transformations, the speaker uses what is perhaps the most concrete symbol of managerial accountability ('the till') that evokes notions about financial transactions, calculations, and the control and security of money. But, when compared with the symbol of 'Christmas' used in the example analysed earlier, 'the till' has nowhere near as much ambiguity and evocative power. We suggest that this difference may be generalized since, in British culture, 'Christmas' belongs to that class of names, words, phrases, or maxims which Graber (1976) labels *condensation symbols,* and which arouse and prepare individuals for mental and physical action. 'Thus a reference to "my country" triggers *a host of informational and affective connotations* about the national unit where a person was born' (Graber 1976, p. 289, emphasis added). But, apart from those who have a special interest in such matters, for example cashiers, the word 'till' is not likely to be a condensation symbol.

To relate these points to a distinction between ritual and myth, rhetoric-as-ritual is characterized by statements that are both complex in structure (the use of multiple juxtapositions of symbols) and content (the use of condensation symbols). By contrast, rhetoric-as-myth is equally complex in structure, but less complex in content (see Figure 8.2). Consequently, the verbal style of rhetoric-as-ritual is relatively florid, whilst rhetoric-as-myth appears less extravagant and, as such, has more the form and impact of plain speaking (see Figure 8.2). Given the distinctions outlined in Figure 8.2, we suggest that the *language of accountability*, with its frequent appeals to 'responsibility', 'integrity', 'reliability', and so on, is likely to produce rhetoric-as-ritual. The *language of accounting*, however, has the ability to order the world in terms of socio-technical categories and, as such, produces rhetoric-as-myth. In other words, the language of accountability surfaces and utilizes the evocative power of ambiguity, whilst the language of accounting helps to create certainty and order by submerging certain types of ambiguity (Barthes 1982, Westerlund and Sjöstrand 1979).

It should be noted, however, that in contemporary, market-oriented societies like Britain, the everyday language of accountability and the technical language of accounting are closely interwoven. Consequently, a number of accounting terms and phrases, for example 'profit', 'loss', and 'the bottom line' are, or become, condensation symbols. Furthermore, the increasingly moral-aesthetic element in the language of accounting is illuminated by those who have commented on the mytho-magico-religious functions of accountants in developed economies. For example, a social anthropologist, Cleverley (1971), writes:

A lengthy, Jesuitical, educational programme, years of conditioning as an articled clerk before he is formally qualified, ensure that *the accountant inhabits a world of which the moral framework is comfortingly rigid. He is the inheritor of the self-righteous certainty which has belonged to the Pharisee, the Inquisitor, the Witch-Hunter. He displays the hallmark of the member of an established priesthood* (Cleverley 1971, pp. 38, 39, emphasis added).

More recently, Gambling (1977) has also pointed to these mytho-magico-religious functions, and suggests that accountants practice a modern form of witchcraft that accommodates the awkward facts that threaten to undermine a culture's values and beliefs. He concludes that:

... a study of what might be called 'the anthropology of accounting' would enable us to understand the part accounting plays in our own society—and maybe even provide insights into less harmful ways of achieving the same results. As it stands, accounting is not a matter of the supernatural, but seems to have something of political activity about it, albeit with a small p!... One might suppose that accounting was a matter of precision of analysis and balancing the books to the last penny. So it is, but viewed from the situation of a more senior accountant, one sees that it is also a matter of assessing how far data can be pushed to accommodate 'political' compromise between collaborators in the enterprise—and still remain in some sense 'true and fair' (Gambling 1977, p. 150).

The rhetoric of bureaucratic control may then be seen to be a linguistic device by which pragmatic 'political compromises' are squared with moral-aesthetic concerns, for example what is 'true and fair'. Furthermore, this political perspective echoes our analysis of the theme of hierarchy commented upon above. This is because one rationale for the existence of power and exchange relationships in social and organizational life is that such structures are absolutely necessary for the proper preservation and allocation of scarce resources.

Thus, to summarize this section, the rhetoric of bureaucratic control uses the language of accountability and accounting to help construct a 'moral environment', where the hierarchical ordering of roles and relationships is equated with the responsible conduct of human affairs, and where 'the right to manage' is extended to become 'the right to manage power and exchange relationships'. However, as discussed in the following section, this fusing of the themes of hierarchy and accountability is reinforced by the theme of achievement.

4. THE MANAGEMENT-AS-ACHIEVEMENT THEME

One of the first things a newcomer to a work organization is likely to be told is that: 'In this place you will be judged by your results.' What is more, this prediction is likely to be accompanied by some sharp observations about how results might be related to rewards. Indeed, several managers have told us that this is what management is really about, i.e. 'Getting the right results through the use of the right incentives.' Hence, in this section, we take the question of the achievement of results first and then discuss issues about the preferred and supposed relationships between achievement, status, reward, effort, and so on. A characteristic view about management-as-achievement is stated in the following letter, where the correspondent asserts that:

> Managers are, or should be, employed by organizations to achieve results and should be evaluated on those results, rather than on how they are achieved.
> If those results are not being achieved then, yes, we need to know which specific behaviour patterns need to be changed (Binnie 1981, p. 52).

[handwritten margin note: Oh dear! The issue of how mgrs manage]

Similarly, Heller (1972), a well-known commentator on managers and management, writes:

> The objective and justification of management lie [*sic*] only in the achievement of results. It follows that any abstract theories of management, and any attempts to describe management in terms other than those of effectiveness, create myths—and that the good manager is a mythical beast. Where does his goodness lie if the results are invisible? So the good manager is the effective one—or is he? (Heller, 1972, p. 3)

Now, Heller not only continues in fine rhetorical style to answer his own questions, but also he rapidly comes to the conclusion that, despite popular opinion

> *There is no absolute criterion of managerial achievement.* A manager is good, and a company efficient, only because others consider the results of their work good: and *the so-called goodness endures only as long as this good opinion—which can be for an indefensible length of time* (ibid., p. 3, emphasis added).

We take up the issue of the idealization of achievement below, but if management is actually the maintenance of the good opinion of others, then the prudent manager would be well advised to improve his rhetorical skills. As Winkler and McCuen (1981, p. 5) observe:

> To Isocrates in 350 BC, rhetoric was 'the science of persuasion'; twenty years later, Aristotle defined rhetoric as 'the faculty of discerning in every case the available means of persuasion'. Richard Whatley, a nineteenth-century British logician saw rhetoric as 'the art of argumentative composition'. Common to all these definitions is the suggestion that rhetoric involves the strategies used by a speaker or writer in attempting to communicate with an audience.

It may not be too cynical to point out that managers are sometimes 'offered' the opportunity to attend 'social skills' training courses. Such courses are often justified on the grounds that, among other things, they will improve managers' powers of communication and persuasion which, it is then explicitly or implicitly claimed, will result in 'personal development' and/or 'the achievement of better results'. But insofar as such training (sometimes termed 'development') does improve a manager's powers of persuasion, taking Heller's view it might be argued that it may also improve the manager's ability to create the illusion of achievement, i.e. other peoples' 'good opinions'.

Talk about achievement, however, is frequently cloaked in the vocabulary of economic exchange and contracts of employment, for example 'effort', 'reward', the 'wage-work bargain', 'pay and productivity', 'incentives', which ensures a regular supply of semantic grist for the rhetorical mill. Indeed, not only does the rhetoric of bureaucratic control utilize ideas about rewards, motivation, performance, and so on, but this usage again illustrates the conflation of the two orders of meaning represented in Figure 8.1. The following example, which has been taken from the correspondence columns of a professional journal, helps to illustrate this point. Here the correspondent asserts that:

Getting a weekly pay-packet stuffed with cash is enjoyable. It represents the work that you've done during the past week, and is a reminder, either consciously or subconsciously, of the reason that you are there—you supply the effort and the firm supplies the wages.
Getting a monthly pay slip on the other hand, is one of the biggest anti-climaxes going. Maybe you are in a job where all job satisfaction completely overshadows the pay packet, but then maybe you're not (ask a few articled clerks). I assume this is why professional people are traditionally paid monthly—the salary being a by-product (supposedly) of the professional's work, and not something to be looked forward to during the week.
    As for encouraging the 'great unbanked' to open a bank account—well, what is so great about a bank account? How many people do you know that pay their monthly pay cheque into their account, only to see it engulfed by the overdraft and the so-called 'generous' credit card facilities? *This type of situation leaves the employee with precious little incentive for the next month's work.* So before a firm switches to cashless pay in order to save £30 p.a. per employee administration costs, I would suggest that it also considers the longer term loss due to lower productivity resulting from the disappearance of that weekly incentive (Paige 1981, p. 37).

The first thing about this communication is that it represents a neat example of written rhetoric. For instance, it poses and answers its own questions, using language that is relatively lavish in symbols (especially financial ones) and allusions. Additionally, it offers a clear warning about the consequences of a given change (in this case 'lower productivity'), which also illustrates the point that rhetoric is frequently used in the direct though covert defence of the status quo. More specifically, the surface message of this letter makes the plausible suggestion that 'cashless pay' removes the concrete representation of the relationship between effort and reward. Perhaps more controversially, this correspondent goes on to claim that, in some way or another, this change damages the incentive to work and, consequently, productivity.

There is certainly something in this assertion, since it has been argued that such changes are manifestations of the fact that we live in an increasingly abstract and alienating society. As Zijderveld (1982, p. 6) writes:

We hear much these days about quantitative limits of modernization. The doctrine of economic growth, for example, can no longer be preached unhampered. Yet, relatively little is heard about the qualitative limits of modernity, except in exercises of journalistic social philosophy ... *Such qualitative limits of modernity have also been reached when the generalization of values and meanings have reached a stage on which society can but be experienced as an abstract society* which apparently controls one's life and limits one's freedom, albeit in a vague and indeterminate manner. This causes an equally disquieting sense of alienation ... *the more abstract a society grows, the larger the chance will be that various groups of people begin to long for re-enchantment* [emphasis added].

This is not to say that an increase in the use of the weekly wage packet would result in a 're-enchantment' with the world. But for many people it is a condensation symbol that seems to evoke a wide range of thoughts and feelings, for instance about social status, equity, 'a fair day's pay', economic security and, possibly, individual and collective achievements. Indeed, in his analysis of wage forms, shop-floor culture and conflict, Willis (1979, p. 198) draws attention to the power of the 'fetishized, brown wage packet'. Put briefly, the whole issue of reward (and punishment) is awash with moral sentiment, much of which is directly concerned with ideas about *acceptable* goal-directed behaviours and their outcomes, i.e.

achievement. It is also relevant to note that in Paige's letter there is the assumption that, whatever the means, effort/performance *should be* related to reward. Thus, what on the surface may appear as a piece of rational plain speaking about incentives, at a deeper level is a vehicle for polyvalent meanings summoned up from the moral-aesthetic domain.

White (1981) has made the point that not only are methods of salary and wage payment systems of economic exchange, but they are also *instruments of authority*. For example, he comments that:

In addition to its rational function as a control system, the administrative system of pay is continually used both by management and by employee groups as a lever to develop or maintain power positions. Over and above the economic significance of the pay system *both for the organisation and for the employee there is a symbolic significance in the pay system.* The condition of the pay system reflects the ascendancy of management or of workers, or the relative importance of various groups of workers. For this reason much effort is invested in the struggle around the pay system, irrespective of the direct economic returns. And for this reason too, *the pay system is a particular focus for managerial and worker ideologies* (White 1981, p. 45, emphasis added).

Now, given this 'functionalist' frame of reference, it is reasonable to consider the relationship between status, effort, and reward (Gowler and Legge 1982). It is often argued that an individual's position in the organization's hierarchy is manifested and maintained by the amount and nature of his rewards, for example pay and fringe benefits. Even if one is not prepared to accept these interpretations, individuals certainly make frequent reference to them. For example, in a letter to a weekly professional publication, a correspondent flatly asserts that 'The pay and salary structures of qualified engineers is [sic] at the root of the professions' [sic] lack of status' (Smith 1982, p. 19). It is often claimed in the rhetoric of bureaucratic control that status should be related to reward, and that both status and reward should be related to achievement. But these relationships are notoriously difficult to establish in terms of definition, measurement and consensus. Indeed, we believe that many would protest that such positive relationships between achievement, status, effort, and reward represent an ideal state of affairs unlikely to be found in the rapidly changing world of practical affairs. But such views return us directly to an issue raised above, i.e. the idealization of achievement.

To adopt or, more precisely, adapt a view from social anthropology, it is possible to treat the principle of achievement in quite another way. First, it may be that the semantic links between achievement, motivation, reward, and so on are restricted to certain cultures. For example, Hofstede (1980, p. 35) contends that:

Differences in categories for thinking about the universe can be found in many fields and are larger for languages that are structurally further apart. Some examples are the way in which the color spectrum is divided (several languages have no separate words for 'blue' and 'green'); the way various aspects of 'time' are distinguished (with consequences for behavior); and the way relatives are classified. *Translators of American literature have noticed that French and many other modern languages have no adequate equivalent for the English 'achievement'*; Japanese has no equivalent for 'decision-making'. Modern linguists struggle with the issue of what, if any, are common basic categories of thought across all languages [emphasis added].

Second, admitting the dangers of ethno-centrism, but moving to a relatively high level of abstraction, it is often asserted that all societies have some form of social differentiation, which is conventionally discussed in structural terms, with reference to age, sex, class, caste, race, and so on. Moreover, there are those who convert forms of social differentiation into forms of social stratification, where such factors influence or even determine individuals' life-chances. As far as the issues debated in this section are concerned, the suggestion that, in capitalist, Western societies, it is the principle of achievement that actually defines and legitimates inequalities in social status and opportunity structures is of considerable interest. Thus Offe (1976), the main spokesman for this view, writes:

... the achievement principle does not operate merely as a norm which ensures equality, but just as much also as a legitimating principle to justify social inequality—it restricts social inequality in the very moment that it propagates a claim for it. The achievement principle sanctions those forms of inequality which have resulted from individual achievement and in this way it is *also* a norm of inequality (Offe 1976, p. 41).

Further, when discussing the social functions of this normative flexibility, he writes:

Our basic assumption is that *the achievement principle is a prescriptive model of status distribution,* providing for formal organizations in industrial societies the sole principle by which social status is legitimated, where status includes both differences in existing status and changes of status by means of occupational mobility (ibid., p. 55, emphasis added).

When this controversial piece of critical theory is looked at from a social anthropological point of view, two distinct, though interrelated, interpretations of the principle of achievement emerge. First, Offe seems to be saying that the principle of achievement not only provides a *charter myth* for the hierarchical structuring of formal work organizations, but also that it 'accounts' for any individual's position or mobility within or between them. Second, to take a broader perspective, there seems a remarkable correspondence between what Offe claims as the social functions of the achievement principle and what *some* social anthropologists claim as the social functions of *totemism*. Totemism, like ritual, myth, and magic, has been the subject of a considerable amount of speculation and controversy. Lienhardt (1964) neatly sums up what might be termed the classical view, pointing out that among traditional societies the recognition of common life is often expressed in 'religious' acts, for example sacrifice and totemism.

Among many peoples, the relationship existing between whole groups of people—notably those claiming common descent and belonging to the same clan is symbolized by a totem. Totems are of many kinds, but are often one or another species of animal, sometimes regarded as an ancestor of the clan. A common totem therefore stands for a community of interests of one sort or another... Among the Australian aborigines, let us say, a clan which has as its totem the kangaroo will pay special attention to kangaroos, and perform ceremonies from time to time to increase their numbers (Lienhardt 1964, p. 181).

However, particularly under the influence of Lévi-Strauss (1964), this view of totemism has been challenged. It is now also seen as a universal *cognitive* device that enables people, particularly non-literate people, to organize their experience of the world into a framework of values and meaning, where the differences in culture and nature are brought into relationship. Worsley (1967, p. 142) summarizes this position:

For Lévi-Strauss, indeed, the problem is not to understand totemism, but to abolish it. Totemism is not a separable 'ethnographic' specimen peculiar to the Australians and some other peoples, but a particular instance of a much more general phenomenon, one indeed that all societies have to face in one

222   PERSPECTIVES ON MANAGEMENT

way or another: *the problem of how men perceive, select, intellectually order, and socially structure the similarities and differences in both the natural and cultural realms respectively, and how connections are established between these two orders* [emphasis added].

Given this view of totemism, it is instructive to consider what Swingle (1976) has to say when writing on the dysfunctions of what he terms the 'mythology of management'. For example, he observes:

The most serious myth that we have to do away with, however, is the myth of the meritocracy. We believe, in our society, that rewarding people simply and non-discriminately on the basis of merit or achievement reflects true fairness and democracy. This myth leads people to believe that the most capable people will be rewarded for their efforts with positions of greater responsibility, prestige, and money. I am always stunned by the naïveté of people caught in such organizations who accept *the myth of meritocracy as a basic tenet of their modern religion*. In all meritocracies someone or some group (even if it is the entire organization) must evaluate achievement and decide on appropriate rewards (Swingle 1976, p. 14, emphasis added).

He goes on to argue that the myth of meritocracy is an outgrowth of the concept of social Darwinism, this being a cluster of ideas, for example the 'struggle for existence' and the 'survival of the fittest', which expresses the popular normative adaptation of the concept of evolution. Thus he comments:

Darwinism related to human social behavior reflects the belief that the strongest, most skillful, [sic] wisest, and most adaptable individuals are those who reach positions of power and influence. As in the jungles, those unfortunate individuals who have some defect of character, intelligence, or strength are found on the bottom of the social ladder (ibid., p. 16).

To summarize this, we suggest that the symbols and meanings of meritocracy, achievement, and so on categorize, justify, and at times celebrate, social, economic, political, and physical differences between men. Moreover, when these differences are expressed and validated in a 'survival of the fittest' form, they mirror the principles and processes that are claimed to 'select' and differentiate all forms of life. Put briefly, social Darwinism relates the order of culture to the order of nature and, as such, meets Lévi-Strauss's main criterion for totemism.

In support of this assertion that certain meanings, symbols, and forms of achievement provide the 'abstract' totemism of contemporary Western societies, it should be noted that ethnographic research frequently associates totems with a variety of patterned avoidances. For instance, Beattie (1974, p. 220) reports:

...a custom of ritual avoidance of the totem is widespread. In Africa members of totemic groups are generally prohibited from killing and eating their totem (if it is edible), though others may do so. A Nyoro believes that if he eats his totemic species he may become ill and perhaps die. He respects rather than fears it; certainly he does not worship it. He uses the same term, meaning 'respectful avoidance', for his relationship to his wife's mother as he does for his relationship to his totem.

In contemporary British society it is not only the symbols of group unity, for example flags, badges, uniforms, and ceremonies, that are the objects of subcultural ritual respect, but also the symbols of and reference to achievement are often accompanied by linguistic and other forms of patterned avoidance. For instance, this may take the form of an ostentatious display of the trophies and tokens of achievement accompanied by an exaggerated expression of diffidence about the acquisition of these prizes. In Britain, when successful people are asked to account for their achievements, they sometimes attribute them to 'luck' or 'good fortune'. This 'luck-labelling' (Fairhurst 1975, p. 181) is often explained in psychological terms. Thus it is said to be a means of coping with the anxieties generated by participation in highly competitive organizational hierarchies, whilst at the same time espousing commitment to co-operative values and behaviours. Obviously, the whole issue of the taboos that appear to surround the question of achievement is worthy of more attention.

It is also interesting to note that the question of the causes of success and failure is of special concern to those social psychologists who are developing attribution theory, i.e. the study of everyday causal explanation of events. As a recent commentator (Bartunek 1981) observes:

Managers are more concerned with examining reasons for behavior than other people. In fact, the need to explain behavior is likely to be particularly strong for managers, since part of their job involves evaluating their employees' performance (Bartunek 1981, p. 66).

and also that

Attribution theorists suggest that we tend to assume that people's behavior is a result of their personality characteristics (such as personality traits, skill or effort) or of external situational characteristics (such as the presence of external rewards or punishments, task difficulty, or luck) (ibid.).

From a social anthropological point of view, however, the attribution of luck may be a taboo that draws attention to the ends of achievement while, at the same time, backgrounding and blurring the means of achievement. In other words, such taboos protect the 'sacred' principles of achievement by deflecting questions about agency, merit, and so on in those circumstances where the 'facts' are especially difficult to determine. This does mean, of course, that 'luck-labelling' may only be used sparingly, since too often a recourse to this form of explanation may raise serious questions, by even the most gullible of people about the 'facts' of achievement.

To summarize this section, we have drawn attention to the idealization of achievement and have argued that the ensuing rhetoric may be analysed in terms of totemism and taboo. Certainly, management is not only said to be about 'getting things done' but also about 'getting things done well', which inevitably introduces the whole complex of meanings, for example 'success', 'competition', and 'performance', that characterize the semantic order of what Offe (1976, p. 40) terms the 'achieving society'.

This approach to the theme of achievement suggests how it is bound up with the theme of hierarchy. For example, people frequently justify their position or status within the managerial hierarchy on the grounds of their achievements. What is more, the rhetoric of bureaucratic control is often used in support of the idea that a hierarchy of roles and controls is absolutely necessary for the achievement of organizational goals.

Similarly, the theme of achievement is frequently conflated with the theme of accountability. For example, during appraisals, assessments, interviews, and so on, managers are required to account for their achievements. Such occasions are likely to be conducted in the language of accounting, and with liberal use of vocabularies of economic exchange and industrial relations, for example with reference to 'effort', 'standards', 'rewards', 'performance', and 'output'. Given this, it is not surprising that, in the managerial subculture, ideas, values, and beliefs about achievement have beome reified into a totem. And, like all totems, it becomes treated with exaggerated respect, even to the extent that a critical discussion of the issue may become difficult.

We also would draw attention to the possibility that all this talk about achievement is yet another facet of the 'right to manage' issue. Put bluntly, in the so-called achieving societies the managerial prerogative is likely to be legitimized by the assertion that the right to control power and exchange relationships should be in the hands of those who have demonstrated 'a good track record of achievement'.

Conclusion

Before embarking upon our conclusions, it is necessary that we enter several disclaimers and caveats. First, this chapter has been an exercise in critical, interpretive anthropology and, as such, is not centrally concerned with 'truth statements' or the vexed question of 'verification'. Although our personal prejudices about management are in evidence, we do not suggest that hierarchy does not reflect excellence or expertise, or that effort is not related to reward. Such questions are dealt with elsewhere in the literature concerned with 'objective realities' and so on, whereas this piece has been concerned with how the meaning of management is accomplished and manipulated through that complex symbolic system we term language.

Second, we have attempted to give shape to this enterprise by focusing upon the rhetoric of bureaucratic control in a context where the term rhetoric is shorn of its negative connotations. However, we have adopted this approach in order to emphasize the view that, amongst other things, the rhetoric of bureaucratic control is used to justify the access to and allocation of scarce resources, i.e. *the* management prerogative.

Third, Figures 8.1 and 8.2 are just an attempt to reduce the complexity of our argument. Obviously, to represent meanings in terms of dimensions, even if they may be curvilinear (see the plain-speaking and rhetoric-as-myth 'dimension'), is like trying to catch sunbeams in a bucket. Essentially, these diagrams are used to help structure our argument, and Figure 8.1 is intended to illustrate the tendency for the rhetoric of bureaucratic control to background or submerge moral-aesthetic meanings. There are, of course, occasions, for example during periods of conflict and crisis, when moral-aesthetic meanings are surfaced, but we suggest that they then tend to take on a techno-social form, appearing as prescriptions, where behaviour is causally related to outcomes, frequently punishments and rewards.

Fourth, as far as our empirical evidence is concerned, we have virtually abandoned method (Phillips 1973) in the sense that the verbal comments, letters, and other sources quoted here have not been selected by any systematic procedure. Thus, as far as we are concerned, there is no way in which any one source can be regarded as more valid than another. Obviously, we must admit bias but, as Silverman and Jones (1976, pp. 23–4) observe:

It begins to look as if there is no 'neutral' ground from which to observe phenomena 'as they really are', or to judge the 'bias' of particular accounts. For each 'observation' constitutes the character of the phenomenon which it claims to speak 'about'. This is what we understand by *reflexivity*. Rather than implying that accounts are 'biased' in particular ways by the social location of the speaker, it suggests that 'bias' (or a common system of accounting) is the only way in which reality may be apprehended. *Without 'bias' there are no phenomena to be discussed* [emphasis added].

These are controversial matters, but if we are to develop our own understanding of management as symbolic action (Pfeffer 1981), and at the same time avoid the scientism complained of by Ross (1982) in the quotation at the beginning of this chapter, it appears that we might fruitfully adopt such interpretive or reflexive approaches.

Fifth, and consistent with the theoretical and methodological opinions stated above, the choice of themes in the rhetoric of bureaucratic control, i.e. hierarchy, accountability, and achievement, is arbitrary. All we can say is that this categorization helps us 'make sense' of managerial language. Nevertheless, given more space, we might have introduced other themes, such as management-as-membership, and extended the material used to illustrate them. For example, the management-as-hierarchy theme would have received further illumination by reference to the vast amount of verbal and written material on the question of 'participation'. Furthermore, a closer look at the logic and language of accounting would have been useful. As Batstone (1977, p. 33) comments:

Accounting systems do not merely foster particular priorities or discriminate between issues, their very language often serves to obscure certain realities of action. In particular, once a variety of terms are substituted for that of 'human being' the notion of 'labour' as a cost becomes easier; it then follows that 'working levels' can be as simply reduced as stock levels. *Such camouflaging rhetoric is easy to find in managerial discussions and reports* [emphasis added].

Each of the themes considered here also involves a 'model of man', and might be explored in order to reveal how the rhetoric of bureaucratic control 'camouflages' different approaches to the problem of human agency. Certainly, the problem of holding people 'personally responsible' for their actions while simultaneously requiring them to conform to what Batstone (1977, p. 6) terms the 'institutional embodiment of purpose', puts rhetorical skills at a very high premium indeed. Hence, it does not seem unreasonable to suggest that the whole question of verbal behaviour might occupy a more significant place on management studies courses than it does at the moment. For example, this approach might treat managerial decision-making—and faking—as a matter for socio-linguistic analysis.

Sixth, given our perspective, we have cast much of our argument in the logic and language of social anthropology, with frequent references to such concepts as myth, ritual, magic, totemism, and taboo. Of course, great controversies have raged, and still do rage, over these terms but, despite the arguments, social anthropology has much to offer, and particularly to those management researchers and commentators who appear unaware of the fact that there is a well-established discipline that regards such ideas as central to its concerns. It is also relevant to note that social anthropologists have been especially interested in symbols and symbolism (Firth 1973), an interest which now appears of increasing concern to management researchers and commentators (Peters, 1978 and 1980, Feldman and March 1981, Moberg 1981, Pfeffer 1981, Broms and Gahmberg 1982, Deal and Kennedy 1982).

To summarize these disclaimers, caveats, and clarifications, they not only serve as theoretical and methodological apologia, but also as encouragement for an interest in what Levy (1981, p. 49) terms 'expressive verbal materials'. We have no doubt that when coupled with interpretive and reflexive modes of analysis such data would be of use to those interested, for example, in marketing, organizational development, and the selection, socialization, and appraisal of employees. This is because in such activities language, and often rhetorical language, is used to explain the past, justify the present, and shape the future.

In addition to these pragmatic intentions, we have a more radical purpose, i.e. to stimulate an interest in the 'deceits' of language, and in the analysis of the relationships between these deceits and social control. For example, in their discussion of interviews, Fowler *et al.* (1979, p. 2) point out that on such occasions:

... there are marked differences between the speech of interviewers and interviewees. These differences express the socially ascribed status of the interviewer, and allow him or her to manipulate the behaviour of the interviewee. There are both practical and ritual (ultimately practical also) functions in these interactions. In practical terms, the interview is a mechanism of *control* of one individual by another; the 'ritual' function is the reaffirmation of the interviewer's right to control the interviewee, and this ritual is part of the legitimation of the roles of 'more powerful' and 'less powerful' which society has ascribed to the participants. *Language with its strong encoding of social meanings is then both a mediator of interpersonal relationships and a force in the perpetuation of the social relationships which underpin them* [emphasis added].

This returns the discussion to the comments of Parkin (1975) cited at the very beginning of this chapter.

Turning to our general conclusions, what immediate propositions emerge from this analysis of management as an oral tradition? First, through embodying and expressing such ideas, management *means* hierarchy, accountability, and achievement. Second, with regard to the management *of* meaning, we contend that:

(a) Management eulogizes 'plain speaking'. But, on examination, examples of apparently 'plain speaking' are revealed as rhetorics disguising and legitimizing values about order and control in industrialized society;
(b) Rhetoric about hierarchy, by surfacing a techno-social justification for delegation and downward-looking relationships, submerges the reality of management dependency on superordinates (Laurent 1978);
(c) Rhetoric of accounting, in an industrialized society, through its myth-making functions, serves to simplify and clarify the ambiguities inherent in an uncertain world;

(d) Rhetoric, by presenting achievement in totemic forms, safeguards and perpetuates its idealization.

Generally speaking, we consider the fact that managers spend a
great deal of time talking is more than a matter for passing
comment, and not necessarily something to be deplored. This
endless talk, especially the rhetoric, may be the way in which social
control is maintained while, in situations of great uncertainty and
complexity, managerial prerogatives are simultaneously accomplished and legitimated. This is not an inconsiderable achievement.
Indeed, this may be what 'achievement' is really all about.
Certainly, some commentators, for example Heller (1972) and Offe
(1976) would appear to lend support to this view. However, in the
course of this analysis, the management-as-achievement theme
grew in significance for us, as the relative length of this section in
the chapter attests.

So, at a higher level of abstraction, our generalizations about the
three themes selected here are as follows. The management-as-
hierarchy theme expresses meanings about social order, whilst the
management-as-accountability theme expresses meanings about the
moral order. And it is the management-as-achievement theme that
cements the social and moral orders into a rational, 'natural' order,
where any other state of affairs would be seen to result in anarchy
and despair

The preferred image of the natural order is produced by the
rhetoric of bureaucratic control, which presents the proper access to
and allocation of scarce resources as a 'neutral' technical business.
But in order to accomplish this, it simultaneously incorporates,
though backgrounds, ambiguous and controversial moral-aesthetic
meanings. Turner (1971) has gone so far as to suggest that the
manager has to acquire the political ability to so manipulate his
verbal and written outputs. Thus he comments:

The overt meaning content of a message cannot normally be ignored, and
the most skilful practitioners of this sort of manoeuvring are those who are
able to link both the hidden and apparent meanings. A successful manager
can be expected to present cases that are both accurate *and* calculated to
advance his own cause (Turner 1971, p. 110).

Finally, in Figure 8.2, we have indicated that the analysis of
rhetoric might be extended to include 'incantation' and 'formula'

(see the terms in italics). Our analysis, though, has concentrated upon Parkin's (1975) crucial distinction between plain speaking and rhetoric-as-ritual. As such, we have emphasized the relationships between language and social control, i.e. how language might be used to exercise power over people. However, the rhetoric-as-incantation and rhetoric-as-formula distinction offers yet another axis of linguistic analysis. For instance, this axis would apply to the body of management research, opinion, and practice that on the surface appears to be concerned with *power over things*. This includes the world of 'management science', which its practitioners might reasonably claim lies squarely in the domain of techno-social meanings, and happily free of the pernicious use of moral-aesthetic meanings. But, as social anthropologists, we would be surprised if this was the case, since the 'technical order' of any society requires some form of symbolic representation. Furthermore, such representations are unlikely to be cast within an inviolate system of unequivocal meanings. Even if this was the case (and some might point to mathematics here), technical designs and choices always require presentation and justification, at which point the moral-aesthetic domain would be likely to make its shadowy appearance. The rhetoric-as-incantation and formula axis must await further discussion. In the meantime, we leave the stage to a member of a 'young managers' programme who, when describing his job in production to other course members, confidently observed:

You often have to make decisions on sparse information. Then you stick to it ... you don't change it ... afterwards you just have to justify it.

REFERENCES

Barthes, R. (1972), *Mythologies,* London, Jonathan Cape. (First published as *Mythologies,* Paris, Editions du Seuil (1957).)
Bartunek, J.M. (1981), '"Why Did You Do That?" Attribution Theory in Organizations', *Business Horizons,* 24/5.
Batstone, E. (1977), 'Industrial Democracy and the Nature of Management' (paper given in September at the Second International Conference on Participation, Workers' Control and Self-Management held in Paris).
Beattie, J. (1974), *Other Cultures,* London, Cohen and West.
Belk, R.W. (1979), 'Gift-Giving Behavior' in *Research in Marketing: A Review Annual* Vol. 2., (ed. J.N. Sheth), Greenwich, Conn., J.A.I. Press Inc.

Binnie, J.H. (1981), letter to Personnel Management, 13/4 (April).
Broms, H. and Gahmberg, H. (1982), Mythology in Management Culture, Helsinki, Helsinki School of Economics.
Burchell, S., Clubb, C., Hopwood, A., Hughes, J., and Nahapiet, J. (1980), 'The Roles of Accounting in Organizations and Society', Accounting, Organizations and Society, 5/1.
Chambers, R.J. (1980), 'The Myths and the Science of Accounting', Accounting, Organizations and Society, 5/1.
Chandler, A.D. (1977), The Visible Hand: The Managerial Revolution in American Business, Cambridge, Mass., Harvard University Press.
Clark, C.R. (1979), letter to Management Accounting (July/August).
Cleverley, G. (1971), Managers and Magic, London, Longman.
Cohen, A.P. and Comaroff, J.L. (1976), 'The Management of Meaning: On the Phenomenology of Political Transactions' in Transactions and Meaning: Directions in the Anthropology of Exchange and Symbolic Behavior (ed. B. Kapferer), Philadelphia, Institute for the Study of Human Issues.
Colville, I. (1981), 'Reconstructing "Behavioural Accounting"', Accounting, Organizations and Society, 6/2.
Crick, M. (1976), Explorations in Language and Meaning, London, Malaby Press.
Davis, T.R.V. and Luthans, F. (1980), 'Managers in Action: A New Look at Their Behavior and Operating Modes', Organizational Dynamics (Summer).
Deal, T.E. and Kennedy, A.A. (1982), Corporate Cultures: The Rites and Rituals of Corporate Life, Reading, Mass., Addison-Wesley Publishing Company.
Douglas, M. (1970), Natural Symbols. Explorations in Cosmology, London, Barrie and Rockliff: The Cresset Press.
Douglas, M. (1973), 'Tacit Conventions' in Rules and Meanings (ed. M. Douglas), Harmondsworth, Penguin.
Douglas, M. (1980), Evans-Pritchard, Glasgow, Fontana.
Drucker, P.F. (1974), Management: Tasks, Responsibilities, Practices, London, Heinemann.
Fairhurst, E. (1975), 'Expectations, Chance and Identity-Stress' in Managerial Stress (eds. D. Gowler and K. Legge), Epping, Gower Press.
Feldman, M.S. and March, J.G. (1981), 'Information in Organizations as Signal and Symbol', Administrative Science Quartery, 26/2.
Firth, R. (1973), Symbols Public and Private, London, George Allen & Unwin.
Fleet, A.H. (1979), letter to Management Accounting (July/August).
Fowler, R., Hodge, B., Kress, G. and Trew, T. (1979), Language and Control, London, Routledge & Kegan Paul.
Gambling, T. (1977), 'Magic, Accounting and Morale', Accounting, Organizations and Society, 2/2.
Golding, D. (1979), 'Symbolism, Sovereignty and Domination in an Industrial Hierarchical Organisation', The Sociological Review, 27/1 (February).

Golding, D. (1980a), 'Authority, Legitimacy and the "Right to Manage" at Wenslow Manufacturing Co.', *Personnel Review*, 9/1 (Winter).

Golding, D. (1980b), 'Establishing Blissful Clarity in Organizational Life: Managers', *The Sociological Review*, 28/4.

Gowler, D. and Legge, K. (1981), 'Negation, Synthesis and Abomination in Rhetoric', in *The Psychology of Ordinary Explanations of Social Behaviour* (ed. C. Antaki), London, Academic Press.

Gowler, D. and Legge, K. (1982), 'Status, Effort and Reward' in *Handbook of Salary and Wage Systems* (ed. A.M. Bowey, 2nd edn.), Aldershot, Gower Press.

Graber, D.A. (1976), *Verbal Behavior and Politics*, Urbana, University of Illinois Press.

Grant, D.M. (1981), letter to *Personnel Management*, 13/4 (April).

Hanson, F.A. (1975), *Meaning In Culture*, London, Routledge & Kegan Paul.

Harré, R. (1980), 'Man as Rhetorician' in *Models of Man* (eds. A.J. Chapman and D.M. Jones), Leicester, The British Psychological Society.

Heller, R. (1972), *The Naked Manager*, London, Barrie and Jenkins.

Herbst, Ph. G. (1976), *Alternatives to Hierarchies*, Leiden, Martinus Nijhoff.

Hofstede, G. (1980), *Culture's Consequences: International Differences in Work-Related Values*, Beverly Hills, Sage Publications.

Hunt, J.W. (1981), 'Who Wants Flatter Hierarchies Anyhow?', *London Business School Journal*, 6/1 (Autumn).

Laurent, A. (1978), 'Managerial Subordinacy: A Neglected Aspect of Organizational Hierarchy', *Academy of Management Review*.

Leach, E.R. (1964a), *Political Systems of Highland Burma: A Study of Kachin Social Structure*, London, Bell. (First published 1954.)

Leach, E.R. (1964b), 'Art in Cultural Context' in *Cultural and Social Anthropology* (ed. P.B. Hammond), New York, Macmillan. (First published in *The Institutions of Primitive Society* (ed. E.E. Evans-Pritchard), Basil Blackwell (1961).)

Lévi-Strauss, C. (1964), *Totemism* (translated by R. Needham), London, Merlin Press. (First published as *Le Totemisme Aujourd'hui*, Paris, Presses Universitaires de France (1962).)

Levy, S.J. (1981), 'Interpreting Consumer Mythology: A Structural Approach to Consumer Behavior', *Journal of Marketing*, 45/3.

Lewis, I.M. (1977), 'Introduction' in *Symbols and Sentiment: Cross-Cultural Studies in Symbolism* (ed. I.M. Lewis), London, Academic Press.

Lienhardt, G. (1964), *Social Anthropology*, London, Oxford University Press.

Mintzberg, H. (1973), *The Nature of Managerial Work*, New York, Harper and Row.

Moberg, D.J. (1981), 'Job Enrichment through Symbol Management', *California Management Review*, XXXII/1.

Offe, C. (1976), *Industry and Inequality: The Achievement Principle in Work and Social Status*, London, Edward Arnold. (First published as *Leitsung Prinzip und Industrielle Arbeit* (1970).)

Paige, M. (1981), letter to *Accountancy* (September).

Parkin, D. (1975), 'The Rhetoric of Responsibility: Bureaucratic Communications in a Kenya Farming Area' in *Political Language and Oratory in Traditional Society,* (ed. M. Bloch), London, Academic Press.
Peacock, J.L. (1975), *Consciousness and Change,* Oxford, Basil Blackwell.
Peters, T.J. (1978), 'Change Tools for Chief Executives', *The McKinsey Quarterly* (Autumn).
Peters, T.J. (1980), 'Management Systems: The Language of Organizational Character and Competence', *Organizational Dynamics* (Summer).
Pfeffer, J. (1981), 'Management as Symbolic Action: The Creation and Maintenance of Organizational Paradigms' in *Research in Organizational Behavior* Vol. 3., (eds. L.L. Cummings and B.M. Staw), Greenwich, Conn., J.A.I. Press Inc.
Phillips, D.L. (1973), *Abandoning Method,* London, Jossey-Bass.
Pym, D. (1975a), 'The Demise of Management and the Ritual of Employment', *Human Relations,* 28/8.
Pym, D. (1975b), 'The Crisis in Authority', *Management Education and Development,* 6/3 (December).
Ross, L. (1982), letter to *Management Accounting* (January).
Silverman, D. and Jones, J. (1976), *Organizational Work: The Language of Grading/The Grading of Language,* London, Collier Macmillan.
Smith, T. (1982), letter to *The Engineer* (December/January).
Stewart, R. (1976), *Contrasts in Management: A Study of Different Types of Managers' Jobs: Their Demands and Choices,* London, McGraw-Hill.
Swingle, P.G. (1976), *The Management of Power,* Hillsdale, New Jersey, Lawrence Erlbaum Associates.
Tambiah, S.J. (1979), 'A Performative Approach to Ritual', *Proceedings of the British Academy,* 65, London, Oxford University Press.
Tannenbaum, A.S. and Cooke, R.A. (1979), 'Organizational Control; A Review of Studies Employing The Control Graph Method' in *Organizations Alike And Unlike: International Inter-Institutional Studies in the Sociology of Organizations* (eds. C.J. Lammers and D.J. Hickson), London, Routledge & Kegan Paul.
Turner, B.A. (1971), *Exploring the Industrial Subculture,* London, Macmillan.
Westerlund, G. and Sjöstrand, S-E. (1979), *Organizational Myths,* New York, Harper and Row.
White, M. (1981), *The Hidden Meaning of Pay Conflict,* London, Macmillan.
Willis, P. (1979), 'Shop-Floor Culture, Masculinity and the Wage Form' in *Working-Class Culture: Studies in History and Theory* (eds. J. Clarke, C. Critcher, and R. Johnson), London, Hutchinson.
Winkler, A.C. and McCuen, J.R. (1981), *Rhetoric Made Plain* (3rd edn.), New York, Harcourt Brace Jovanovich Inc.
Worsley, P. (1967), 'Groote Eylande Totemism and *Le Totemisme Aujourd'hui*' in *The Structural Study of Myth and Totemism* (ed. E. Leach), London, Tavistock Publications.
Zijderveld, A.C. (1982), *Reality in a Looking-Glass: Rationality through an Analysis of Traditional Folly,* London, Routledge & Kegan Paul.

9

Perspectives on Management

MICHAEL J. EARL

This collection of perspectives on management is intentionally diverse. Thus it would be foolish, and arrogant, to seek to synthesize the collection in this end-piece. Nevertheless, it is possible to discern some recurring themes and to identify some interesting gaps by way of conclusion.

First, some doubts are raised about the very phenomenon or activity of 'management'. Johnson, referring to central government, seems to ask whether 'management' isn't a case of 'old wine in new bottles', an attempt, perhaps, at professionalizing what was formerly called 'administration'. Indeed, in interpreting current debates, he sees the reincarnation of PODSCORB, an acronym which has a singularly barren and mechanical ring about it in the 1980s. Stewart, of course, raises fundamental queries about the models of management of the PODSCORB genre, since studies of managerial behaviour do not paint a picture of rationality, planning, and pursuit of organizational goals, but rather of informality, reactivity, and political processes. Such behaviour may surprise or even disappoint the lay observer for it sounds anything but managerial; indeed, to administrative or economic man, it may sound like mismanagement! Yet Stewart is not alone in painting a non-traditional picture of management. Gowler and Legge, in addressing the meaning of management, and Earl, when he argues that at the organizational level accounting serves *as* management, see much of the oral tradition and political behaviour of managers as management by symbolism, an activity observed by cultural anthropologists in primitive societies where 'management', as such, may be an alien concept. So, as I queried in the Introduction, are modern managers and students of management guilty of the reification of management? Or have reformers, management consultants, and those who might be dubbed 'management scientists' created and propagated models and methods of management which quite plainly do not fit the social structure and processes of the organizations for which they were designed? Or, to be even more blunt and extreme, is management overplayed and overdone? The answer to the last question is probably obvious, once we consider the likely consequences for most socio-economic organizations were there to be no attention to formal management at all. Business would probably fail through poor cost control, inadequate financial stewardship, inattention to planning, and so on. Organizations and their members might be impoverished because of unconcern with the needs and development of human resources. And, whilst some unstructure, confusion, or rebellion is to be encouraged in organizations, anarchy is not. The important question therefore is probably not whether management exists, is necessary, or is in need of improvement, but how management can be achieved in its pursuit of some balance of social and economic imperatives and desires. To begin with, most managers and management academics would argue that management is an activity in its own right; it cannot be residual, intermittent or *ad hoc*—or if it is, the costs must be recognized.

Central government is an exemplary case. Principals in government are expected to be, as Johnson points out, servants of ministers, policy analysts, stewards of democracy, and so on. They are recruited, developed, and promoted according to such values; management ability is not a key quality sought in civil servants. Indeed, when the issue of management in government raises its head nationally, negative perceptions abound. Management is then seen to be about administration, cost efficiency and even O. & M., partly as a result of the contemporary clamour for productivity, accountability, and creation rather than consumption of wealth, partly because central government has little tradition of formal management as others have experienced it, and partly because of the quite reasonable suspicion that 'good business practice' might not fit in public service and government. Yet most civil servants do not claim that 'management' is an irrelevance; it is just that conventional models of, and full-time attention to, management seem inappropriate. This attitude is not unusual elsewhere, for example in professional organizations and specialist departments. Here management often is only seen to be important when there is a perceived management problem. Professionals and specialists frequently consult with business-school academics when they have a staff turnover problem, an apparent motivational vacuum, difficulties in controlling projects... or when some external pressure troubles them. They seek a solution in the hope that, once the problem is solved or removed, they can resume their work as professionals or specialists and forget the nuisance of managing. Likewise, in central and local government, research tends to show that management techniques, for example budgeting, fail or disappoint not because of irremediable design faults, but principally because the administrators or officers involved have not supported, learnt about, participated in, driven, adapted, dramatized... in short, managed the technique. Of course, the career structure, the incentives, the resources, and so on may impede the management task, but such infrastructure too has to be managed. In short, the breakthrough required is probably either an emotional or imposed commitment to the concept of management, accompanied by high expectations of the results, but not expecting too much too quickly. Then, in due course, the administrators and officers may develop both relevant management models and an appropriate infrastructure within which to manage. Such an analysis would suggest that, in a sense, management is what managers do, for it is only managers who can put the management into any situation, system, or technique.

Mathias, of course, presents a similar argument in his exploration of the entrepreneurship debate. Entrepreneurship is the activity of entrepreneurs. However, whilst we recognize an entrepreneur (or indeed a manager) when we see one, we find it very difficult to analyse the concept of entrepreneurship (or indeed management), despite the fact that we commonly attribute economic success or failure to abundance or scarcity of it. Furthermore, controversy exists over the origins of entrepreneurship and the conditions that beget entrepreneurs. Interestingly, I suspect that we can only speculate on what, if anything, fosters 'good managers'. It could be opportunity or it could be threat; it could be formal education or it could be experience, it could be... Alternatively, 'good managers' in fact may be born: that is to say management, like entrepreneurship, may be an independent variable. Academics who research, study, and teach management presumably would prefer that this were not the case. Fortunately for such scholars, the one factor that often seems to explain the difference between high and low performance in management tasks and situations is the degree of management—for example employment of planning and control techniques, creation of visibility and consciousness, frequency of meetings, amount of support and commitment, appropriateness of resources and organization, and so on—that managers put in. Thus management, at least in some situations, is not in danger of being overdone.

However, if management is in part a matter of commitment and application and is, in the sense employed above, what managers do, it may be important that management does not become reified. At the very least neither management theory nor management practice should become too complex or too clever. Concepts, techniques, and methodologies, if they are to be adopted in the real world and if they are to adapt to changing circumstances, probably need to satisfy three criteria. They must be understood by managers if they are to be diffused and implemented. They must be generalizable, not necessarily in the sense of being universally applicable, but in the sense that it is known when and when not they are likely to be effective. And they must be robust, that is validated by research or by proven practice. Such criteria may create an argument for simplicity, but they are not a charter for the simplistic. Certainly, we should shun over-elaborate models, elegant but idealized techniques, and theories which cannot be interpreted for use. Conversely, universal laws should be suspected, easy but untested and ill-researched prescriptions scrutinized, and local, unidimensional or 'modern' solutions handled with care. Yet, it should also be recognized that management research is still in its youth, so that frameworks for analysis are more likely to be developed than meta-theories, so that organizations and managers can contribute as much, if not more, to research and experimentation as can academics, and so that descriptive and classificatory research may be as valid and necessary as the pursuit of models, theory, and principles.

Indeed, it is interesting to observe in the contributions by those writing at the micro-level—Stewart, Earl, Tricker, Gowler and Legge, and, to an extent, Hay and Mathias—that normative, maximizing, and rational models and paradigms are absent. The more the 'black-box' of the firm is opened up and the actual behaviour of managers studied, the more the old models of management, for example those based on neo-classical economics or even scientific management, do indeed seem to be misfits, as suggested earlier. Empirical studies in the field seem to suggest that managements and managers do 'strange things', adopt simple rules, behave like non-managers, act politically, and even seek to limit, or work around, formal systems and procedures. This poses problems for both theorists and practitioners, for yet again, it becomes difficult to know that 'management' is or should be. On the one hand, organizations seem to survive, cope with, even thrive on these behaviours; perhaps they depend on them. On the other hand, most organizations seek to maximize some objective function, need some formality, and would welcome techniques that seem to improve efficiency or effectiveness. One way to resolve this conflict is, of course, to recognize that in purposive organizations we need to seek some balance between social and economic goals and controls, between formality and informality, between structure and process ... and so on. However, whilst this seems a likely prescription for effective organizational performance, we are not yet able to confirm it. What we might conclude, though, is that in an applied social science, such as management studies, while a diversity of research and research methods is required, empirical work particularly should be encouraged. For only in this way shall we learn what management really is and begin to develop theories of management which meet the criteria outlined in the previous paragraph. Furthermore, Mathias and Hay hint that, especially in seeking to understand the functioning of manager-controlled firms, industrial economists and economic historians might adopt a similar research strategy, perhaps working with academics from management studies.

Yet, how much empirical research into management and organizations is there? One can safely say not enough, because would-be researchers find that empirical work in the field is time-consuming, demanding, and often poses uncomfortable questions of methodology. Furthermore, empirical research is not the route to regular and frequent publications and it is not easily done on ever-decreasing research budgets and in the face of ever-increasing teaching and administrative duties. It may even be unfashionable, since it is sometimes qualitative rather than quantitative, inductive rather than deductive, broad rather than precise, descriptive rather than analytical, phenomenological rather than 'scientific', and interpretive rather than hypothetico-deductive. Yet in management studies, and in other social sciences, some of the most influential and seminal work over the years has been based on empirical fieldwork.

Given the constraints that do exist on such research programmes, however, what other approaches may be effective? My own instinct, or perhaps prejudice, is that management academics must not lose touch with managers (and vice versa). Frequent discourse with managers does help to keep one in touch with current issues, develop a sense of relevance, have a feel for what is practical and practicable, see research opportunities and, above all, appreciate and understand the realities of management and organizational behaviour. Unfortunately, we often create impediments to this process. Management education all too easily can become a one-way communication exercise, presenting and promoting current theories, techniques, and issues. There are at least four ways of coping with this.

One is to use the case method of teaching, which in the UK is nowadays slightly suspect, but which can provide vicarious experience of real-world situations with which managers can identify and from which teachers cannot easily escape by abstraction. Second, an even older mechanism, that of tutorial or seminar discussion, can help to open up discussion, encourage challenge, and both address specific problems and develop general concepts. We often find in Oxford that it is in individual tutorials or in small group seminars with managers that the most illuminating episodes in management education occur. It is on these occasions that managers say 'Yes, but it isn't really like that is it?' or 'It is far more complex than you suggest' or 'That sounds fine, but how do we implement it?' or (the lesson that we constantly have to relearn) 'Things take much longer to achieve than you seem to think.' (More supportive expressions also are heard, such as 'I had never quite seen it that way before' or 'Now we have tried to apply it to my situation, it makes much more sense' or 'I never thought that standing away from the problem and seeing what theory and research said about it could be so valuable.') Third, another alternative is available which provides a bridge between empirical research and education, namely action-oriented and problem-solving approaches to management development.[1] Project-learning not only can take the classroom into the factory or office, but provides opportunity for experimentation and validation, and encourages learning by more socially interactive means—perhaps more in keeping with the managerial idiom. Finally, management consultancy can provide opportunities for teachers and researchers to tackle real-world problems in real-world situations, and to test and diffuse their ideas and techniques. It also allows managements to tap, and perhaps influence, the ongoing development of the body of knowledge in management studies. It is not unusual, however, for academic institutions to query the legitimacy of this activity. There is an ambivalence and anxiety about consultancy in management studies which would seem strange in medicine, law, and the applied sciences.

To return to the descriptive research, showing managements and managers to be not as they are often thought to be: this has immediate value. It warns us against naïve implementation of normative models and against unthinking application of management techniques which are either implemented in ignorance of the social context in which they are supposed to work, or designed on erroneous assumptions about managerial and organizational behaviour. However, it need not warn us against seeking change, or working for whatever notions of improvement are extant at any time. But it does, as Fox suggests in his more macro-level of analysis, remind us to assess the costs—social and economic—that we may incur in the process. Indeed, at both the macro- and micro-levels, it is all to easily forgotten that we are the product of our history—although I do wonder whether those who are today most involved with management, or management study, in fact are somewhat more cautious than their predecessors in seeking and introducing change. It may be significant that this volume does not contain one reforming or revolutionary piece (although there are many ideas for action), and in the management literature at large I would venture to suggest that the picture is not too different. Yet, as I argued in the Introduction, management in the UK has a 'bad press' and at the macro-level there are radical ideas available from both the Right and Left. Is perhaps management by its very activity and purpose conservative, or is there a recognition that management is both conditioned and constrained by its wider social, political, and economic environment?

Such conclusions may be realistic, but they are somewhat surprising. After all, on the one hand business managers are thought to be concerned with innovation, and on the other hand recent business performance, on most evaluative criteria, would suggest the need for change. Furthermore, some would argue, perhaps deterministically, that new information technologies are forcing major changes on, or offering new opportunities to, management and organizations as an information society, or a post-industrial society, emerges. Conversely, others would argue that organizations are mini-societies, microcosms of the society of which they are a part, and only change as society changes. They reflect the values, display the culture, and embody the power and class dispositions of society at large. Indeed, organizations in industriaal society may have become the principal generators and distributors of status, income, and power. Yet, if this is so, and if the working population is larger than it ever has been (on average), if work organizations have been the principal medium of occupational structure and mobility, if entrepreneurs are significant executants of change, and if large organizations have commanded key resources, surely organizations can choose to innovate, bring about social change, in short influence society—not least if new, technologies are available to help?

Indeed, social experiments, often with economic purposes in mind as well, have been attempted at the level of the organization. One or two, by now well-known, firms have introduced broadly based participative forms of management. Worker co-operatives have been founded both in distressed industries and in new and small firms.[2] Application of information technology and redesign of jobs have been attempted using systems design methodologies based on democratic principles.[3] Examples of these innovations exist in the UK as well as in more-publicized European countries. Nevertheless, the political, social, and economic environments do seem to influence the rate of organizational change. For example, the Bullock Report[4] in the UK probably was too political an exercise to lead to any serious consideration of industrial democracy in the workplace. The scepticism and conservatism of trade unions in the UK, again the product of our social history, often seem to retard many apparently positive attempts by management to improve industrial performance and to innovate in general. And the economic recession of the early 1980s seems to have done very little in the cause of socially enlightened management; not only are many managements hardening their attitudes on pay and jobs, perhaps through necessity, but they are not thinking beyond tomorrow and considering the future consequences for either industrial innovation or social equilibrium. Thus, in the UK at least, reform and major change in work organizations seem likely to be a slow process—and, as Fox suggests, there may be in this as many advantages as disadvantages.

Another omission throughout the volume, apart from implicit attention in Mathias's paper on entrepreneurship, is the subject of risk. It is often thought that managers are risk takers, that business is about entrepreneurship, and that in general management is in the risk business. Yet none of the contributors has referred directly to risk and risk-taking from their particular perspectives of management. So it may be important to ask whether managers or businesses indeed do take risks. In one sense, they clearly do so whenever they make a decision into the future. On the other hand, they perhaps take calculated risks, in that they implicitly or explicitly attach probabilities to outcomes, much as in Knight's more precise definition of risk.[5] They will rarely jump into uncertainty where probabilities are unknown.

In practice, of course, we tend to train managers not to take risks—or, more precisely, to avoid risk. We insist on risk analysis, devise risk reduction strategies, develop tight monitoring systems and prepare contingency plans. In other words, the very professionalism of management is perhaps the act of risk reduction and risk avoidance. Second, the separation of ownership and control, which Hay, Earl, and Tricker all seem to accept, perhaps has diluted the entrepreneurial spirit. Decision-making and risk-bearing have become diffused so that, as Galbraith argues,[6] the technostructure (managers and their aides) of large corporations is motivated by security rather than profit. 'Organisation man' is not attuned to risk and return. Indeed, promotion, security, and status may come more from not making mistakes, rather than breaking new ground—or at least such may be the case in manager-controlled rather than owner-controlled firms. These managerial behaviours would suggest that Schumpeter's model of economic development may be valid.[7] To paraphrase, the management function maintains a steady-state economy, the entrepreneurial function creates the discontinuities.

However, senior managements concerned with survival or growth of their particular business, rather than with any macro-economic steady-state, may become concerned from time to time about risk-averse managerial behaviour. They may feel that management technologies all too easily become a battery of risk avoidance measures. Indeed, some firms are now querying whether their planning and control systems drive out risk and entrepreneurship altogether. There is certainly evidence that much organizational information-processing exists to provide answers, not learning, and rationalization, not ideation.[8] Corrupting Toffler's model of futures[9] therefore, it may be that the combination of management science and organizational politics too rapidly closes down possible futures through probable futures into what the organization deems to be the preferable future.

So far, the rationales for risk avoidance have been endogenous. What about external factors? First, economic uncertainty in recent times—inflation, unemployment, fluctuating interest and exchange rates—may have foregrounded risk and backgrounded return in decision-making at large. For example, firms seek ever shorter pay-backs on investment projects and many graduates entering business, I am told, appear to seek posts which offer security of employment rather than experience or opportunity. Second, as business and government organizations grow larger, their managements may become more remote from the stimuli of the market place, that is from consumers. As a result, entrepreneurial wit, flair, and ability may be being removed genetically from us. Third, hard work and seeing things through may have gone out of fashion. It may have become too easy to say 'no', to opt out, and to eschew responsibility. If any of these trends are in evidence, then risk-taking will diminish. However, all these forces, both endogenous and exogenous, may apply only in large organizations. It may well be that it is the *small* businessman who is the entrepreneur and that it is he and his managers who take most risks. And this set of papers probably has been concerned more with management in large organizations.

In the Introduction, it was pointed out that none of the papers was written by a practising manager. It is interesting to note that in the literature at large there has been no recent, major work by a manager, administrator, or businessman. Where, one might ask, is today's equivalent of Sloan?[10] Is it possible that the development of management studies has reduced the opportunities for such works? Maybe today's Sloans are, as the previous paragraph would suggest, so risk-averse that they would not entertain such exposure! If there are any populist management writers today, or gurus, they are likely to be on the fringe of management, an example, perhaps, being

Drucker.[11] Even among those on the fringe, or those engaged in management research, the doyens no longer produce grand theories of management as did, say, Fayol[12] or Barnard[13] in earlier years. This again may reflect the development of management studies which, in the desire to have a research base, advocates caution in offering prescriptions and, inevitably, factors management into 'researchable' proportions. Indeed, the absence of grand theories may also be a recognition of the need for theory development to meet the three criteria suggested earlier in this paper. Nevertheless, the literature can seem somewhat dry and dusty by being deprived of such works.

An argument can certainly be made for more integrative work and writing on management. As organizations, economies, and societies become more complex, as the rate of change quickens, and as technology brings management activities closer together, the specialist management student may have less to offer the real world and be less able to cope. Furthermore, management and management problems are far from being unidisciplinary and neatly packaged phenomena. Just as Mathias argues in the case of entrepreneurship, management is a multi-variate activity which operates in a variety of specific institutional contexts and thus requires to be analysed in all its many relationships. Yet the different social sciences seem often to be developing separate and distinct languages, methodologies, and concepts. Moreover, in seeking to apply them in the study of management, there may also be differences in value positions which are difficult to resolve. Yet, perhaps this volume has demonstrated not only the need for multidisciplinary and interdisciplinary research in management studies, but also the possibilities. Four illustrations may support this claim.

First, because of the rapid and sometimes modish transfer of concepts and methods between the social sciences, commonalities do exist. For example, Hay employs the theory of agency in discussing the divorce of ownership and control. Earl refers to the same construct in discussing financial reporting to owners, and it is also being applied to analysis of internal control systems, such as budgeting. Now, it may well be that the elegance of agency theory and its assumptions will not be able to cope with the complexities of management situations, especially management behaviours, but it does seem to be worth bringing together work and workers on agency theory development, not only for the sake of management studies but for other social sciences too.

Second, reference already has been made to the political threads that connect the papers of Stewart, Earl, Tricker, and Gowler and Legge. There would seem to be considerable opportunity for, and return from, greater application of political science to management and organizational studies. The same might be said of the contribution of social anthropology. Indeed, calls are beginning to be made for anthropological research into management and management technologies, these often, it appears, being pleas for interpretive and observational methodologies and for broadly based frameworks, as much as anything. Were this to happen on any scale, it might well be that management researchers would find the problems as interesting and challenging, the results as strange and imprecise, and the discovery of 'answers' as elusive and difficult as both Mathias and Hay suggest economic historians and economists would. But these are not good reasons for aborting new fields of enquiry.

The contributions of Fox and Mathias, as well as hints in other papers, also point to the need for a bringing together of historical and contemporary studies of management and organizations. Given that we are products of our history, it is likely that past events and environments can partly explain contemporary management phenomena. It is also possible that study of previous periods in the evolution of business, or of management, entrepreneurship, accounting, and so on, would provide generalizable insights into, or even theories of, the dynamics of change in management practice, the social and economic origins of certain management behaviours, and the effectiveness of different industrial or administrative policies. It may also be the case that management processes and behaviour in general can be studied just as effectively, in some cases more effectively, by historical methods as by live fieldwork. For example, the work of Chandler[14] has furthered our understanding not only of the role and shape of business in the economy, but of internal administrative systems also.

Finally, many research topics lend themselves to interdisciplinary attack. Tricker, in discussing corporate governance, differentiates it from management. Now clearly, there is substantial overlap between the two activities as he describes them, but there are also important distinctions, particularly in the areas of accountability and regulation. These issues of corporate governance would seem to be suited to study by, at the very minimum, lawyers, accountants, economists, management theorists, sociologists, historians, and political scientists. (Indeed, Tricker's research group aims to create a network of corporate governance scholars.) Much the same set of disciplines and scholars could stake claims in the study of entrepreneurship, as Mathias describes it. Certainly, management studies in general, by its applied nature, presents many opportunities for interdisciplinary scholarship and research.

Thus, in the call for more integrative research, these four illustrations suggest that historical studies have contemporary value, social science theory development could benefit from co-ordination, other disciplines and methodologies should be applied to management study, and several management issues are susceptible to interdisciplinary attack. In addition, in earlier discussion of management education and development, two other integrative intiatives were supported; namely, the fusion of research and education and the collaboration of researchers and management, through the media of action-learning and consultancy research. All these suggestions come from a writer with the perspective of management studies. There may be equal benefits to sister disciplines from more interdisciplinary or multidisciplinary research. Two examples are offered. Hay raises one question that is of concern to industrial economists, namely 'what determines the degree of managerial activity to overcome organizational slack and X-efficiency'. An accumulation and synthesis of the many unconnected researches into management control, strategic planning, and organizational behaviour might produce some systematic evidence on this question. In contrast, Mathias doubts whether today's emerging body of knowledge on management decision-making and techniques is helpful to economic historians who are studying management as it operated under earlier institutional structures and economic systems. Whilst Mathias's caution is clearly necessary and sensible, I would be less dismissive of the benefits that might emerge from interfaces between contemporary and historical studies of management and business. One often feels that there are administrative inertias that connect different eras, that some things in management do not change that quickly, and that perhaps history can repeat itself. Above all, whilst we want to avoid creating branches of study which are too large to tackle, we occasionally might test whether the frameworks and models of one discipline can stand up to the data of another.

Such concern for integration may be an appropriate way to close this volume. It perhaps reinforces just how 'messy' is management studies. The concept of management is problematic, the delineation of management studies is not clear, management behaviour is complex, and perhaps surprising, and particular areas of management have many dimensions to them—indeed, several contributors have found it difficult to keep to their brief. All these traits are probably inevitable in an applied social science, especially one in its youth. Consequently, whilst management theories need to be understood, generalizable, and robust, the study of management should remain eclectic, empirical, integrative, and in touch with managers—in both education and research.

NOTES

1 See, for example, R.W. Revans, *The Origins and Growth of Action-Learning*, Bromley, Kent, Chartwell-Bratt (1982).
2 See, for example, T. Eccles, *Under New Management*, London, Pan Books (1981).
3 See, for example, E. Mumford, *Values, Technology and Work*, The Hague, Martinus Nijhoff (1981).
4 Lord A. Bullock, *Report of the Committee of Inquiry on Industrial Democracy*, Cmnd. 6706, London, HMSO (1977).
5 F.H. Knight, *Risk, Uncertainty and Profit*, Chicago, Ill., University of Chicago Press (1921).
6 J.K. Galbraith, *The New Industrial State*, London, Hamish Hamilton (1967).
7 J. Schumpeter, *Theory of Economic Development*, Cambridge, Mass., Harvard University Press (1949).
8 M.J. Earl and A.G. Hopwood, 'From Management Information to Information Management' in H.C. Lucas Jr. *et al.* (eds.) *The Information Systems Environment*, Amsterdam, North-Holland (1980).
9 A. Toffler, *Future Shock*, London, The Bodley Head (1970).
10 A.P. Sloan (Jun.), *My Years with General Motors*, London, Sidgwick & Jackson (1965).
11 See, for example, P. Drucker, *The Practice of Management*, London, Heinemann (1955).
12 H. Fayol, *Administration Industrielle et Generale*, Paris, Dunod Frères (1925).

13 C.I. Barnard, *The Functions of the Executive*, Cambridge, Mass., Harvard University Press (1968).
14 A. Chandler, *Strategy and Structure: Chapters in the History of the Industrial Enterprise*, New York, Anchor Books (1966).